DEEP VENTURE

DEEP VENTURE

A Sailor's Story of Cold War Submarines

GARY PENLEY

PELICAN PUBLISHING COMPANY
Gretna 2012

The word "Pelican" and the depiction of a pelican are trademarks
of Pelican Publishing Company, Inc., and are registered in the
U.S. Patent and Trademark Office.

Library of Congress Cataloging-in-Publication Data

Penley, Gary, 1941-
  Deep venture : a sailor's story of Cold War submarines / Gary
Penley.
     p. cm.
  ISBN 978-1-58980-870-6 (hbk. : alk. paper) 1. United States.
Navy—Submarine forces—Biography. 2. Submariners—United
States—Biography. 3. Marine engineers—United States—Biography.
4. Amberjack (Submarine : SS-522) 5. United States. Navy—
Sea life—Anecdotes. I. Title. II. Title: Sailor's story of Cold War
submarines.
  V63.P39A3 2011
  359.0092—dc23
  [B]
                             2011030264

The names of some people in this book have been changed for reasons
of privacy.

Printed in the United States of America

Published by Pelican Publishing Company, Inc.
1000 Burmaster Street, Gretna, Louisiana 70053

To Bob Lee and Ralph Kennedy.
Fair winds and following seas, my mates,
on your eternal patrol.

"Miles away, creeping along deep,
we could still hear the booms.
Nothing on earth sounds like a depth charge."
                        —Six-Day War, June, 1967

Contents

Part Three: Snafu

Acknowledgments

I thank the following people for their invaluable contributions to this book:

Norman Bessac, Captain USN (Ret., deceased); C. D. Summitt, Captain USN (Ret., deceased); Ralph Kennedy, ENCS (SS) USN (Ret., deceased); "Van" VanBuskirk (deceased). Although these men are now deceased, all were alive when I began writing this book and all made personal contributions that aided in its completion.

Robert Rawlins, Captain USN (Ret.); John MacKinnon, CDR USN (Ret.); James Ennes, LT CDR USN (Ret.); the Ralph Kennedy family; Fred Birch; John Collins; George Penley; Jim Diers; Dave Tanis; DeWayne Catron; Danny Dawson; Fred "Whitey" Kutzleb; Bob Cantley; Rich Dominy; Gary Reynolds; Jim Barnes; Richard Sellers; Ben Rathke; Pat Gurr; Joseph Lentini; Fred Swets; Stan Kolodzie; and Luis Urrea.

A special thanks to Doris Baker, whose encouragement, advice, and candid analyses will never be forgotten.

And to Karen, who makes dreams come true.

This is no bull.

This is a statement that all sailors use when beginning a sea story—to remove any doubt of the truth of what they are about to tell, no matter how outlandish or unbelievable their tale may seem.

I heard this line countless times during my seven years in the navy, and so I use it to begin my story.

It is a sea story, and in this case, the line applies because every word is true—the story of how a kid from the prairie became a sailor and then a submariner, joining a bunch of devil-may-care guys who dared the depths to place themselves in harm's way.

We were young then, and all a little crazy.

We had to be.

Prologue

High above the water, on the loftiest decks of the tender, the crew strained against the rails. One hundred and thirty pairs of eyes turned seaward, probing the fog, each straining to be the first to catch sight of the sub. Then an arm flew out, a finger pointed, and a man cried, "There she is!" A cheer went up as the ghostly outline appeared out of the mist.

She rode low in the water, dark, her nose plunging through the choppy seas like a great leviathan, her shadowy silhouette revealing the machine of destruction that she was.

After the initial cheer, we all grew quiet, gazing at the deep-diving warship that would be our home for the next three months.

A great sense of pride and honor welled up in me at the big sub's approach, and a familiar knot of dread.

Part One

From the Prairie to the Sea

Chapter One

Welcome to the Navy

Even a kid from the prairie could recognize the color—battleship gray—but I'd never seen it on a bus.

The year was 1960, and submarines were the last thing on my mind when that gray bus pulled up in front of the station. In fact, at that moment I couldn't even have said exactly why I'd joined the navy, except that my father had been a sailor during World War II, followed by my older brother in the 1950s, and without giving it much thought I had simply planned on joining after high school.

There were about thirty of us, lolling around the San Diego bus station that September afternoon, little more than kids— seventeen, eighteen, or nineteen at the most—and hailing from all over the country and every walk of life. Though we were all tired, dirty, and rumpled from long bus rides, a few of the guys sat up straight, as if trying to sit at attention. Others leaned back or slumped sideways in their seats. Some lay stretched out on the hard benches, asleep.

A tall sailor strode in the front door and stopped among us, his hands on his hips. Standing straight as a main mast and stiffly dressed in a snow-white uniform, he was a first-class petty officer. None of us knew that at the time, of course— or even what a first-class petty officer was. And he was a "squared-away sailor," another term we weren't familiar with yet. We soon figured out that he was our bus driver, and that's all we knew.

"Welcome to San Diego," the petty officer said with a wide

smile. Then clapping his hands to rouse the sleepy ones, he said, "Grab your bags, boys. You've got a date with the navy."

The petty officer seemed friendly enough, but something in his smile looked suspicious, as if he might be aware of a huge joke that the rest of us were not. And even in my groggy state, I felt pretty sure the joke wasn't on him.

The recruiters who signed us up had told us not to take much baggage, because we'd be sending it all back home as soon as we were issued uniforms. Our driver continued to grin as we picked up our small bags and boarded the drab bus.

With no one saying a word, our land ship headed through San Diego. We stared out the windows at brightly painted signs advertising tattoo parlors, uniform shops, pawn shops, and bars with names such as "The Anchor," "The Forecastle," and "Safe Harbor." Palm trees, by the hundreds, lined the streets. I'd never seen a palm tree.

We began to catch sight of portions of the bay, long piers jutting out into it, and navy ships, all the same color as our bus. One of the guys got brave enough to say something: "That one looks like a destroyer."

Another fellow piped up: "I think that might be what we're riding in. Is this a bus or a destroyer?"

Everyone laughed, including the driver. The petty officer joining in our laughter boosted our ebbing confidence, and soon everyone started making wise cracks, attempting to bolster our young fear with vocal bravado. Suddenly we were a bunch of tough, funny guys, on our way to being tough, funny sailors.

The front gate of the base loomed ahead, a high arch spanning it connected wide pillars on either side that housed the marine guards. The bus stopped at the gate and the petty officer swung open the door. A marine guard in an impeccable dress uniform leaned in and looked back at us, disdain obvious on his square-jawed face.

"Just another load of fresh meat," the driver said. With a wry smile the marine nodded, stepped back smartly, and waved us through.

"Boy, he looked like a tough one," one of the would-be sailors behind me said.

"Sure did," another stated. Everyone on the bus broke into

laughter—everyone except our driver, that is, the first-class petty officer.

The driver abruptly stopped the bus and turned his head, nailing us with an icy glare. "All right, we're on the base now. Knock off the crap."

We knocked off the crap.

I had grown up in a patriotic family, but on a cattle ranch in the middle of nowhere, and consequently had never seen a military base of any kind. As the bus started moving again, I saw rows and rows of barracks, each one exactly like the next—long, narrow, two stories high, and pale yellow in color—stretching as far as one could see. Then a parade ground came into view, acres and acres of asphalt, also seeming to reach forever. We would learn that this vast expanse of pavement was affectionately known as "the grinder." And we would learn how it had earned such a name.

The base was a busy place. Companies of men—hundreds of them—marched back and forth across the grinder. Others stood in formation at strict attention, listening to men in khaki uniforms bark orders at them. Some companies were clad in dungarees and some in whites, all with heavy-duty belts around their middles, leggings that covered their calves, and rifles on their shoulders.

A number of companies were involved in strenuous calisthenics, reacting to orders from stiff drill instructors standing on raised podiums and growling into microphones, their gruff barks issuing from loudspeakers that carried across the grinder into our bus, and into our tender ears.

The recruits would drop down onto the pavement to do fast pushups, jump back up for a series of deep-knee bends, fall on their backs with their hands behind their heads in a blur of high-speed sit-ups, then bound up once more for even speedier jumping jacks. A number of companies were made to count loudly along with the exercises, their shouting cadence also carrying rudely into our bus.

Some of the calisthenics consisted of strange, muscle-twisting exercises involving the long rifles the sailors carried. I liked that. The idea of having my own rifle was cool; or at least it seemed so at the moment.

Our bus jerked to a stop in front of a large building—the

Receiving and Outfitting Center—commonly referred to as R &
O. Here would begin our indoctrination into the navy. High on
the front of the R & O Center hung a large sign that spelled
out a poignant message. The bulging letters, outlined in coiled
rope, anchors, and ship's propellers, made my young heart skip
a patriotic beat.

WELCOME ABOARD.
YOU ARE NOW MEN OF THE
UNITED STATES NAVY.

As our driver left the bus, I stared at the sign and thought how
proud my grandfather would be if he were still alive.

My reverie was quickly broken. The meanest man in the
world—a chief petty officer—stepped onto the bus. Built like
a bridge pylon and dressed in stiffly starched khakis with a
flat, visored cap squared over a hard, scowling brow, the chief
crossed his arms, clenched his teeth, and scanned the lot of
us as if he might be preparing to breathe fire through the bus
and incinerate us all. Sound vanished, movement stopped, the
universe stood still. I began to sweat—from my forehead, my
armpits, and every other fold in my young body. Maybe the man
was already breathing fire.

Then the chief opened his mouth and welcomed us to the
navy. "All right, maggots, grab your bags and get your sloppy
butts off this bus. Fall into formation out there, if you got any
idea what that means, and face that sign." He pointed at the
hallowed sign on the front of the building.

We squeezed past him as we left the bus, tripping, catching
our bags on seats, and melting under his gaze with every
stumbling step. Outside, afraid to set our bags down and afraid
not to, we lined up side by side facing the big sign. The chief
stepped in front of us, put his hands on his hips, thrust his head
forward in a predatory stance, and barked, "Is that what you call
a formation?" A few of us shuffled around and tried to straighten
the line. It didn't work. The chief shook his head in disgust, then
whirled and pointed up at the sign.

"In case some of you can't read, that says, 'You are now men
of the United States Navy.' Sounds pretty good, don't it?" Some
of us smiled and nodded. The chief did not.

"Let me tell you something," he growled. "That's a buncha

crap. There ain't a man among ya. There might be a few men here by the time you leave this place, but there ain't one of ya that fits that sign today—not a one."

I thought to myself: *Gee, I've only been in the navy a few minutes, and already I'm learning things. For one, I know not to take signs literally; and two, I can tell that a rich vocabulary is not going to be a requirement.*

Then, the unthinkable: the chief turned his steely eyes directly on me.

"What are you grinning at, son? Think something's funny?"

"No, I . . . I wasn't grinning," I lied.

"You weren't grinning?" he replied.

"No, I wasn't."

"No I wasn't what?" he growled.

"I wasn't grinning, and I don't think anything's funny . . . Sir."

"That's good," the chief said, "because I didn't say anything funny. If I do say something funny, you can grin. In fact, you're supposed to. But since I didn't, you couldn't have been grinning. Right, son?"

"Right, sir," I said.

With that the chief turned his attention to some other luckless recruit, and I began to think again, this time without grinning. I was learning more and more, and already I had something to be thankful for. I was thankful that I had used the bathroom before we left the bus station.

We were shuffled off to the side; again lined up in a shoddy, meandering formation; and threatened with bodily harm should we attempt to do anything besides breathe. From here, we watched more busloads of young maggots arrive and receive their welcome from Chief Fire Eyes, including, of course, the requisite explanation that there wasn't a man among them. Following each welcome, the chief would have the new guys join us—an ever-growing crowd of maggots—until we numbered approximately eighty.

Chief Fire Eyes stood in front of the large group, hands on his hips, and informed us that: one, we all looked like crap; and two, we were going to become a company. Company 496 would be our name. We all looked at the chief, the thought that he would be our company commander settling on us like a sentence of prolonged evisceration. Then a tall black fellow in the front line demonstrated what I considered to be either extreme courage or a symptom of mental illness. He spoke to the chief.

"If I may ask," the young sailor said, "are you going to be our company commander, sir?"

"No," the chief said sarcastically, "and you may all thank God for that." We all did.

Fire Eyes then informed us of another military custom that we would follow without fail. "Your company commander, whoever he may turn out to be, will be known as your Commanding Officer, or C.O. Whenever you do meet him, and each time that he comes into your sight, you will jump to attention and holler—I repeat, holler—'Attention on deck!' And you will remain at attention until the C.O. tells you otherwise, which he will do by saying, 'At ease.' Or, he might say, 'At ease, maggots,' or something similar."

Another chief petty officer showed up from somewhere, this one short and dumpy with a thin mustache and a loud mouth meant to make him sound ten feet tall. The high pitch of his voice pretty well screwed up his act, however, that and the fact that he waddled when he walked. I wondered if the little chief suffered from the small-man syndrome, and I also wondered if he'd ever had a date that he didn't have to pay for. I chose not to ask him either of those things.

"This is Chief Wimberly," said Fire Eyes. "He's going to show you where to put your bags in a barracks, and then he's going to take you to the mess hall. Remember your table manners, if you got any, and eat all you can hold. You'll be needing it."

I glanced at the short, fat chief and thought: *Wimberly? Even the poor guy's name sounds wimpy.* I hoped he'd be our company commander.

With Chief Wimberly calling cadence, we made our way to the mess hall, still dressed in civilian clothes, "civvies" as such clothing would forever after be known. Recruits from other companies would look at us, laugh, and holler, "Hey, look at that: R & O." We weren't allowed to return their insults, or even cast our eyes in their direction.

Our "march" to the mess hall seemed at least a mile and, according to Chief Wimberly, was the worst display of troop movement in military history. We had difficulty keeping straight faces as he dressed us down in his squeaky little voice, but I noticed his squat body had a firmness about it, and he stood as straight as a bulkhead on a battleship as he assured us that we would soon become better marchers—far better—whether we liked it or not. My desire to have him as company commander began to waver.

The mess hall, a sprawling one-story structure, was the largest building I'd ever seen. Inside, a number of cafeteria-style chow lines and a great number of long tables were designed to serve thousands of recruits at the same time. An endless background noise invaded our ears as we stepped inside—metal trays sliding out of metal racks; metal silverware hitting the trays; a nonstop murmur of voices; and a constant shuffle of feet, bodies, and chairs as young recruits grabbed seats, quickly gulped down tons of chow, threw their silverware onto their trays, and jumped up to leave. And a strong odor—a mixture of hot food, cooking oil, soap, steam, cleanser, and bodies. A unique smell—neither offensive nor appealing—that I would find permeating every mess hall in the navy.

We picked up silverware and heavy aluminum trays divided into six compartments, then started down the chow line. A company of recruits, now in their third week, had mess hall duty for seven days straight—not a fun job. They stood behind the chow line, dumping food onto our trays from large metal ladles and forks that looked like spears.

The recruits—both those serving food and the ones being served—had their heads practically shaved and were dressed in navy dungarees or white uniforms. In great contrast, our company still wore civvies and sported cool haircuts: sideburns, ducktails, flattops, and the like. We thought we looked much better than the rest of them. In fact, from our viewpoint they looked pretty funny. Those in uniform had a different opinion, however. We were just R & O, and as such were greeted with smirks, jeers, and sneers as we made our way through the chow line and found seats at the tables. Some of the uniformed recruits got up and moved if we sat near them. I thought I might get spat upon, but I didn't. I appreciated that.

As for Chief Fire Eyes cautioning us about table manners, it must have been his idea of a joke. As I sat eating with my right hand only, napkin on my knee and left hand in my lap, being careful to keep my elbows off the table, a recruit several seats to my left hollered one word: "Ketchup." From somewhere down the table to my right, a bottle of ketchup came flying by. Sliding upright on its bottom, the hurtling bottle was caught in the waiting hand of the fellow who had ordered it. Raising my head and looking around the room, I observed that, although most were at least putting their silverware to some sort of use, the term "table manners" did not apply. Very funny, Fire Eyes.

The last place one passed through before exiting the mess hall was a steamy, smelly room called the scullery. Here, the leftover food was dumped into garbage cans, after which the trays, silverware, cups, and glasses were steam cleaned and stacked on metal racks to be wheeled back out to the chow line. An unfortunate group of third-week recruits worked in the scullery—a sweaty, stinky job without a modicum of dignity attached to it. And the worst job there—indeed the worst job on the entire base—was performed by a single sailor, a hapless oaf known as the dirty tray man.

The dirty tray man was covered in sweat, grime, and splotches of leftover food. He always looked exhausted, and he never smiled. What caused this chronic condition? He stood over a barrel-sized garbage can fitted with a flat wooden lid that had a sizeable hole through it. As each sailor passed by on his way out of the mess hall, he'd throw his utensils into a deep pan and toss his tray to the dirty tray man. The dirty tray man would quickly beat the tray on the wooden top to shake the leftover food down into the can. Bits of airborne chow filled the air in front of him, flying upward and sticking to his clothes, arms, hands, and face. After knocking the biggest gobs of chow off the tray, he'd throw it to the guy working next to him, who would then send it through the steam-cleaning machine.

The dirty tray man had about two seconds to accomplish this task, because the next sailor in line would be impatiently waiting to toss him another tray. I never felt impatient at that point, however. I actually wished we could pass through the scullery at a slower pace, because the dirty tray man was fun to watch. And I always wondered what the poor slob had done to get himself assigned to such a job, though I sorely hoped I would never learn the answer.

The uniformed companies marched in formation to the mess hall, but after they finished, they were free to walk back to their barracks on their own. Not us R & O guys; we had to line up once more and march back to the Receiving and Outfitting Center to the squeaky cadence of the spherical Chief Wimberly. After that we lost him, because he turned us over to yet another chief who could have been a twin to Fire Eyes, the one who had given us our initial welcome.

By this time, we were learning to march considerably better, or so we thought. Fire Eyes II lined us up and started us at a fast pace toward the door to the barracks where we had left our baggage. As we neared the double set of closed doors, marching six abreast, we thought the chief was never going to give us the order to halt. He did—at the very last second—ensuring that the guys in back couldn't stop in time to keep from jamming the ones in front up against the doors and the side of the building. Amidst a mass of flattened bodies, flailing arms, bruised noses, squashed faces, and banged shoulders, loud hollering and cussing erupted, to the huge delight of the chief. He then told us to "fall out," as if we hadn't already.

In the barracks, Fire Eyes II stood on the top of a table so that he could tower over us all and collectively scan us with his fierce glare while filling the long room with his bull-like roar.

"This is where you're going to sleep tonight," the chief hollered, loud enough to have been addressing a company three barracks away. "You can pick whatever bunk you want. You'll find a pillow on it, but you'll have to make the bed up yourself. Mommy ain't here to do it for you any more. There's stacks of sheets and pillowcases on these tables, and blankets, in case some of your tender bodies get cold. There's towels and washcloths too, so don't forget to shower before you hit the sack. I'd advise you to wash your dirty butts till they shine."

I wondered if the chief's "advice" constituted a direct order, and if we were allowed to wash the rest of our bodies as well. I also wondered where the navy found these rabid lions. Were all chief petty officers like the three we had met that afternoon, or were these handpicked for the delicate job of handling new recruits?

Four of us had decided to join the navy together. Four kids who had known each other all our lives and graduated from high school in the same class. Two of the four, Richard Lacy and Joel O'Rear, had lived in the little town of Lamar, in the southeast corner of Colorado. The other two, Nelson Brookshire and myself, had been raised on ranches several miles south of Lamar. We had ridden a school bus to town, however, so we all knew each other well.

We had joined on the Buddy Program, a deal in which the navy guaranteed that we would be assigned to the same company in boot camp. And, as promised, we were starting out in the same company: Number 496. We would soon learn, however, that there were no guarantees as to when an individual *finished* boot camp, or in what company.

Our temporary barracks, like all the others on the base, consisted of a long room with narrow beds lined up on each side—double-deck metal bunks jutting out perpendicular to the walls. Large rectangular tables, with benches on either side, filled the middle space between the rows of bunks. Tall windows without curtains let in the light. Nothing but paint, thick and off-white in color, adorned the walls. Nonexistent would best describe the décor, but the floors and walls glistened, even the ceiling. It may have been the cleanest room I had ever set foot in.

There were a few others from Colorado as well, guys from various towns and cities that we had gotten to know a bit on the bus trip from Denver to San Diego. That first night, the four of us from Lamar chose bunks next to each other, as did others who had joined on the Buddy Program—guys from places I had only heard of: Georgia, Louisiana, Mississippi, Texas, New England (was that a state?), and even New York, which until then I had thought of as just a big city instead of a state.

We got out clean clothes, if we had any left, began undressing, and headed for the showers, some embarrassed about this public display of their naked bodies and others too tired to care. I noticed that most guys appeared to be scrubbing themselves all over, so I stopped worrying about the order from Chief Fire Eyes II to just concentrate on washing our butts.

Boot camp 1960. Center: *Gary Penley.*

After showering and making up our bunks, some of the guys crawled into bed and promptly fell asleep, but many of us felt the need to talk. We sat on the edges of our bunks or at the tables and rambled on and on, mostly about home, how we felt about the navy so far, and what the morning might bring. I especially wondered what sort of demented chief petty officer we would meet next.

And speaking of chief petty officers, after we had chatted for a while, a gigantic chief opened the door at the center of the barracks and stepped in. He was tall and well built, neither fat nor thin, just a greatly oversized human. After he stood long enough to let us get a good look at him, the big chief reached over and switched off the lights. He spoke briefly into the darkened room—only one sentence, in fact—but it was concise, to the point, and impossible to misconstrue.

"Hit the sack and shut up!"

Chapter Two

Boot Camp: The Test

Although I felt wrung out and wasted that first night, I found that I couldn't sleep. I lay awake for hours, listening to the other recruits snoring, tossing in their bunks, and a few talking in their sleep. Vivid memories took me back home, to my childhood, to my mother, and to her father. My grandfather, whom I had called Dad, died just two years before I joined the navy. He and my mother had raised me out on that wild prairie, with neither electricity nor running water. Since all my friends in town had television, indoor bathrooms, and lots of time to play, as a kid I had thought life was tough on the ranch, and in many ways, it had been. Now I longed for it, and for Dad, as never before.

Finally, exhausted both mentally and physically, I slept.

After a short, troubled sleep, Chief Big Man, the giant that had bid us sweet dreams the night before, threw open the barracks door, switched on the lights, and issued our morning wake-up call. "All right, maggots, drop your cocks and grab your socks. Roll your young carcasses outta them racks—now!"

As I was sitting up, trying to brush the cobwebs out of my mind, I looked at my high-school friend, Joel O'Rear, and said, "I wonder how long we're going to be maggots?" Joel, a polite, soft-spoken fellow whose innocent face belied a core of courage and moral sinew, just smiled and shook his head.

Chief Big Man, who was standing half the length of the barracks away, hollered at me. "If you keep running that mouth, you'll be a maggot a damn sight longer'n you wanta be, sailor!" I ducked my head, wishing I could somehow become invisible. Had I spoken louder than I meant to, or were these chiefs endowed with superhuman hearing as well as bestial natures?

Then something I had missed dawned on me: the big chief had called me "sailor." In spite of everything that seemed negative at the time, that single word lifted me out of my exhausted gloom. Sailor. That was my goal, and though the chief had likely used the term out of habit, and probably hadn't even meant to, I had been called a sailor. Maybe I wasn't going to be a maggot so long after all.

Chief Big Man marched us to the mess hall for breakfast, where we again endured the loathing and disdain reserved for the contemptible R & O. Passing through the scullery on the way out, despite strict orders to the contrary, I hesitated a moment to observe the redoubtable plight of the dirty tray man. Fascinating. Perhaps that particular job existed only to put all others in perspective.

Chief Big Man did not march us into the wall as Fire Eyes II had the night before, and once we were all inside the barracks, he left without a word. As we stood around our bunks, wondering if we should talk, not talk, move, not move, go to the bathroom or go in our pants, the big chief returned. Another chief, of average size and not particularly mean looking, walked in with him.

"Attention on deck!" Big Man roared. In their haste to jump to attention, two or three recruits who were seated on bottom bunks slammed their heads against the metal rails of the bunks above them. Simultaneously and without success, both chiefs attempted to suppress a smile.

The newcomer standing beside Big Man was the sharpest-looking chief we had seen. Somewhere in his mid-thirties, brown hair neatly trimmed in a not-too-short military cut, hat cocked to one side over a perfectly symmetrical face, the man was a good-looking sailor, handsome even.

"This is Chief Loibl," Big Man said. "He's your C.O. From this minute till the day you graduate from boot camp, you belong to him, body and soul."

Following this endearing introduction, Big Man turned to Chief Loibl. "They're all yours, Chief."

"Thank you, Chief," said Loibl, and Big Man did an about face and strode out of the barracks.

Our new C.O. scanned us all with a cool gaze, then said, "Good morning."

"Good morning, sir," we said, in quite imperfect unison.

"At ease," the chief said. "You can sit down on one of the benches if you want to, or you can stand up, but gather around close so you can hear me. And listen up.

"My name is Loibl. It's spelled L-o-i-b-l, but it's pronounced like noble. You don't have to worry about that, though, because to you my name is Sir, and nothing else. Everybody got that?"

"Yes, sir," we said loudly. A few guys jumped to attention, then slowly sat back down, embarrassedly figuring out that the move had been unnecessary.

The C.O. went on. "We've all got jobs to do here. My job is to make men out of you. Navy men to be specific—sailors. I'm a good sailor, and that's what I intend to make of you. Understood?"

"Yes, sir!"

"Good. Boot camp won't be easy—not for any of you—because I don't intend to make it that way. You'll find I'm not too hard to get along with, though—unless you try to mess with me."

Loibl stopped talking and looked around the room, his eyes seeming to meet everyone's at once. "Some of you will try to mess with me—it always happens—and when you do, you'll find out what I mean.

"Now, as you know, boot camp is supposed to last nine weeks. You probably haven't heard this yet, but it's only nine weeks long if you don't screw up. There's lots of ways to screw up, and if you do, you can be set back to a previous week. For example, you could be in your seventh week and get set back into a company that's just starting their third. If that happens, you'll never see this company again, and you'll lose all that time.

"And, if you're a scrounge, and can't keep your butt clean, or if you decide you don't like to take orders, or if you think you're too tough for this company, or not tough enough, we've got a place for you, too. It's a special company called 4013—the scrounge company. If you get sent to 4013 you get treated like an animal, and you've got to work like an animal—with damn little sleep—to get out of it and back into a regular company. And however long you spend in 4013 doesn't count as boot camp time at all. It's just lost. Sound like any fun?"

"No, sir!"

"Good thinking. Now I want you all to look around you; take a good look at the guy next to you, because he may not be there in a few days, or a few weeks. He may be gone and you'll never see him again."

A terrible silence fell over the company, unlike anything we'd experienced since our arrival. We all looked at the ones nearest ourselves—quick looks, embarrassed, afraid to let our eyes meet theirs. As I glanced at my hometown buddies, my heart leaped into my throat. I'd known them since early childhood, and until that moment, I hadn't realized how vital their presence was to me—a tangible link to my rapidly receding past. I'm sure all the other recruits who had joined on the Buddy Program felt the same ache, the same fear.

A weak performance in boot camp portended a dark potential that none of us had known. We were young, and we were going be tested—to find out what we were made of—with serious consequences if we fell short.

With Chief Loibl's words resonating in our minds like a gong heralding the end of life as we knew it, he stared at us all. Neither meanness nor empathy shone in his eyes—only determination.

Finally, when the air engulfing the crowded recruits grew unbearably tense, the C.O. spoke again. "Okay, so now you know. This is not a game. It's more serious than anything you've ever done. But don't stand around moping about it. All you have to do is listen, keep yourselves clean, do what you're told, and you'll get through it.

"Now get those hang-dog looks off your faces and listen up; we've got a lot to talk about and a lot to do before your tired butts hit these racks again."

The C.O. continued to talk for some time, but most of us were already disobeying orders. Instead of listening, we were thinking about the possibility of ourselves or one of our buddies being set back or sent to 4013, the scrounge company.

We would learn more about Company 4013, and occasionally get a glimpse of the pathetic bunch marching on the grinder. In regular companies such as our own, a selected recruit marched in front, proudly displaying the company flag on a high pole known as the guide-on. Company 4013 also displayed their flag wherever they went, except to carry 4013's guide-on or to march behind it had nothing to do with pride; it was all about degradation.

Those assigned to the scrounge company were made to wear their white hats turned down like rain caps and to keep their eyes directed down toward their feet at all times. They worked and drilled to extremes beyond exhaustion and underwent inspections nearly impossible to pass. Instead of sleeping the night away, they were roused every hour and put through a series of strenuous calisthenics. And the sadistic chiefs— several, instead of one—who commanded 4013 made the rest of the C.O.s look like Samaritans.

Haircuts: the first order of our first full day. We had all been dreading what we felt to be the ultimate in dehumanization. However, even before we began our march to the barbershop, our feelings about losing our locks had undergone a drastic change. Why? Because in leaving our proud manes in the past we would take a major step toward losing our disgraceful status: R & O.

This change of heart about losing our hair amazed me. Somehow it seemed to smack of brainwashing. Is that what we were all involved in? An exercise in mass brainwashing? Probably so, but I didn't care. As the barber sheared off my long, flowing sides and carefully trained ducktail in less than a minute, unlike Samson, who lost his strength along with his hair, I felt stronger: a step closer to becoming a sailor.

My buddies pointed at my bald scalp and laughed, and I did the same to them.

It was during these first experiences as a company that we began to know each other and to adopt the military tradition of using last names only. First names hardly seemed to count and were seldom used except in the case of good friends.

Although we had all been given physical exams before signing our enlistment papers back home, here we underwent a complete new series, more rigorous and, since there were eighty of us, more embarrassing. The entire company was made to undress and stand around the outer walls of a large room, all facing inward toward each other. There were no secrets left.

Although we tried to keep our eyes averted from one another, one little guy, named Hailey, couldn't help being noticed. If ever a recruit looked like he didn't belong in basic training, it was Hailey. Only inches past five feet tall and skinny as a sparrow, Hailey's boyish body appeared to be hairless except for the scant brush of blond the barber had left on his scalp. With skin so fair as to appear anemic, his narrow shoulders drooped, his knees sagged, and he stared at the floor, his posture alone depicting more than simple shyness. His eyes, which never met anyone else's, looked tired and drawn, and even when he marched, he moved with an exhausted plod. Hailey had no physical stamina whatsoever, and it didn't take a psychiatrist to recognize a gross lack of confidence and self-esteem. The little fellow looked as if he had never ventured beyond his own backyard, and here he was in boot camp.

Having lived all of my nineteen years in rural Colorado, I had met only a few black people. We had several in Company 496. Christophe, the fellow who had dared to speak to Chief Fire Eyes minutes after our arrival, reminded me of Harry Belafonte. Christophe hailed from New Orleans and, besides being movie-star handsome, charming, and exceptionally bright, he stood well over six feet and was built like a prize fighter.

Christophe and a black friend, Encalarde, had joined together. Encalarde towered over the rest of us, too—all six feet, three inches of him—but even for so tall a fellow, parts of Encalarde's body were out of proportion.

Time dragged while we stood naked and waited for a team of doctors to come and examine us all. As the eighty of us stood around the perimeter of the room, our big toes touching a straight line painted about two feet from the wall, we directed our eyes up at the ceiling, down at the floor, at some imaginary spot in space, or out a window—anything to ensure that we didn't appear to be looking at the bare bodies of our companymen.

In the midst of this uncomfortable silence, I heard a tittering begin—suppressed giggles and inhalations of air: low expressions of awe. The guys on the far side of the room were grinning at something on our side, and I sensed that the ones standing to my left were looking to their left and downward. What on Earth could they be staring at? I wondered, but I kept my eyes trained upward toward the ceiling. Then the fellow on my immediate left tapped my hand to get my attention. When I glanced in his direction, he motioned me to look beyond him, at someone, or something, down the line.

As curiosity overcame embarrassment, I turned my head, following the staring eyes of others with my own. Expecting to behold some bizarre spectacle such as oversized genitalia or some sort of physical deformity, my searching eyes stopped where the others were transfixed: on Encalarde. The guys were not staring at any part of the tall man's torso, or at his privates, but farther down, at his feet—the most humongous pair of feet I had ever seen, or ever hope to see again in this life.

Earlier that day I had noticed that Encalarde's hands seemed large even for so tall a man, but his feet defied reason. They simply could not have been as big as they appeared, but the truth was in the seeing. Size 15EEE they turned out to be.

Encalarde's gargantuan underpinnings served to lighten the moment for everyone; he was even grinning himself. And when the first doctor passed by, looking us each up and down carefully, he stopped in front of Encalarde and stared at his feet in disbelief. Then the doc shook his head and said, "My God, son, when I saw those things on the end of your legs I thought they were breathing on their own."

Following the physicals, we put on our shorts and pants, no shirts, and lined up for a series of four inoculations: two in each arm. A short, skinny fellow named Selley had a great propensity to talk, often in derogatory terms to his companymen. With a pinched face and narrow eyes that were not to be trusted, Selley had already become known for possessing a mouth that never stopped. In the rapid series of shots, the mouthy recruit found something he couldn't talk his way out of, the first in a number of such predicaments Selley was to encounter in boot camp.

Four desks were situated around the periphery of the inoculation room. A hospital corpsman—the naval equivalent of a male nurse—sat at each, a number of syringes and dozens of needles arranged in front of him. Moving around the room in a clockwise rotation, we shirtless recruits would stop at the first desk, receive a shot in the left arm, then move to the second desk, do an about face, get another in the right, step to the third, about face, another jab, and so on.

As Selley came through the door—talking, of course—his offensive voice started rising in volume, and after the first shot, he began talking even faster than usual. On his way to the second desk, his words shot out faster and faster and he began to stray out of line, weaving toward the open space between the line of recruits that ringed the room. Every eye was on him as his incessant babble became incoherent. Wandering aimlessly in the center of the room and chattering like a monkey on amphetamines, Selley stopped and began to reel in place, as if his feet were nailed to the floor and his body caught in a crosswind. His eyes rolled up in his head, his voice trailed off into a gratifying nothing, and he fell like a stone.

Even the corpsmen grinned when Selley hit the floor; some of us laughed out loud. As the line continued to move around the room, and around Selley's unconscious body that lay untended between us, somehow the sting of the shots seemed less painful.

Uniforms. Finally, we were to be issued navy clothing, the badge of a sailor. We all lined up for this procedure, of course. By now we had begun to laugh about lining up for everything, wisecracking that it looked like we'd be standing in line for half of our military careers, little realizing that in years to come our facetious prophesy would turn out to be more reality than joke.

Again, rather than feeling humiliated at losing our familiar civilian clothing, we were happy to see it go. We would proudly don our uniforms, never again to be chastised and belittled as novice R & O.

Our new clothes didn't fit; all too big. Our pant legs, baggy and loose, had to be rolled up several inches, and our flaccid shirts hung on us like entrants in a scarecrow contest. Our white navy hats, which should have been perching on our brows at a cocky angle as we had envisioned, touched only the tops of our slick scalps, drooping down over our ears like an inverted soup bowl balanced atop a fencepost. You could slap your buddy's hat sideways and it would spin on his head like a tilt-a-whirl, a short-lived form of recreation that Chief Loibl put a stop to.

We were also issued seabags in which to store our personal gear, and we would learn the hard way why we were all issued outsized clothing—because when we washed them, by hand, they shrank several sizes. Along with shoes, which did not shrink, a few garments in our seabags were actually issued to fit: dress blues, which had to be dry cleaned instead of washed, and our heavy navy peacoats.

And as for shoes, when the outsized Encalarde stepped up to be fitted, the petty officer whose sole job was to measure feet stared at his in disbelief. After every sailor who worked in the clothing warehouse had come over to have a look at Encalarde's feet, the officer in charge was notified that they had found a sailor with feet larger than any shoes the navy owned. After the dismayed officer came to see for himself, Encalarde was allowed to keep his civilian footwear while the navy had two pairs of custom shoes made for him.

Shortly before being issued navy clothing, our company of green recruits had been moved out of the temporary R & O quarters and into a permanent barracks. Unmistakable pride lit up our faces as we moved into the second story of one of the long buildings. Never mind that the barracks looked exactly like all the others on the base; this one was ours.

Feeling cockier with each new step toward sailordom, we felt sure that after donning our new dungaree uniforms and shipping our civvies home, we would finally look like a real company. Senior recruits—that was my thought.

However, the best laid plans . . . As we marched along, bent double and grunting under the weight of heavily packed seabags, which we lugged by means of canvas straps that cut into our shoulders, our bulbous pant legs rolled up as high as six inches, our outsized shirts pulled around our waists and tucked into our pants in ungainly folds, our white hats tottering on our bald heads like trash can lids, we didn't exactly resemble a gathering of old salts.

The other companies still hollered "R & O" at us.

But not to worry: rifles came next. Oh, to be issued my rifle. I had grown up shooting guns of all kinds, and could not wait to get my hands on that beautiful piece of artillery, to hold it, caress it, become one with it.

The armory overwhelmed me—row upon row of racked rifles. I'd never seen so many firearms in all my life. Then a petty officer handed me one; it was heavy, about ten pounds, and when I raised it to my shoulder, it had a good feel. Instinctively, I knew this rifle would shoot well; that is, until I discovered it was not a rifle at all. Once upon a time, it had been a rifle—back in World War I—but the ancient barrel had since been plugged and the action rendered useless. The pieces, as we were instructed to call them instead of rifles, could neither be loaded nor fired. A guy standing next to me muttered something about it being the worst piece he'd ever had.

So, my "rifle," along with thousands of others that recruits carried nearly everywhere they went, was no more than a weight to be used in drills to build up our bodies—more a barbell than a firearm. Oh, I *would* learn to hold the piece, in more positions than I enjoyed; and I would become one with it, because the damnable thing and I were inseparable from that moment on. I never again felt the urge to caress it.

We soon learned how to wash our clothes and, surprisingly, they shrunk to fit quite well, finally ridding ourselves of the last vestiges of R & O. And though every day was long and strenuous, with each one I felt closer to becoming a real sailor. But I dreaded the nights. I still could not sleep. However exhausted, sore, and stiff my body felt at the end of the day, when the lights went out I lay in my lower bunk for hours, listening to the sounds of seventy-nine other guys sleeping.

Experimenting with lying in a hundred different positions, forcing myself to lie in a single position, and trying to will myself to sleep, all without success, I strove to figure out what could be bothering me badly enough to keep me awake half the night under such exhausting conditions. I didn't talk to anyone about the problem, not even my buddies from back home. In time I would learn the answer to my dilemma, but for the moment, even though I was a member of a large group of fellows my age all living in the same environment and all subject to the same changes, challenges, and stresses, something inside me felt very alone. A nightly battle being waged within myself, or maybe with myself.

A few days after receiving our uniforms, everyone in the company was given a battery of tests. The tests, which took several hours to complete, covered mathematics, electronics, mechanical aptitude, command of the English language, and other minor subjects. One test was called the GCT: General Classification Test. The GCT was the navy's equivalent of the IQ, and unbeknownst to us at the time, was the weightiest score of all, the most important in meeting the qualifications for many navy schools.

Chief Loibl extolled us to do our best on the tests, because our scores would follow us through all of our years in the navy. They would affect our eligibility for schools, our future assignments, and ultimately our entire careers, both inside and outside the military. The C.O.'s advice turned out to be more prophetic than I would ever have dreamed.

After finishing the tests, we wouldn't learn the results for another week or so. That didn't really matter; we were kept too busy to worry about them anyway.

Now that we had had our physicals and inoculations, been issued our gear, and got the testing behind us, drills began in earnest. As the short, mustachioed Chief Wimberly had warned us the first day, we learned to march, and march, and march. And when we weren't marching, we were standing in formation on that endless field of asphalt: the grinder.

Standing on a high platform in front of us, a drill instructor—a chief, of course—would glower at the lot of us while barking orders over a loudspeaker. We recruits, along with our beloved World War I pieces that would not shoot, would practice a lengthy set of drills week after week, day after day, and hour after agonizing hour. These drills—surely invented by some warped individual whose parents had kept him locked in a closet between regular floggings with a rubber hose—made no sense whatsoever. We endured the daily agony, however, twisting and bending our bodies to the endless, repetitious, mind-grating growls of the drill instructors, right up to the final day of boot camp.

We also practiced a garish, strutting thing called "Right shoulder arms and pass in review," a maneuver in which the company marched in a large oval on the grinder to get into position, then high-stepped past the podium, snapped our eyes to the right, and presented arms—an exhibition that consisted of saluting the drill instructor with our harmless rifles. We engaged in this inane spectacle until the mere mention of it was likely to induce nausea or an involuntary bowel movement.

For now, the answer as to why we were spending a dispropor-tionate amount of time performing nonsensical drills lay several weeks in our future. In the meantime, we continued to hone these useless skills, and wonder what they were all about.

Although it seemed we had no time for anything else, somehow we managed to do far more than just march and practice military drills. We also learned to scrub our clothes, by hand, on great concrete wash tables, and suspend each garment from a clothesline in a very meticulous manner, tying it to the line by short lengths of white cord called clothes stops—the same cord by which our pieces hung from the bottom rails of our bunks at night.

Like the clothes that hung just so-so on the lines, our pieces were tied to our bunks in a certain manner, and if the C.O. found a piece hung a half-inch off center or tied by a nonregulation knot, the guilty recruit was made to sleep with his piece, clinging to the cold metal barrel and hard wooden stock in an amorous manner as if he couldn't wait for the lights to go out. A perfect memory refresher; I don't recall anyone ever sleeping with his piece more than once.

Learning fire-fighting techniques was loads of fun. We had to put out raging fires—real ones—and breathe in smoke and ash until just before our throats became totally clogged and we died. And in a chamber filled with tear gas, which we entered after donning gas masks, we were ordered to remove them and stand in place without wiping our eyes until the instructor allowed us to stumble blindly out the door. The instructor came out last, removing his gas mask only after he had closed the door to the chamber and waited for the air to clear. He seemed to enjoy his job.

We went to the firing range one day—and one day only—to learn to shoot real rifles. Much more fun than tear gas and flames.

Most of us thought we knew the meaning of the word "clean," but the navy taught us a whole new definition. Every morning after breakfast, we lined up on the grinder for a personnel inspection. A chief, or sometimes two or three chiefs, always from different companies than our own, would walk down the line, stop in front of each recruit, and give us a thorough once-over from head to toe. Our white hats had to be free of even the slightest discoloration around the inside band—so pristine that when we wore them to the mess hall for breakfast we gently balanced them on our heads without pulling them down snug. Pulling your hat down would cause a slight ring to form on the inside—a ring nearly invisible to the naked eye, but not to the microscopic vision of the inspecting chiefs.

They even inspected our "weapons." As if the apex of lunacy had not been to issue us those refugees from the scrap heap in the first place, they trumped their own insanity by requiring us to keep the things looking like new, and they carefully examined them to see that we did.

And most of us thought we came to boot camp knowing how to shave. Not so. We got dunned if even a bit of fuzz could be seen in open sunlight—a problem for many recruits, because fuzz is about all their young faces would produce.

Every shoe had to be spit-shined, with one exception: Encalarde's. The inspecting chiefs all considered themselves quite witty, and the tall African American's whaleboat feet never failed to catch their attention and to elicit comments. And not a single one of them ever noticed that his giant shoes were not spit-shined. Encalarde got a daily laugh out of foiling the inspectors, and the rest of us vicariously enjoyed our role as accomplices in his little game.

Failing a personnel inspection generally invited some imaginative form of punishment. A particularly forgetful individual was once caught at inspection with a full pack of cigarettes stuck inside the waistband of his pants—an infraction so major as to border on insanity. Chief Loibl stood the young recruit in front of the company, at attention, and lowered a large trash can upside down over his head. We then watched the fellow smoke twenty cigarettes inside the inverted trash can, standing at attention with his arms at his sides as he puffed each one down to a miniscule butt, at which time he was allowed to move his arms enough to switch to a new one, light it from the burning butt, then snap back to attention and smoke that one down without removing it from his mouth. When the entire pack of cigarettes was thus consumed, the C.O. removed the trash can from his head and ordered him to rejoin the ranks. The recruit's face was ashen, colorless, and he was unable to move from the spot where he stood. Reeling on his feet, he made it back to his place in formation only with the aid of two of his buddies.

Each morning while the company was enduring the daily personnel inspection, our barracks was undergoing a white-gloves inspection by another group of fanatical chiefs. To fail a barracks inspection was to ensure mass punishment for the company.

We generally passed our barracks inspections with few problems, but the company in the barracks below us didn't fare so well. Wimberly, the short chief who had marched us to chow that first day, was C.O. of the company that occupied the ground floor. With his thin mustache, black glowering eyes, and diabolical methods of punishment, Chief Wimberly became known as Little Hitler.

One day when Wimberly's barracks-cleaning crew neglected to empty the trash cans prior to inspection, and failed as a result, he ordered the guilty group to climb inside a dumpster and stand at attention while the rest of his company poured the contents of the trash cans on their heads.

Another infamous incident that showcased the satanic imagination of Little Hitler involved several sets of dungarees found hung on the clotheslines in a nonregulation manner. After lights out in the barracks and his company was sleeping, the round little chief quietly removed the errant sets of dungarees from the clotheslines and tossed them onto the concrete patio, which still held a film of standing water from a scrubbing earlier that evening. After strewing the dungarees across the wet patio, Little Hitler got his company out of bed, made them dress in full uniform, run outside, and fall into formation. He then proceeded to march them back and forth over the clothes until they were thoroughly sopped, twisted, and filthy.

The patios were kept well lit at night, and when we heard the marching going on below, several of us crept out of bed and watched in wonder as Little Hitler's company tromped back and forth over their own clothes. Chief Loibl was tough, but Wimberly made him look like a scoutmaster.

Our most difficult inspection was one that occurred not daily but about every week or so—the bag inspection. A procedure that required a great amount of memorization as well as skill, the bag inspection involved every piece of gear that we owned. Everything—down to your navy-issued soap dish and the soap itself—was laid out on your bunk in a specific manner. The clean sheet on your mattress, upon which every piece lay, had to be stretched tight enough to bounce a fifty-cent coin that an inspecting chief was sure to drop on it.

Every piece of clothing, every handkerchief, towel, wash-cloth—anything made of fabric—had to be folded in one way and one way only. And all the individual items, whether fold-able or not, were spaced in a maddeningly exact arrangement that covered the bunk from one end to the other.

There were no written instructions for laying out a bag inspection, or even a diagram to consult. A chief whose job was teaching this dubious art came into the barracks one day, told all eighty of us to gather around one bunk, and do our best to watch as he showed us how to stretch the sheet as taut as a circus tent, fold each and every piece neater than our grandmothers could have done, and lay them in a measured arrangement that would have warmed the heart of every obsessive-compulsive patient in a mental ward. The entire lesson, which the instructor covered just one time, took several hours to complete.

Hailey, the pale, skinny recruit who lived in a perpetual state of exhaustion, couldn't resist a chance to grab some rest. While the chief was explaining the hopelessly meticulous procedure, Hailey sat down on a bench behind the crowd of recruits who were standing tall in order to observe the chief's lesson. His head slowly dropping to the table, Hailey fell sound asleep. Several of us noticed him sleeping, and a couple of us tried to wake him up, but he just rolled his eyes and closed them again.

A few days after the chief's lengthy instruction session, we had our first bag inspection. Since all eighty of us had to be inspected, several chiefs came in together—about four or five of them—and spread themselves throughout the barracks. Knowing that a bag layout was a complicated task to learn, in general the chiefs weren't too tough on us. When one of them found something wrong, he would point it out and show the recruit how to correct it. If he found three or four things wrong, he'd likely get gruff with the errant sailor-to-be and maybe a bit sarcastic.

When the entire company was involved in some kind of procedure—any kind—the inspecting chiefs, or our own C.O., tended to single out someone for special treatment: most commonly a public butt chewing. The individuals they singled out tended to vary somewhat, to ensure that no one was allowed to escape unscathed. Some recruits, however—the ones who became known as screw-ups—got swooped upon with terrible regularity.

We were still pretty green the morning of our first bag inspection, and most of us hadn't yet learned how the singling-out process worked. Some unfortunates went all the way through boot camp without figuring it out. The more observant among us, however, started to see a pattern forming that very day, the moment a chief caught sight of Hailey's bag layout.

Having slept through the instruction period, Hailey had attempted to arrange his gear with virtually no knowledge of where to begin. His layout looked absolutely windblown, and with his bunk being a top one, it stood out for all the world to see. Each piece of clothing was lopped over and around itself in a semi-square pile to which the term folded did not apply, and the entire array lay on the sagging sheet in such a haphazard manner as to make the greenest recruit cringe at the sight.

Hailey stood at drooped attention, his eyes downcast as the inspecting chief stopped, rested his hands on his hips, and surveyed the catastrophe before him. Slowly the chief's eyes wandered over the bunk, from one end to the other, then at Hailey, then back at the bunk. With his eyes coming to a slow simmer and his head beginning to shake in astonishment, he turned and hollered at the other chiefs.

"Hey, come here and take a look at this one!"

The other chiefs moved toward Hailey's bunk like sharks to blood.

They stopped short, surveying the scene in disbelief. All eyes in the company focused on Hailey, standing at the end of his bunk, neither moving nor looking up. Then the chiefs began to shake their heads, and as one, they turned and looked at Hailey.

"Is this what you call a bag layout?" one of them barked.

Hailey replied in a mumble, his answer inaudible.

The chief roared. "Look at me when you talk to me, son, and speak up, so I can hear you." Then he repeated, "Is this what you call a bag layout?"

Hailey raised his head and looked at the chief, his eyes neither afraid nor defiant, simply distant, dead. "Yes, sir," he said in a toneless voice.

The chief smirked and laughed, and I felt something rise in me that I knew I had to quell: an ingrained hatred of sarcasm.

The chief picked up a gruesomely folded piece of Hailey's clothing—a white jumper—and holding it by the collar, shook it out until it hung straight. Then he picked up another twisted mass and held it out to Hailey. "Look at this," he said. "My dog can scratch up a rug and leave it in better shape than that." Laughing at his own joke, the chief threw the two jumpers against the wall next to Hailey's bunk. They settled to the floor in a heap.

At that point, all the inspecting chiefs descended on Hailey's gear. With two or three standing on either side of the bunk, they picked things up, piece by piece, shook them out, made sarcastic remarks, and slung them to the floor with the rest. When the shapeless pile of clothing grew to around two feet high, one of the chiefs ordered Hailey to sit on it.

Hailey trudged over to the pile, sat down on it, leaned forward with his arms hanging between his legs, and looked at the floor. The chiefs gaily continued to throw clothing, washcloths, shoes, etc. in his direction. Soon Hailey was nearly covered—underwear hanging from his head, pants draped over his drooping shoulders, towels slung across his lap, socks all over him—a terrible thing to watch.

Hailey's lifeless face never changed expression, and he never looked up.

Chief Loibl, our C.O., was not one of the inspectors. He was standing in the barracks, but merely as an observer while the other chiefs evaluated his company. Loibl's face remained expressionless as he watched the sideshow of Hailey's humiliation.

Hailey was a screw-up of the first degree, and we all knew that his actions would bring disfavor upon the company as a whole. Nevertheless, I began to feel empathy for the little guy—a rare emotion in the survival world of boot camp—and I sensed that many of the others felt the same.

Chief Loibl kept Hailey in the company for another week and gave him a second chance to pass a bag inspection. He was the first to go to the scrounge company, 4013.

Being average height and size—5'11" and 160 pounds—I concluded it would be easy to keep a low profile in boot camp. Follow orders, don't make waves, and slide on through. Impossibly naïve.

Sometime during the second week, it came my turn to be singled out. We were standing in formation, at attention, when the C.O. walked up behind me and barked in my ear—something about the way I was standing, holding my piece, or some such triviality. As I jerked to even more rigid attention, Loibl went on, loudly, "That 74 GCT is screwing you up, Penley!"

We hadn't yet gotten our test scores, but the C.O. had them. I hadn't known until that moment that my GCT score was 74, nor did I realize the significance of it. The GCT had a maximum score of 75.

Chief Loibl had either simply found a reason to make it my turn to be jumped on, or, fearing that my high GCT might be an indication of arrogance, he decided to attack a potential problem before it started.

The tirade continued. "Are you listening to me, Penley? Do you think you're smarter than the rest of us?"

"Yes, sir!" I replied.

"Yes, sir, what?"

"Yes, sir, I'm listening to you, sir."

"Do you think you're smarter than the rest of us?"

"No, sir!"

"No, sir, what?"

"No, sir, I don't think I'm smarter than the rest of you, sir."

"That's good," Loibl said, "because you've got the same job to do here as the rest of us, and you'd better damn well get with it."

"Yes, sir," I said.

The C.O. was pretty smart himself. Now the rest of the company knew my GCT, and they too would be watching for me to act arrogant. Peer pressure, which tended to invoke self-policing within the company, was part of Loibl's scheme. In a few short sentences, he had instilled a bit of doubt, forcing upon me the task of proving that I could pull my own weight and be one of the guys. Thanks a lot, sir.

Although I had completed high school, my grades were anything but sterling. In fact, my grandfather's death had affected my attitude so badly that it took me an extra year to graduate. My buddies from back home—Lacy, O'Rear, and Brookshire—all knew about my high-school record, and they were as surprised as I was to learn my GCT score.

A couple of days after the C.O. confronted me—practically accusing me of being intellectually arrogant—we all received our test scores. Richard Lacy, a straightforward, no-nonsense guy whom I had known since we were little kids, never failed to speak his mind. After we were given our scores, Lacy cornered me in private.

"Penley, do you know you have the highest GCT in the company?"

"I figured I did, after what Chief Loibl said," I answered.

"Everybody's talking about it," he said. "You've probably got the highest GCT on the whole base."

Oh no, I thought. Considering the C.O.'s attitude, my test score might end up being more of a liability than anything else.

"Well," I said to Lacy, "you remember what a screw-up I was in high school, so nobody needs to worry about me being a brain of some kind."

"Yeah, I know," he said, shaking his head. "I never knew you had any smarts at all."

I looked at him with a wry grin. "Neither did I."

Along with drills, body-building exercises, washing clothes, and inspections, we had regular classes to attend—military regulations, law, ship design, armament, shipboard living, rules of the sea, and other basic information needed to become sailors. At the end of each week, we all took a written test that covered the most recent classes. Failure of these tests was one way a recruit could get set back.

I found the tests easy, and most of the other guys in the company did too. In fact, because of the C.O.'s warning about appearing arrogant, at times I purposely marked some questions wrong to ensure that my weekly score would not stand out.

In general I was doing well, but instead of sleeping and getting the rest I needed, I was still fighting the nightly battle within myself. Then one night as I lay in bed, somewhere between the second and third weeks, I began to think—to take an inventory of my life, and of myself.

My grandfather, the man I had called Dad, carried the rawhide name of George Blizzard, and no name could have fit him better. Despite having only a third-grade education and raising a family through years of hard times, including the Great Depression, Dad had doggedly pursued a lifelong dream of becoming a cattle rancher. At the age of sixty-eight, flat broke, he gave it one last try. I was two when Dad was sixty-eight, and I watched him and helped him as, through his seventies and early eighties, he built up his ranch, working harder and taking more financial risks than most men ever dared at any age. A real-life John Wayne.

I was sixteen when Dad died, and he had done it. He owned four thousand acres of grassland, a herd of cattle, and didn't owe a penny to anyone.

I had never been a good student, and when Dad got cancer, a year and a half before he died, Mom and I had to run the ranch without his help. My less-than-average grades dropped even further. And after Dad was gone, and Mom and I moved to town, my attitude suffered a crisis that I nearly didn't survive. I went wild—fighting, drinking, racing cars, wrecking cars—generally becoming irresponsible, uncontrollable, and a danger to myself and others. Hence, the extra year spent finishing high school.

And here I was in boot camp. In the time since Dad had died, I'd never really looked back and thought seriously about my growing-up years, or the confusing, upsetting period since his death. I was still too young to appreciate how unique my childhood had been and too immature to properly assess it all, but somehow my situation, and the internal battle in which I found myself, demanded that I look back seriously over those years and face what had happened—that I try and come to grips with my past.

Just lying there thinking about my own world and where I had come from, I began to feel a calm, an absence of agitation that I had not felt in years, and although I didn't fully realize it at the time, a self-confidence that I had never known.

I could do anything those chiefs ordered me to do, and it certainly wasn't hard to figure out what they wanted; they screamed it in our ears every day. And yes, they were tough, but if they thought they could get to me with their growling, swaggering, and posturing—I'd grown up with a man who ate guys like them for breakfast.

I rolled over in my bunk, and fell sound asleep.

Chapter Three

Boot Camp: The Fun

When reveille sounded the next morning, I sat up in bed and shouted through the barracks. "Drop your cocks and grab your socks! You guys want to be sailors, don't you?"

Every bleary eye that could focus on me appeared to question whether I was undergoing some sort of seizure or had simply gone berserk. Until then I had been keeping up with the others reasonably well but not with any special enthusiasm. Feeling an unusually ravenous appetite, I was dressed in minutes and eager to head out into the predawn darkness for our waking-up march to the mess hall. And as for wise-cracking—practically an organized competition among recruits—no one could compete with me that morning.

Nelson Brookshire, a hometown friend who went about life in an unflappable, eternally good-natured manner, just smiled at me. Joel O'Rear laughed out loud. Richard Lacy, the quiet one, sat down beside me at breakfast. After waiting for me to finish telling a joke, Lacy leaned over and said, "What's going on with you, Penley?"

"I'm having fun," I replied. "All these hard-asses are trying to do is teach us something, and find out if we're wimpy enough to be broken."

Lacy chuckled. "You just now figuring that out?"

For reasons I'll never fully understand, I felt as though I had experienced some sort of rapid metamorphosis, an instant adjustment, and from that day forward, boot camp became fun—at times, hilarious. Why? Because the poor slobs who could never learn to stop banging their heads against that disciplinary wall and laugh off the BS—and boot camp was full of them—provided nonstop entertainment for the rest of us. It was the best show in town, and it was free.

I became a clown—a red, white, and blue, regulation navy clown—but a clown nevertheless. I even caught Chief Loibl looking at me occasionally, not with concern, but simply with interest and sometimes a faint smile—a touch of amusement that I wasn't supposed to see. I worked hard, studied hard, and stopped intentionally marking some of my weekly test questions wrong. I aced most of the tests, but the C.O. never again mentioned my GCT score. In fact, he seemed to pretty well leave me on my own from that point on.

Going to sick bay was an experience that, if one was not sick to begin with, he would be—provided he survived the ordeal. Having heard horror stories from other recruits who had run this medical gauntlet, I vowed never to go there.

Sick call was held in the morning shortly after breakfast, and uniquely, it was something the company C.O. could not keep you from attending if you wanted to go. In order to prepare for sick bay a recruit had to pack his ditty bag—toothbrush, toothpaste, soap, extra skivvies, socks, etc.—in case he was sent to the hospital.

A strange, embarrassing malady began to bother me. My nipples got sore. They would sting as my T-shirt rubbed against them, and considering our nonstop physical activity, the rubbing became a constant irritation. My nipples grew red and continued to get sorer and sorer. Finally, with great trepidation, I decided to take my problem to sick bay. I didn't tell Chief Loibl why I needed to go and, thank God, he didn't ask.

After returning from the mess hall that morning, I packed my ditty bag—a small canvas sack that hung over the shoulder—and headed for battalion headquarters. A window in the side of the headquarters building served as a check-in point for recruits going to sick bay.

It was a cold morning, but not cold enough that the C.O.s would allow us to wear our coats. As I approached the sick bay check-in window, I saw a dozen or more recruits standing around outside with ditty bags hanging over their shoulders. They were shivering, coughing, blowing their noses, or just plain looking miserable.

Inside the window stood a first-class hospital corpsman—an older sailor, sour looking, red eyed, and obviously suffering from a hangover. The corpsman suspected every individual reporting to sick bay of being a wimp who could not take the rigors of boot camp, or worse, of being a malingerer who was just trying to get out of work for the day.

Since I neither looked nor sounded sick, the corpsman gave me a highly suspicious look and asked pleasantly, "And what might be wrong with *you?*"

Trying hard to maintain contact with the man's accusing eyes, I said, "My nipples are sore, sir."

He didn't say a word for a while, just stared. Then, with a degree of cynicism that would have invoked the envy of a criminal prosecutor, he asked, "Your *nipples* are sore?"

"Yes, sir," I said. "They've been sore for several days, and my clothes rubbing against them makes them hurt all the time."

The corpsman shook his head, wrote down my name, serial number, and company, and told me to go stand with the rest of the ditty-bag brigade. After a few minutes, he called me back to the window and pointed at the waiting recruits. "Line up that bunch of slackards," he said, "and march their worthless butts down to sick bay."

I gathered the group of sickly recruits into some semblance of formation and began marching them toward sick bay. What a sight we made—a makeshift company of guys marching along, coughing, hacking, spitting, limping, or supporting an injured arm with the other—and me stepping along beside them calling cadence. America's finest we were not.

At this point, I was beginning to doubt my sanity, and certainly my judgment, at having decided to participate in sick call, especially with the particular problem I was experiencing. My concerns proved not unfounded as we reached the infamous boot camp sick bay.

It was still cold and, with typical military reasoning, we were required to wait outside, seated on metal folding chairs.

A second-class corpsman—a pudgy wiseacre who was trying to compete with the older one at battalion headquarters for the cynicism award—sat at a desk, also outside, facing the group of sicklings. The corpsman would motion each of us to come up, one at a time, and thrust a thermometer in our mouth. When he had thus taken and recorded all of our temperatures and we were again seated on cold chairs in the cold air, he began to call us up individually and ask about our ailments. To some he simply handed a package of pills, droned out some instructions, and sent them back to their seats. Others, whom the corpsman decided needed to see the doctor, were told to sit back down and continue to wait.

Then came my turn. The corpsman called me up to his desk, looked me up and down, and asked what my problem was. "My nipples are sore, sir," I said, keeping my voice low in an attempt to conceal this information from the others.

The corpsman looked incredulous. Leaning back and knitting his hands across his ample middle, he spoke, loudly. "Got something wrong with your tits?"

"I . . . guess so, sir," I answered.

"What's wrong with 'em?" he asked, a smirk on his face and unkind humor in his eyes.

When I haltingly explained, he managed not to laugh out loud and told me to sit down and wait to see the doctor. The others were all watching me as I returned to my chair. I did not look at them.

The corpsman was still grinning as I walked past him to go inside and see the doctor. The doctor turned out to be a young officer who appeared knowledgeable and maybe even polite, a possibility that gave me a momentary spark of hope. But, as the events up to that point had so aptly demonstrated, this wasn't my day.

When I explained my problem, for what seemed the thousandth time that morning, the doctor looked at me as if I might have just told him that my genitals had taken flight. He told me to remove my shirt and T-shirt, then bent down and began to scrutinize my nipples. The word uncomfortable does not begin to describe my feelings at that moment.

The doctor flattened his palms and, laying them an inch or so beneath my nipples, began to push upward, first with one hand and then the other. "Does that hurt?" he asked.

"No, sir," I answered. "It only hurts when something rubs directly on them." Oh, God, I prayed. Don't let him touch them.

He didn't. He straightened up, looked into my eyes, and asked gruffly, "What are you doing, son, growing breasts?"

"I . . . hope not, sir," I stammered.

After grinning wryly at his own joke, the doctor looked thoughtful for a moment, and then to my utter surprise, he came up with the answer. "You guys wash your clothes by hand, don't you?" he asked.

"Yes, sir," I replied.

"And you rinse the soap out of them by hand?"

"Yes, sir."

With that he picked up my T-shirt and rubbed the fabric between his fingers. "This shirt feels stiff," he said, "like maybe you didn't get all the soap rinsed out of it. That could be why it's irritating your nipples."

Instantly, I knew he was right. "That's it, sir. I'm sure that's what's been making them sore."

The doctor smiled—an act I wouldn't have guessed him capable of—and said, "Rinse out your T-shirts better and see if that works. If it doesn't, come back and see me again."

"Thank you, sir," I said.

I turned to leave, insanely happy to be doing so, and walked back outside to join the waiting crowd. Sidewise chuckles and half-hidden grins masked nothing as I returned to my cold chair. Several laughed out loud when the corpsman asked me if the doctor had got my tits fixed up.

When everyone had either gotten pills from the corpsman or seen the doctor, I was again ordered to march the sick, the lame, and the lazy back to battalion headquarters. Although most of my temporary company didn't feel well, and some were in pain, I had a difficult time maintaining discipline within the afflicted ranks. I guess it's hard to take a guy seriously when you know he has a problem with his tits.

Back at the window, I again faced the first-class corpsman. His breath smelled like putrid whiskey and he still looked hung over. Along with a red mushy nose and lines in his face that looked like forty miles of bad road, the old corpsman had a long string of hash marks on the left forearm of his uniform, each of which represented four years in the navy. After the harrowing morning I had suffered at the hands of the base medical team, I badly wanted to ask him why he hadn't made chief in all those years. Fortunately, I managed to suppress that suicidal temptation. Just imagining the look that such a question would have wrought on his face made me feel better; something in me still wishes I had asked it.

The corpsman waved his arm out the window, dismissing us. "All right," he said wearily, "get outta here."

Running was not allowed unless one was ordered to do so, but I whirled and charged back to the barracks like a wild animal released from a cage, knowing that I would not return to sick bay if my nipples turned green and fell off.

As the weeks went by, we spent more and more time on the grinder, often doing drills along with other companies or watching them march close by. Occasionally we saw 4013, their ragged, humiliating flag proceeding them, their hats down over their ears, their eyes on the ground. We always looked for Hailey, but with their hats turned down, an individual face was difficult to pick out.

We lost other members of our company to 4013, but since they were mostly slobs who couldn't keep themselves clean enough to pass inspections, we didn't much care. We never saw them again, never spoke of them, and soon forgot their names. But not Hailey. Strangely, although we hadn't seen the little guy since he'd been sent to 4013 in about the second or third week, we talked about Hailey a lot and wondered how he was doing. Whenever we passed the scrounge company, we'd all compare notes to see if anyone had caught sight of him. No one ever did.

A popular punishment among C.O.s was called the duck walk—a painful, stiffening endeavor for the offender but highly entertaining for spectators. Duck walking consisted of squatting as low at the knees as possible, folding your hands behind your head, and propelling yourself forward in a three-foot-high position. This forced the bent legs, the body, and the folded arms to oscillate right and left as well as forward and back as the hapless individual waddled along behind the rest of the company. Errant recruits were sometimes made to duck walk behind their marching company for an entire day.

One chief ordered a fellow to duck walk in great circles around several companies that were practicing drills together on the grinder—not only making a long trip with each round, but this creative C.O. required the guy to quack as he went. The recruit's loud quacking added a considerable measure of levity to the otherwise monotonous drills, especially after his voice began to crack and he really did sound like a duck.

Even the mess hall could be fun. One had to be careful about having fun in the mess hall, however, because a chief petty officer was always assigned to eat there with the recruits. His presence alone—seated by himself at a small table near the end of the chow line—served to ensure order and a somewhat quieter atmosphere. A single recruit, his only assignment being to serve the chief, stood directly behind him at parade rest, waiting to bring him a cup of coffee, a second helping, a bowl of dessert, or whatever else the man might desire.

Sitting alone at his table, the chief looked like the king of the mess hall, and that was the idea. Whenever he looked up from his plate, he surveyed the room like a predator. Recruits hardly dared look in his direction, and nobody ever spoke a word to him.

Since all the guys who worked in the mess hall on any given week belonged to the same company, it didn't do to get on their bad side. At lunch one day, I got into an argument with a server behind the line concerning the size of the portion of food he had spooned onto my tray. This argument started a chain reaction. The server passed a furtive look to the next guy down, who also gave me a very small portion of what he was serving. Soon, all the servers saw what was going on, and each gave me an extra small amount as I passed by his station.

I began to tire of the servers' little game.

The last recruit, at the end of the chow line, was dishing out peas. Reaching into the deep tray, he spooned out exactly four peas and deftly dropped them onto my tray. "Is that all the peas I get?" I asked him.

"Yep," the server said with a wicked smile. "That's all you get."

The hallowed chief's table, and King Chief himself, sat only about fifteen feet from where I stood at that moment.

"Okay," I said to the smug recruit, then turned and headed directly for the chief's table. The chief hadn't noticed the cute game the servers had been pulling on me, and, intent on eating his lunch, he didn't see me coming. The pea server, however, along with the rest of his company, immediately noted where I was heading. They stopped their serving and stood frozen in place, watching me like a covey of quail about to take flight.

The chief was a large, rotund man with a red puffy face and a heavy scowl. I walked up to his table, holding my tray in front of me, and said, "Excuse me, sir."

"Yeah?" he said, wiping his mouth with a napkin and glowering up at me.

"Is this all the peas I'm supposed to get?" I asked, pointing at the four tiny green balls dwarfed in a compartment of my tray.

"Hell no!" the chief said. "Who told you that's all the peas you could have?"

I turned and pointed at the kid behind the line, whose countenance had taken on the look of a terror-stricken primate braced for the charge of a rhinoceros.

"He did," I said righteously. "He told me I could have only four peas."

And the rhino charged. Jumping to his feet and throwing his napkin on the table, the chief stomped up to the server of peas. I dutifully followed along behind, holding my half-filled tray before me.

The chief bellowed. "Did you tell this guy he could only have four peas?"

The recruit reeled, as if the very force of the chief's voice might blow him off his feet. "Yes . . . sir," he said meekly.

The chief leaned forward in a menacing stance. "Just who do you think you are, maggot?" And the chief went on and on and on. He didn't just chew the server's butt out; he chewed around it until it fell out.

When finally the chief began to wind down, he turned to me and said, "Step up here, son, and tell this little butthead to give you all the peas you want."

I didn't have to tell the kid anything; he readily dished me out a spoonful that couldn't have held another pea. Before the chief turned to leave, I said, "Excuse me, sir. There is something else."

"What's that?" the chief asked.

Saying nothing, I simply held out my tray and pointed at the other small portions I'd been given back up the line. The chief went livid—again. Pointing an arm up the line, he said, "Go on back through again, son, and get you some more chow." Then he hollered, nay, roared, at the line of servers. "Give this man all the food he wants, or I'll have every one of you on report!"

With that the chief huffed back to his table, and I began making my way through the chow line a second time, in reverse. Grinning broadly, the line of recruits waiting to be served all stepped back to give me room. And I, moving backward through the line and occasionally asking for more than one heaping spoonful, was probably served the largest tray of food in naval history. I smiled and thanked them all for their generous servings. They did not smile back.

I believe the King Chief witnessed another indiscretion in the mess hall but chose to disregard it. Selley, the talkative, offensive guy who had entertained us all by passing out during our initial inoculations, never seemed to learn the merits of keeping his mouth shut.

Medina, a small Hispanic fellow in our company who spoke perfect English, was Selley's opposite. Polite and mannerly, Medina went about life doing the best job he could and never bothering a soul. He smiled often and nodded to others in greeting, but as opposed to Selley's constant yammering, Medina spoke little.

The differences between Selley's and Medina's mannerisms—incessant talking versus a polite silence—came to a head one day in the mess hall. There was no reason for this ever to become an issue, and, as was generally the case when a meaningless conflict arose, Selley started it.

I happened to be sitting next to Medina that day, the young Latino being a pleasant fellow to eat with. Though I normally tried to avoid sitting anywhere near Selley, he chose a seat directly across the table from Medina.

The three of us ate in silence for a few strained moments, and then, as predictable as the sun rising in the east, Selley shot off his mouth. "Medina, why don't you ever talk?"

Medina didn't answer.

"Don't you know how to speak English?" Selley asked with a smirk.

Medina continued eating, totally ignoring Selley.

This lack of response delighted Selley. With a gleeful smile, he continued to badger Medina in the same racially slanted manner. Medina continued to eat.

When Medina's tray was still about half-filled with food, and Selley's insulting mouth running at full tilt, the little Hispanic quietly laid his silverware on the table, picked up his tray, and flipped it toward Selley, flinging its contents across the table with perfect aim.

In an instant, Selley looked worse than the dirty tray man: food splattered all over him, large globs stuck to his face. He did stop talking for a moment, and then, looking down at himself incredulously, he said, "I can't believe it. . . . I can't believe it. . . . I can't believe you did that!"

Looking across the table at Medina, who was smiling and gathering up his silverware, Selley pled for an answer. "Why did you do that?"

I looked around to check out the chief's table and saw the King Chief looking in the opposite direction; purposely, it appeared. Undoubtedly he had figured Selley out for himself and was probably trying not to laugh out loud.

Shaking his head in amazement at Medina's silent retaliation, Selley wiped the food off his face and continued babbling about it. Without breaking his smile, Medina stood up, picked up his tray, and walked away. I followed him out, laughing so hard I nearly fell down.

The rural Colorado boys—O'Rear, Lacy, Brookshire, and myself—kept our noses reasonably clean, none of us getting set back or sent to 4013. By the last weeks, when it became apparent that those of us left in Company 496 were going to make it all the way, the four of us started calling ourselves "The Big C."

Everyone in the company began to feel more confident in those final weeks, even a little cocky, and sometimes it cost us.

No one was supposed to talk after lights out in the barracks, and no one ever had. Then one night a couple of guys could be heard talking, albeit quietly, down near one end of the long room. Someone spoke up and said, "Hey, you guys, knock off the crap and go to sleep."

This tough talk prompted some other wise character to pipe up, loudly. "Yeah, knock it off, maggots, and get to sleep."

Another chimed in—trying to sound even meaner than his predecessor—and the game was on. Most of the guys in the company were speaking out gruffly, one after another, each trying to outdo the one before him. Then an especially rough voice said, "You guys knock this crap off and get to sleep!"

"Boy," said a recruit from his bunk, "that one sure sounded mean."

The lights came on. The chief on night duty filled the barracks door. "You damn right that sounded mean!" he roared. We all froze in our bunks. Busted, big time.

The chief bellowed again. "Okay, if you guys got so much energy, pile your butts out of those racks and let's see if we can use some of it up."

We all jumped up and stood at the ends of our bunks, at rigid attention, attired in nothing but our skivvies. "Hit the deck," the chief said. "We're gonna start with pushups, and since you're all feeling so talkative, you're gonna count as you go. And I better not see a one of you even try to slow down till I say you can."

We went through a series of high-speed calisthenics, while counting loudly, for about forty-five minutes. Finally the chief stopped us. Again we stood at attention, but now we were panting, our skivvies soaked in sweat.

"Okay," said the chief. "Do you kiddies think you can go beddie-bye now and go to sleep?"

"Yes, sir," we all said in unison.

"I couldn't hear that very well," the chief said.

We responded with a window-shaking volume, "Yes, sir!"

"Good night, kids," the chief said, smiling as he switched off the lights and closed the door.

Chief Loibl became furious about something one late afternoon. I don't recall the nature of the transgression, or how many of us were actually guilty, but we all paid the price. And I learned something about having grown up in the country and working hard as a kid.

The C.O. marched us over to an edge of the grinder and stood us at attention. After royally chewing out the entire company, he ordered us to hold our ten-pound pieces in front of us, arms outstretched, for about a half-hour. Then, as we were beginning to think that this static holding exercise might constitute our entire punishment, Loibl told us to start pumping our pieces and counting off as we went.

Pumping your piece consisted of thrusting the heavy rifle out at arm's length in front of you, snapping it back to your chest, thrusting it high over your head, and bringing it smartly back down to your chest, counting at the top of your lungs with each movement—One! Two! Three! Four! One! Two! Three! Four! This four-motion piece-pumping exercise was repeated as rapidly as possible, with everyone standing at attention all the while.

With Chief Loibl standing off to the side, hands on hips and glowering at us, we pumped our pieces as the shadows of dusk began to move in, and continued as darkness fell and the big lights surrounding the grinder came on. Still we pumped.

We'd been going for hours now, and many began to visibly weaken. Tom Gunn, a good-natured country boy not much bigger than I, continued to pump his piece and shout the numbers as though it were no bother at all, and to my surprise, I did the same.

The night wore on, and even the biggest and strongest guys began to waver from side to side as they thrust their pieces over their heads. Some staggered forward as they pushed the heavy rifles out in front of them. Their voices began to crack as they shouted out the numbers. The C.O. hollered at them and made them straighten up, until it became impossible for them to remain standing at attention.

Some guys started to cry and finally began falling down. Loibl made them get up and continue pumping.

Tom Gunn and I remained at attention, pumping our pieces with vigor and trying to outholler one another.

When a recruit fell to the grinder a second time, Loibl would let him stay down. Finally the entire company, save Tom Gunn and me, were on their knees or their backs, tears running down their faces. To Chief Loibl's chagrin—and probably to his amazement—Gunn and I kept it up. We two country boys were having a contest and exchanging an occasional grin as we pumped and shouted.

The C.O. stood and watched as Gunn and I, standing among our exhausted, humiliated, and bawling companymen, continued our competition. Finally, when Loibl had let the two of us go for another forty-five minutes after the last man had fallen, and some of them had actually gone to sleep on the pavement, the C.O. shook his head and said, "Okay, I guess that's enough for tonight."

Gunn and I exchanged a mental high-five that Loibl didn't appear to appreciate.

Despite the many lessons Selley was dealt in boot camp, he never did learn to control his mouth. Following the incident in the mess hall when Medina showered him with a tray of food, Selley decided it was my turn to undergo a dose of insults. The time and place he chose to turn on me made sense I suppose, but, as usual, it didn't work out exactly as Selley had planned.

The company was standing at parade rest on the grinder, our ever-present pieces held by the barrels in front of us, the butts resting on the pavement at our feet. Selley was standing directly behind me, and Chief Loibl off to the side, only about fifteen feet away. Even with the C.O. standing so close, Selley began to bad-mouth me, under his breath so the chief couldn't hear.

"Think you're pretty hot stuff, don't you, Penley," Selley whispered at my back. "Think you're a big man, huh? Think you're smart, don't you?" On and on Selley went, and if Chief Loibl heard any of his remarks he didn't let it show.

The C.O. heard me, however, as did the rest of the company. When I got my fill of Selley's crap, which didn't take long, I turned my head around, looked him in the eye and said, loudly, "Selley, if you say one more word, I'm going to swing this piece and knock your teeth out."

Selley's jaw dropped, his mouth hanging open but blessedly silent. As I turned back around and again assumed parade rest, every man in the company fought to keep from laughing aloud. Chief Loibl remained expressionless, his eyes to the front.

Sometime near the end of our long nine weeks, Chief Loibl called me into his office. *Oh, my God*, I thought. To be called into the C.O.'s office usually meant something dreadful—being set back to another company, sent to 4013, or any number of horrible fates the imagination might conjure.

After I walked in, saluted, and stood at attention, the C.O. said, "At ease, Penley. Have a seat if you'd like to."

After I sat down, Chief Loibl offered me a cigarette, lit it for me, and then looked me coolly in the eyes. "I understand you're getting orders to Engineman School," he said.

"Yes, sir, I am," I replied. Because I had made high scores on my initial tests at the recruiting center, I'd been guaranteed a school of my choice.

"Why did you choose Engineman School?" the C.O. asked. "You're going to be working on diesels, air compressors, and all kinds of machinery in the engine room. With your test scores you could have gotten into electronics, sonar—anything you wanted."

"I grew up working on mechanical things, sir. In fact, we didn't even have electricity on the ranch until I was twelve. I guess that's why I chose to be an engineman."

"Well, I think you should have taken something more technical," Loibl said. "But that's done now, and it can't be changed."

"I know, sir," I said.

"If you ever get a chance at one of the navy's high-powered

schools on down the line—and you probably will—jump at it," the C.O. said.

"I will, sir."

Then the chief smiled, stood up, and shook my hand. "Good luck, Penley, and remember what I said."

"I will, sir. Thank you."

"You're welcome. Now go out there and be a good sailor."

C.O.s generally tried to hide their soft side, if they had one. I had figured Chief Loibl for a good guy; now I knew for sure. A year and a half later, I'd have reason to thank him again.

Boot camp companies competed with one another on scores of different endeavors—seamanship, whaleboat races, inspections (of course), scholastic averages, marching form, and various types of sports. Not only was competition between companies encouraged, it was mandatory. Whenever a company won a particular event, they got a star sewn on their company flag and a thin banner to fly above it on their guide-on.

The outstanding companies, those that excelled in multiple competitions, became well known and could be seen blocks away—seven, eight, or even a dozen stars on their flags and an equal number of banners flying above them.

Company 496 was not comprised of overachievers. I think Chief Loibl was just happy to see us get by in any sort of reasonable shape and had given up on us ever winning a thing. Our pitifully plain flag remained devoid of stars; our humble guide-on boasted no banners. Then one day, to the C.O.'s great surprise—shock, actually—we won something.

I happened to be standing guard duty at the barracks when the company returned from the competitions that day, and the C.O. was standing within earshot of me. Here they came, heads high, chins out, strutting, a single star adorning the flag, a lone banner flying high atop the guide-on. Winners all and proud.

Standing with his hands on his hips and staring in disbelief, Loibl watched their grand approach. "Well I'll be damned," he muttered. "They won something."

On the average, 496 wasn't a particularly intelligent company nor did we excel at sports that required any skill, but we offset our deficiencies with brute strength. The single competition in which we bested the others was the Tug-of-War. When Chief Loibl heard that, he shook his head, looked up at our proud little banner, and laughed.

Some companies had rows of stars on their flags and a long string of banners, and some had nothing at all. Not 496—we were winners, and it showed. For several weeks, until graduation, we proudly marched under our single star and our lone banner. Our strongman victory, displayed for all the world to see, did not appear to swell Chief Loibl with pride. I suspect that, more than anything else, it gave the other C.O.s a reason to goad him.

We never did learn a sane reason for most of the things they made us do in boot camp. Looking back, however, one can detect a modicum of logic in the overall picture—just a tiny bit. A chief once summed it up best while inspecting a kid's bag layout. The chief looked at the recruit's questioning face and said, "Son, if we can get to where we trust you with your socks, maybe we'll be able to trust you with a wrench."

A few weeks before we graduated, we finally learned what all the drills were about and that strutting, parade-like thing called "Right shoulder arms and pass in review" that resembled the halftime entertainment at a high-school football game. Someone in a graduating company had to explain it to us, because no rational being could have figured it out on his own. The sole purpose of the drills that we practiced with our pieces until we could, and often did, recite them in our sleep was to provide a grand display for our graduation ceremony. That was it; nothing more.

The day we discovered the purpose of the drills to be as ridiculous as the drills themselves, we learned an invaluable lesson—a senseless philosophy that everyone in the military must accept without question from time to time: "There's no reason for it; it's just the way it's done."

Regardless of all the seeming nonsense we had endured to get there, we couldn't have been prouder on graduation day. They had given us something, and that something was good. You couldn't be a man unless you'd been a maggot, and we would never again be maggots. Now we really were men of the United States Navy. We were sailors.

Bounding out of our bunks for the last time that morning, we packed our seabags and donned our dress blues—the hallmark of a sailor. Along with several other companies, we were going to graduate and gain a second stripe, one that had already been sewn onto our uniforms. That day we went from lowly seaman recruits to seaman apprentices—not exactly a lofty position in the ranks, but we felt like admirals.

Just before we left for breakfast, Chief Loibl walked into the barracks and said, "Good morning, *men*." We hardly knew how to answer; we'd never been ten feet tall before.

The graduating companies marched to breakfast ahead of all the others, and in the mess hall we basked in the admiration and jealousy of the recruits who still had long weeks ahead of them. As we were leaving the mess hall, an incredible thing happened—a wonder that dwarfed all the other events of the day.

Filing out through the scullery for the last time, we handed our trays to the dirty tray man, and looking across the filthy trash barrel that separated us, somehow he looked familiar. He looked like Hailey! If it was Hailey, the kid was only in his third week, and saddled with the worst job on the base.

We stopped and stood in the steamy scullery, trying to figure out if this sweaty, food-spattered recruit really was our former company mate.

It was Hailey, all right, but not the Hailey we had known.

I don't know how many heartbreaking times the little guy had been set back or how many miserable weeks he had spent in 4013, but today his movements were swift and confident, his eyes bright and lively. He had found something within himself, and the Hailey that we had known a couple of short months ago didn't exist any more.

Hailey looked up from his work and noticed us. He threw back his food-spattered head and laughed. "Hi, boys," he said. "Congratulations! I'll be following you out of this place one of these days."

A human metamorphosis had taken place. Several of us reached across the trash barrel and shook his greasy hand. Not knowing whether to laugh or cry, I said, "You're a good man, Hailey, and you're going to make a hell of a sailor."

"You bet I am," he said. "Maybe I'll see you somewhere out there again." Then without breaking his smile, he turned and grabbed the next dirty tray.

And so we left Hailey in the scullery—the dirty tray man, but a man who had climbed a higher mountain than we and found himself.

Out on the grinder with the rest of the graduates, bedecked in shining dress blues trimmed in white hats, white belts, and white leggings, we stood before the base commander, the battalion commander, and our good C.O. The time had come to demonstrate our expertise—for the last time—at executing those damnable drills.

Chief Loibl was standing at the front of the podium when we strutted past and the senior instructor growled that grating, overworked order: "Right shoulder arms and pass in review." Grinning in spite of himself, Loibl looked up at our little Tug-of-War banner, flying high and proud, and saluted it.

We rushed to the armory, where we gleefully surrendered our pieces, and then to the barracks to shake Chief Loibl's hand. We gathered up our seabags, never again to march in formation, endure those body-bending, mind-boggling drills, or carry another rifle that would not shoot.

A swarm of busses waited to carry us to various destinations— the airport, the bus station, or families waiting outside the gate. The four of us hometown buddies, "The Big C," gathered together and shook hands, oddly ill at ease. We weren't the same guys we had been nine weeks ago, and suddenly we didn't quite know what to make of one another. I was proud of them, though— proud of us—and I knew they felt the same.

We were young and filled with bravado, more afraid of what lay ahead than we dared let show. But the world that we had found was a golden-haired lady with fire in her eyes. Dangerous but irresistible, she lured us on.

Chapter Four

Waiting and Wondering

We finished boot camp around December 1, and I went back to the high plains of Colorado for a two-week leave. My mother, along with a group of old friends, greeted me at the little bus station in Lamar. Mom acted as if I had been made an admiral, maybe a four-star. She managed to show me off in uniform to several of her lady friends before we got to the house and I was able to change into civvies, but afterwards I refused to wear my uniform any more and be paraded around town like some sort of returning hero, which I was not.

I was anxious to wear civilian clothes, especially my cowboy boots, and run around with my old buddies and have fun the way we had in the past. My clothes and boots felt like welcome old friends, but strangely, my hometown buddies did not. We all expected things to be the same as before, but they weren't. Or, more specifically, I was not.

We drank beer, participated in the small town pastime of "dragging Main Street," raced cars on country roads, chased girls—mostly to no avail because of the sequence, the beer having preceded the chasing—and disrupted the local movie theater as we always had. I can't say I truly enjoyed it, though. To me, everything we did felt like the last act of a long-running play, a sad encore to a once joyful production that had burned itself out.

Alone, I roamed the big ranch where I had spent my tumultuous growing-up years, land that my mother still owned. I climbed windmill derricks and looked far out over the endless sea of prairie. I walked miles along the wooded creek where I had swum, fished, and hunted as a boy. I knew every tree, every bush, every rock, and the location of every deep pool.

I visited Dad's grave, and after that, I was anxious to get back to the navy. I was happy the day I left.

As promised, I received orders to Engineman "A" School, which was located at the Great Lakes Naval Training Center north of Chicago. However, due to a school backlog when I finished boot camp, I was given a nine-month delay and sent to Keyport Naval Torpedo Station in Washington state, a small facility that test-fired torpedoes. During World War II, a number of torpedoes had run erratically after being fired, resulting in several misses on enemy ships. And even worse, two torpedoes had circled back and sunk the U.S. submarines that had fired them. Because of these wartime tragedies, all torpedoes were now test-fired and monitored for efficiency before being released to the fleet.

Hidden in tall pine woods fifteen miles from the large base at Bremerton, Keyport was a place few people—even career sailors—had ever heard of. Along with an unknown number of civilian technicians, the little base housed eighty-seven navy personnel. While the civilians worked in buildings separate from the naval section of the base, the entire military facility was located in one building—enlisted men's barracks, petty officer's barracks, chief's quarters, officer's quarters, laundry, kitchen, mess hall, gymnasium, bar, pool hall, brig, a number of offices, and even a small bowling alley, all in a single three-story structure.

Dominating a broad grassy knoll surrounded by woods and overlooking a narrow bay—a small inlet of Puget Sound—the tall brick building was solid as a battleship. If we had had any women—Waves—stationed at Keyport, which we did not, even more facilities would have been necessary within this all-purpose structure.

Several young sailors just out of boot camp arrived at Keyport at the same time: Rathke, Flowers, Coulter, Jim Pickett, and myself. All were waiting for some sort of school in the mechanical field, and all had the same nine months to wait. Our placement as future mechanics of one sort or another designated us as fireman apprentices instead of seaman apprentices. Same difference—we were still just E-2s, the lowest rank outside of boot camp, and, as the E-3s were eager to point out, lower than whale crap, which lay at the bottom of the ocean.

Since these self-anointed high-rankers, E-3s, were not petty officers and therefore had no authority over us, we wasted no time in pointing out that if we were lower than whale crap, then evidently they *were* whale crap.

All of us lower-than-whale-crap guys were put to work as apprentices in the Boat Machine Shop. Down the hill from the main building, the machine shop was situated at the head of a long pier that extended a hundred yards or so out over the bay. The far end of the pier was covered, housing a number of sizable navy boats. Keyport's operation required ten or twelve large cabin boats—some designed for firing live torpedoes, some for retrieving spent torpedoes, and smaller craft that were designated as target boats. The machine shop had to keep this small fleet in running order, which meant overhauling diesel engines and replacing parts as needed.

The Boat Machine Shop measured about sixty feet long by thirty feet wide. A glassed-in office dominated one end of the shop while a tool-and-parts storage room occupied the opposite end. In between, diesel engines hung from portable derricks or rested on heavy stands. Wide windows on one side looked out onto the long pier that led to the boat sheds.

Most of the civilian machine shops I'd seen were greasy pits with grimy parts strung everywhere. Not in the navy. One could have eaten off the floor of the Boat Machine Shop, and in the evening before we knocked off work, every tool was put away and every spare part wiped clean and stacked neatly by the engine to which it belonged. Then, without fail, we swept every square inch and mopped it.

Several veterans of World War II were still in the navy in 1961, men and women who had stayed to make it a career for twenty or thirty years. These veterans were generally highly respected, and most of them deserved the respect. Some, however, abused their exalted position, feeling they could get away with anything short of murder, which they could. Chief Tallman, the chief in charge of the Boat Machine Shop, was that type of WWII veteran, and, in the opinion of most who worked for him, a little crazy too.

A tall, stout man with a hard face who wore his hat cocked and didn't particularly care for his job, Chief Tallman could be fair at times and a decent leader; other times, it was best to keep quiet and give him plenty of room. His eyes told the tale: sometimes they were hard and piercing—cop's eyes; other times they were cool and friendly, but they could change in an instant. Talk was that he had undergone too much shelling during the war and had two ships torpedoed out from under him. Chief Tallman was a friendly grizzly: stroke him when it was okay, but watch the eyes and know his mood, and never, ever, get on his wrong side.

I didn't like the machine shop, mostly because of the petty officers we had to deal with. Besides Chief Tallman—whose fiery unpredictability made working there tantamount to tiptoeing through a minefield—we had a pudgy, fat-cheeked first-class engineman named Denny. Although he preferred to be formally known as Dennis, it didn't work out; everyone above and below him called him Denny. Denny was basically a good guy, but with a one-dimensional brain that occupied a position on the lower end of the spectrum, we wondered how he could possibly have made first-class.

When Denny thought Chief Tallman was in a good mood—a variable that he was incapable of assessing—he spent most of his time in the chief's glassed-in office that dominated one end of the machine shop. From this vantage point, Denny could help the chief look out over the shop while doing his best to suck up to him, not realizing that Tallman openly referred to him as "dumby" when he was not in the office. The chief might have been crazy, but he wasn't stupid.

Besides the chief and Denny, we had a second-class engineman who not only hated engines but all things mechanical, and an E-3 fireman named Belder who had been in the navy for six or seven years. Why was Belder only a fireman? Because he had been court-martialed and busted down from second-class, a loss of two stripes in one fell swoop. A round-faced, balding little man with a weak countenance, Belder dressed in badly worn, multipatched dungarees that he should have been court-martialed for wearing. Greasy, untidy, and a terrible example of a sailor, Belder had one thing going for him: because of his years of experience, he was the only man besides the crazy chief who knew anything about engines.

Belder taught me something—not about engines, but about myself.

Belder did most of the hands-on supervision in the machine shop, and we fireman apprentices listened and learned from him. And although he was only an E-3 with no real authority, we essentially took orders from him.

Although Belder and I seemed to have gotten along well for quite some time, for reasons I never understood, he turned on me. He began to find fault with nearly everything I did, and instead of trying to teach me the correct way to do something, he chose to ridicule me in front of the others. Belder's badgering became sarcastic, and he made fun of me. Regardless of the fact that he couldn't get any laughs out of the other apprentices, he seemed to be having great fun at my expense.

I endured all this in silence for about three weeks, until the day it became impossible.

Belder had been on me all morning, and when we broke for lunch, instead of going to the mess hall with the rest of the guys, I went upstairs to the barracks and sat down on my bunk. Mad as hell, I was trying to think and trying to control myself. I had learned that on rare occasions my temper could reach an extreme level, a level that I didn't even know existed in me until the age of fifteen. And up to this particular day, sitting on my bunk thinking about Belder, I had reached that manic level of rage only twice before in my life. I was close now and knew I had to be careful.

Belder lived off base and, bringing his own lunch from home, ate by himself in the machine shop every day. So I knew where he was.

I had always had some problem dealing with authority, I suppose because Dad, my grandfather, had been such an authoritarian himself—a part of him that I had not revered. My attitude toward authority hadn't caused me any trouble in boot camp for two reasons: 1) I had learned to consider the whole thing a huge, ridiculous joke, and 2) except for other recruits, everyone in sight had outranked me. However, the situation with Belder seemed far more serious.

The more I thought about my present predicament, however, the less it seemed to differ from boot camp. Seated there alone on my bunk, I arrived at an answer for dealing with authority—a personal philosophy that would serve me through all my years in the military, and in the civilian world as well. This philosophy boiled down to the bedrock premise on which the military operated. Simply put, if a person outranked me, then by definition, he held authority over me, and I could live with that. However, if he did not outrank me, then God help him if he tried to overstep his bounds. Belder may have been a petty officer in the past, but since he no longer wore those stripes, he had no authority over me, and no right whatsoever to talk down to me.

Jim Pickett, another apprentice in the machine shop who had become my best friend, came up to the barracks looking for me after he finished his lunch. Finding me sitting on my bunk, hands fisted on my knees and gazing at the floor, Jim sat down beside me. After several silent minutes, he looked over and asked, "What you thinking about so hard, buddy?"

"Belder," I said.

"I figured so," Jim answered. "He's sure been riding your butt lately. Why's he doing that?"

"I don't know," I said, "but it's going to stop—today." With that I stood up, threw on my white hat, and started for the door.

"Where you going?" Jim asked.

"To talk to Belder."

"Be careful," my friend warned. "Don't get too carried away."

Belder was seated on a bench eating a sandwich when I walked into the machine shop. "Hi, Penley," he said cheerfully. "What's up?"

With my jaws clenched tightly, I didn't answer. Although I had felt such a rage only twice before in my life, Belder acted as though he couldn't even tell I was mad. Maybe he couldn't.

I spoke with difficulty. "You've been . . . riding me a lot lately, Belder. Why is that?"

The little greaseball smirked, a self-satisfied humor in his eyes. "Riding you? I haven't been riding you."

I stepped closer, very close, and looked down at him. "The *hell* you haven't. You know what you've been doing. You've been riding me every day and making fun of me." My jaw quivered; my body shook.

Belder stopped eating, and he stopped smiling. Looking straight up into my face, he said, "If I've been riding you, Penley, I didn't know it."

"Bull!" I screamed. "You know exactly what you've been doing and so does everybody else. And I'm not taking any more of it! Understand?"

Eyeing me closely, the little guy nodded. "I understand."

I whirled and stomped out the door, walking halfway down the long pier that adjoined the machine shop. I stopped, leaned on the rail, and tried to cool off. After all the other guys had come back from lunch, including Chief Tallman and Denny, I walked back to the shop and silently went to work. None of them said a word; Pickett had told them I'd gone to talk to Belder. The chief and Denny knew nothing of our exchange, nor had they seemed aware of the way Belder had been treating me.

Belder was even dumber than I thought. A few minutes after I started working on an engine, he told one of the other guys to go pick up a part and bring it to him. Then he said, for all to hear, "Penley thinks I've been picking on him, so I'm not going to tell him to do anything."

I lost it. I screamed across the shop like a madman. "I didn't say you were *picking on me,* Belder. I said you've been riding me, which you *have,* and I'm not taking any more of it!"

Everyone stood still, looking back and forth from Belder to me. Chief Tallman and Denny did the same, staring out the windows of the office.

I walked straight to the chief's office. Stopping in the doorway, I looked at the chief and Denny, trying to gain control of myself. When I could speak, I told them what had been going on between Belder and me and about the talk we'd had during lunch. The two of them listened quietly until I finished. The chief looked out at Belder, then back at me. Then he spoke. "You're right, Penley. Belder doesn't have a bit of authority over you, and he damn sure hasn't got any business riding you all the time." Denny nodded in agreement.

"Take it easy," the chief told me, "and go on back to work." Then his eyes darkened and he stood up and yelled, "Belder, get up here—now!" I thought the chief might kill him before he finished chewing on him, and Belder probably wished he would.

Gary Penley, Keyport, Washington, 1961.

Young Salts, Keyport, Washington. Left to right: *Ben Rathke, Gene Warner, Jim Pickett, unknown friend.*

All the guys grinned as I walked back through the shop. The silent applause was deafening.

Belder had found his proper place, and I had found mine.

A few weeks after the incident with Belder, during which time he and I had ceased to acknowledge one another, Chief Tallman put me to work in his office straightening out the files. Theoretically, files were kept on each boat and each engine in Keyport's fleet, but as I quickly learned, the chief's file cabinet was a hopeless jumble of mislabeled, misfiled, and misplaced records. The fact that I had no experience as a file clerk didn't matter; a chimpanzee could have demonstrated more talent at the job than the chief or Denny possessed.

I found the filing job incredibly boring, but I got along better with Chief Tallman than most people did, and he was fun to watch.

Tallman wasn't the only WWII veteran at Keyport. Chief Zimmer, the chief cook, had also served in the big war. Short, white-haired, swaggering, and snarly, Zimmer ruled the mess hall with a loud bark that everyone knew to be far worse than his bite. The twinkle in his eye, even when he barked, spoiled his tough act, revealing the good guy that dwelled only a millimeter beneath the gruff façade. Chief Zimmer and Chief Tallman were buddies, and God help the world when the two of them got together.

Chief Tallman was late for work one morning, an unusual occurrence for a punctual old salt such as he. Chief Zimmer was overdue at the mess hall, too. As the shop clock ticked farther and farther past 8:00, and then past 8:30, even Denny began to look worried. Finally, a little after 9:00, we heard Tallman's car careening to a stop in his parking slot behind the shop.

Through the windows that lined the pier side of the machine shop, we could see the two chiefs making their way toward the shop door at the far end of the building. They were taking a lot of steps but making little headway, their course encompassing the entire width of the pier due to their zigzagging like a wartime convoy avoiding enemy subs. Actually, what the chiefs were doing couldn't really be called zigzagging; staggering would be the proper term. Chief Tallman's hat, normally cocked over his brow at a jaunty angle, teetered precariously far back on his head. Zimmer's hat was gone.

Denny and I were standing in the office, watching the show as the two came into view, as was everyone else in the shop. "Oh, my God," Denny muttered.

The two heroes plunged through the door nearest the office, Tallman first, with Zimmer grasping his shoulders like a vessel in tow. Both were in uniform, khakis, and both rumpled and covered in dust. Zimmer's uniform took first prize; not only was it dusty and wrinkled, all across the crotch and down the front of both legs, it was also sopping wet and covered with dirt that had congealed into mud.

They had been out drinking all night and, heading back for the base that morning, had stopped beside the road to relieve themselves. While carrying out this mission, both had lost their balance and tumbled into the ditch. Evidently Chief Tallman had finished his job by the time they fell, but Zimmer had continued to pee in his pants while rolling in the dirt.

After they made it into the shop and wobbled to a stop just outside the office, they pulled themselves upright with great dignity and looked at Denny and me. Tallman reached up and straightened his hat. Zimmer tried to do the same but discovered his hat was missing in action. Then Tallman looked out at the sea of amused faces staring at them from the shop. "What you guys lookin' at?" he hollered. "Ya look like a buncha jaybirds sittin' on a fence. Get to work!"

The chiefs looked back at Denny and me, then looked at each other, grinned foolishly, and nearly fell down laughing.

Mr. Kurtz, a full lieutenant, was a "mustang," an officer who had come up through the enlisted ranks before earning a commission. A navy diver, Mr. Kurtz was in charge of the Diving Locker and a number of divers on the base. A wise old sea dog, the lieutenant didn't miss much. One day as we passed in a hallway of the main building, Mr. Kurtz stopped me and asked, "What's going on with your boss down there, Penley?"

I knew who he meant, but I feigned ignorance. "Which boss is that, sir?" I asked.

Mr. Kurtz also knew that I knew who he meant, but he patiently said, "The chief, Chief Tallman. What's going on with him?"

"I . . . uh, don't know, sir," I said. "I don't work directly with the chief very much."

The crafty lieutenant knew I was lying, but he let me off the hook. After giving me a look that told me I wasn't fooling him a bit, Mr. Kurtz smiled and said, "Thank you, Penley. Carry on."

"Aye, aye, sir," I said, saluting him smartly and scooting around a corner like a mouse who had barely escaped the grasp of a cat.

Mr. Kurtz let me off another hook as well—a hook that I almost entangled myself in. If a man was allowed to, he could enter into training to become a navy diver. Regardless of rank, the divers all slept and lived in a separate building, the Diving Locker, and besides being the most fearless bunch I had ever seen, they had a spirit among them, a camaraderie that appealed to me.

Having been disenchanted with the Boat Machine Shop ever since my arrival, I decided to approach the diving officer about the possibility of training to be a diver.

Mr. Kurtz was the toughest officer I had come across at that early stage of my naval career, but he was congenial and polite as long as one wasn't foolish enough to cross him. One day I knocked on the lieutenant's door and was invited to come in and have a seat. Leaning back in his chair and folding his hands behind his head, he asked, "What's on your mind, Penley?"

"I wanted to ask you about diver training, sir," I said.

Mr. Kurtz leaned forward, resting his elbows on his desk, and stared at me for a long moment before he spoke. "So you think you want to be a diver?"

"Yes, sir. I've been thinking about that quite a lot, sir."

"We're not talking about scuba diving, you know. We're the real deal here: navy divers—hard-hat diving, deep stuff, in a full suit of gear."

"I know, sir."

"And that's what you think you'd like to do, huh?"

"Yes, sir. I think so."

"Well," said Mr. Kurtz, "I know you've got a clean record—never been in any trouble—so that won't be a problem. And I know you're pretty smart, too. And hell, it doesn't take a lot of brains to be a diver, anyhow."

We both laughed.

"It takes some other things, though," Kurtz said. "Maybe I ought to tell you about a few of those."

"All right, sir," I said, sitting up straight and listening closely.

"Let me tell you the first thing that happens when we start to train a diver."

"All right, sir."

"The first thing we do is suit you up in full diving gear and bolt a hard metal helmet over your head. I imagine you've seen one or two of them; they've got air hoses coming out of them and a glass plate that covers your face."

"Yes, sir."

"A guy up topside lowers you down on a cable, because the diving suit has heavy weights on it that make you sink like a rock. And the helmet that we send you down in the first time doesn't have a face mask. It's covered over with black paint, so you can't see a thing."

"The glass plate is painted over, sir?"

"That's right, it's painted black."

I wanted to make sure I had this straight. "So the face mask is totally black and doesn't let any light in at all? And you do this on your very first dive?"

"That's right," Mr. Kurtz said. "No worry, though; after you get down so deep there's not much light anyway."

"How . . . deep do you go on that first dive, sir?"

"Oh, I don't know," he said casually. "How deep do you want to go?"

I paused, fidgeting in my seat while the diving officer fixed me with a gaze that would melt iron. "Well, Penley," he repeated, "how deep do you want to go?"

"Sir," I said, "I believe I've already gone as deep as I want to go."

Mr. Kurtz stood up, smiled, and shook my hand. "Thanks for coming in, Penley."

"Thank you, sir," I said. Doing an about face and hurrying out of his office, I ended what may have been the shortest diving career in the navy.

Although fighting is outlawed on military bases, the younger enlisted men at Keyport often got into fights with one another—fights which took place out of sight so that no one would get in trouble. What this amounted to was an ambush by the one who started it. And no one ever reported these incidents, because to do so would label one as a snitch and would invite another ambush.

A seaman named Crowe—a big, blond-headed ass who swaggered instead of walked—loved to beat up on others and loved the reputation he gained from doing so. I watched him closely and noticed that he picked his fights carefully. And, because he wasn't smart, Crowe generally gave clues as to whom he had his sights set on.

Jim Pickett, who was smaller than Crowe, ambushed Crowe one day and challenged him. The bully simply walked away as if Pickett didn't exist and that ended any problem for Jim.

Since I was also smaller than Crowe and less confrontational than Pickett, I took notice when the big guy began watching me—sizing me up—and then one day he mentioned something to the effect that he thought he could "whip my rear."

"You could be right, Crowe," I said. "You might well be able to whip my rear, but if you do, you'd better never go to sleep in the barracks again." Crowe never spoke to me again, about anything.

Having taken all I could of the Boat Machine Shop and the tedious job of filing clerk, I requested to go to work on one of the torpedo-testing boats. A lesson, as it turned out, in being careful what you ask for—you might get it. Chief Tallman went to bat for me to help me get the job, and I was assigned to the crew of a target boat. When the chief told me this disquieting news, I did some quick research on what the job entailed. Most importantly, I wanted to know whether the torpedoes we'd be testing were equipped with live warheads. Happily, I learned that they were not.

Regardless of the torpedoes being put on "safety," it took me awhile to get comfortable with the term "target boat."

Of the three types of boats used in testing torpedoes, the target boat was the smallest and the slowest. Whereas the torpedo firing and retrieving boats were seventy-two feet long and powered by eight big engines—sleek, throbbing monsters that sliced through the water like Goliath's saber—and had a hold below the main deck where the crew could take refuge from the weather, the humble target boat was only about twenty-five feet long, equipped with two diesel engines and a small space beneath the deck used only for storing gear. All of the craft were navy gray, but somehow the target boat seemed the grayest. Squatty and low, it hugged the water like a flat-bottomed rowboat and would make less than half the speed of the big ones.

Our little boat boasted a crew of three: a coxswain, a seaman, and an engineman—me. The coxswain, a petty officer, was the man in charge. We also carried a fourth, a civilian technician who ran the sonar and torpedo-tracking gear. Due to the soupy Puget Sound fog, the incessant rain, and the fact that we had nowhere to get in out of it except to crouch behind the narrow back-sloping windshield—inadequate cover for one man, let alone four—we dressed in rain gear more often than not.

What does a target boat do? Not much. Being a target is not a difficult job. Interesting at times—as any victim of a sniper could tell you—but not difficult.

Target boat on which I dodged torpedoes.

Homing torpedoes are designed to detect the noise made by an enemy ship's propellers and/or engines, home in on this noise, and blow off the propellers and maybe the entire stern of the ship. Our job was to run far out into the middle of a large bay, tie our bow to a buoy, and make ourselves a target for homing torpedoes. We did not leave our engines running for a second after tying up to the buoy.

The civilian technician would lower instruments into the water from the stern. Suspended on a cable several yards beneath the boat, these instruments generated a noise that simulated a ship's propellers, or screws as they were known throughout the navy. After the firing boat shot a torpedo at us from more than a mile away, the technician would listen on earphones while turning dials and watching needles on a black box that monitored the accuracy of the torpedo's run.

Our coxswain was a second-class boatswain's mate named Randy, a career sailor with no family who had been around the world more than once and promoted up the ladder and busted back down so many times he couldn't keep track of his own service record. His surname was actually Randall, but the formality of such a name connoted everything that Randy was not. A gaunt sailor with a withered face who had abused himself for too many years, Randy got so drunk every night that he probably couldn't remember his real name himself. That's where I learned to drive a boat, on those mornings when Randy was too hung over to do the job himself.

Randy knew I was green the morning I stepped aboard as his new engineman. Sizing me up through eyes so bloodshot they looked like they might begin to bleed, he said, "Think you can keep this thing runnin' for me? Fix her if she breaks down?"

"Damn betcha I can," I said.

Randy looked startled at my reply, then he threw back his head and laughed. He knew I was bluffing, but he liked it. I laughed with him, and prayed to the god of engines to help me keep them running.

Randy called the civilian technician "Boss," not out of respect, but as a semifriendly sort of sarcasm. Boss was an unassuming middle-aged fellow who never offended anyone. I don't think Randy disliked him; he just didn't care for civilians in general.

Seaman Johnson, a big, easygoing fellow with droopy eyes and a hangdog face, did whatever he was told and seldom said a word to anyone. I had made fireman by then, and since he was a seaman and likely destined to become a boatswain's mate, he should have been running the boat instead of me, but because I wanted to learn, Johnson didn't seem to mind if I took the helm in the morning. And Randy couldn't have cared less who took over his job as coxswain; the old salt was fast asleep on the deck, his back braced against the gunwale.

This wasn't exactly how I had pictured "going to sea," but it promised more excitement than keeping files in a machine shop.

Torpedoes were referred to as fish, and for obvious reasons, all boats in the bay shut off their engines before a homing fish was fired. The moment it was fired we received a message over the radio: "Fish in the water." Randy, Johnson, and I would stand around wondering what the technician was doing and what the torpedo was doing as well.

The three of us would scan the surface of the water constantly, because torpedoes were known to do strange things. Instead of homing in on our sonar gear, sometimes one would head off in a different direction, traveling on its own until it ran out of fuel and floated to the surface. Others would take a high-speed dive and bury themselves in the mud on the bottom; these were retrieved, often with great difficulty, by the divers. The most exciting were torpedoes that broached and ran on the surface. This was not a good thing. Exciting but not good.

When a torpedo decided to run on the surface with a mind of its own, we had no way of knowing where it might go before it ran out of fuel, and we didn't dare start our engines to try and run away from it. Being a homing torpedo, it would do its best to chase us down if we made any noise. And even without a warhead attached, a torpedo slamming into your screws at a speed of thirty or forty knots could do major damage, probably sink the boat.

A torpedo surfaced one foggy day shortly after it was fired. Knowing that it had most of its fuel left and a long way to run, we started looking for it in earnest as soon as the alert came over the radio.

We couldn't see the rogue torpedo, and neither could either of the other boats. In a moment of gross stupidity, the coxswain of the retriever decided to go looking for it. He started his engines, headed across the bay, and soon found it, running in his own wake. Directly behind the retriever, the torpedo was closing fast on its stern, homing in on its screws. Too late to shut the boat down and stop, the coxswain kicked his engines to full throttle and brought it to flank speed, trying to outrun the wild fish.

We could hear his racing engines out in the fog, but we couldn't see the boat. Then the coxswain's frantic voice came over the radio. "I found it! It's chasing me!"

Randy keyed the mic and gave a sympathetic reply. "Why'd you start your engines, dumb ass?"

Audible but not visible, the race continued. Whining engines out in the fog, waves hammering the hull of the speeding retriever. Then everything got louder and visible. The big boat came roaring out of the fog, headed in our direction, the torpedo churning along in its wake about sixty feet behind.

Randy, who had been grinning at the other coxswain's plight, panicked. Jumping up and down and waving his arms like a man gone insane, he screamed, "Turn! Turn that thing! Get the hell outta here! Ya lost your mind?"

The coxswain wheeled his big boat to the left, throwing a wide fan of water as it heeled into the turn, but he turned too fast. Following the sound, which travels as the crow flies, the torpedo jumped the wake and tried to cut him off. It nearly succeeded. The coxswain whipped the heaving boat back to the right just in time to avoid the torpedo's noise-seeking nose. After losing most of its lead, the retriever plunged away and out of sight, both it and the relentless fish lost in the fog once more.

Randy, having lost his hat and shaking convulsively, pointed in the direction the death-defying race had disappeared. "That guy's crazy! Just crazy!"

Johnson and I couldn't help but laugh, and Randy, suddenly realizing what his maniacal reaction must have looked like, picked up his hat and grinned. "Shut up," he said.

At last we heard the big retriever slow down and knew the pursuing torpedo had finally run out of fuel. Randy couldn't wait to get back on the radio. "Did you guys manage to outrun that big fish?" he asked, chuckling. "Looked like it about had ya when ya came by here."

"Yes, we outran it," the other coxswain answered peevishly. "No thanks to you."

"What'd you expect me to do?" Randy said. "Rev up my engines and draw it off of you? Only an idiot would start his engines with a live fish in the water." He laughed into the mic.

Randy's penchant for panic seemed to have the opposite effect on Seaman Johnson and me, and it helped keep boredom at bay. Everything had gone without incident one lazy day until late in the afternoon when we lost track of a submerged torpedo.

When we knew a fish was in the water, we kept an eye on the technician as he monitored its run. We could tell by his mannerisms when things were cool and when they weren't. That afternoon, the technician began listening intently, turning dials, and thumping gauges. We watched him closely. After a minute or so, Randy asked, "What's the matter, Boss?"

"I don't know," Boss said. "I can't hear the fish; lost track of it altogether."

"Where the hell *is* it?" Randy said, his voice cracking.

"I told you I don't know," Boss said. "Something's either wrong with the equipment or with the fish. Where is it? Your guess is as good as mine."

We all searched the surface anxiously, especially Randy. He was leaning across the steering wheel, peering over the front of the boat when the torpedo surfaced. The big fish exploded out of the depths on our starboard side, leaped out of the water with its propeller spinning wildly, flew up and over the bow, and dove back into the water on our port side. With a great splash, it disappeared.

The torpedo had gone airborne, jumped completely over the boat without touching it. Randy whirled around to look at us, his eyes the size of the steering wheel. His lips were moving, but no words would come.

Choking back my laughter, I said, "I think I figured out where the fish is, Randy."

Knowing we had caught him in yet another panic, Randy

grinned sheepishly and said, "You're a damned Einstein, Penley."

Randy was at least twenty years older than me, maybe more, and I liked him better than anyone I worked for at Keyport. I hope he didn't ever have to retire; all he had was the navy and alcohol.

I was too green to fully understand at the time, but what the crew of our little base lacked was cohesion. Except for the divers, who were an entity unto themselves, the feeling of being a crew did not exist. It was every man for himself. And as I would learn, no organization, especially the military, can operate with any degree of efficiency under such conditions.

We were not a crew, we were not shipmates, and nobody seemed to care.

Returning from liberty one Sunday evening, I boarded a navy bus in Bremerton that would take me to Keyport. Along with its regular route, the bus also made stops at ships that were anchored or tied to piers in the area. On this particular night, a nuclear submarine happened to be tied up a few miles outside Bremerton, and a number of the sub crew boarded the bus with me.

The submariners were laughing and joking and calling out nicknames, which elicited laughs from everyone, including the men at which the lighthearted gaffs were aimed. Sitting near the front of the bus, I listened and watched the crew interact with one another. There was a oneness about them, a brotherhood. This was the first time I had seen a real "crew" of sailors.

One of the submariners, a petty officer, noticed me quietly watching them and pointed at me. "I'll bet that guy right there could be a submariner," he said to the others. It was a compliment and quite unexpected.

I smiled at the petty officer and said, "Thanks." I didn't think much about it at the time, nor did I realize the prophetic aspect of his comment.

I was happy to be leaving Keyport the day I boarded the train for the Great Lakes Training Center in Illinois.

During my nine months at the little base, I had seen several men court-martialed, reduced in rank, and even sent to the brig. And all were deadbeats who had deserved it. One was a petty officer who threw a dog out of a second-story window and laughed when the poor animal broke its leg on the sidewalk below. It was my turn to laugh when he lost his stripes for the cruel act. Several sailors had endured vicious beatings simply for the pleasure of the base bully, and my wallet had been stolen from my bunk by one of my "shipmates."

I learned things at Keyport—some positive, some negative—and I had some fun, especially on the target boat. But always something had been missing. It wasn't the navy I was looking for, whatever that might be.

Chapter Five

Off to School and God
Knows Where

Five of us—Rathke, Flowers, Coulter, Jim Pickett, and myself—
all who had worked in the Boat Machine Shop at Keyport, on
a long, long train ride from Seattle to Chicago. Tremendous
glaciated mountain ranges with wild rivers plunging down steep
crevasses in a rush to escape the heights that gave them birth,
pine forests so dense one couldn't see into them, wide stretches
of prairie that reminded me of home. It was on that trip that I
began to dream of returning to Colorado and starting up the old
ranch when I got out of the navy.

Steaming through a string of northern states that had been no
more than names to a Colorado country boy—Idaho, Montana,
North Dakota, Minnesota, Wisconsin and, after the better part of
three days, Illinois.

The whiskey we had brought with us smoothed the train ride
considerably and, surprisingly, didn't get us in trouble with the
conductor. I'm sure he knew, but he just grinned a bit and shook
a warning finger at us when he walked by.

Jim Pickett passed out, as was his habit when under the
influence, and I did my best to keep him sitting semi-upright
as if he were leaning against the window asleep. I also strove to
keep him in a nonslobbering status, this not accomplished with
overwhelming success.

We didn't talk much about our upcoming schools, and I didn't
think the other guys were particularly concerned. As opposed to
my abominable scholastic history, they had all finished twelve
years of school with no problem. With that terrible high-school

record plaguing my past, however, when I wasn't asleep I worried the entire trip.

Dad had sold all the livestock shortly before he died, and then when Mom and I moved to town she lost control of me, and I lost more than my grade-point average and an extra year of my life finishing school. When my class graduated and I didn't, I acted as though it didn't matter to me, and I pulled off my apathy act pretty well. Deep inside, though, in that secret place where I hid my true feelings, I had never felt so worthless.

If I wanted to complete high school, I had to go back and finish with the class behind me—the group I had always been a year ahead of—a humiliation I didn't know if I had the nerve to face. In an attempt to get out of facing the shameful situation, I talked with the navy recruiter, a chief, about joining that summer.

I was eighteen at the time, and by law I didn't need my mother's permission to join. The chief, a pleasant fellow and, as it turned out, a conscientious one as well, questioned me at length about my growing up and my recent losses. Then, off the record, he let me take a short exam—a sort of preliminary GCT given to prospective recruits.

After grading my test and laying it face down on his desk, the chief looked at me with a new concern in his eyes. "My job is to recruit men for the navy," he said, "and I could help fill my quota by signing you up. But I don't want to do that, not yet anyway. I'm going to advise you—and I mean *strongly* advise you—to go back and finish high school. Then come and see me again and I'll be happy to sign you up. If you finish school, it'll help your navy career immensely and probably your entire life."

I took the chief's advice and, laying a huge amount of self-pride on the table for all to see, went back and finished high school. When I returned to the recruiting office the following summer, the chief immediately remembered me. Reaching in his desk, he pulled out the test I had taken a year earlier. Smiling, he said, "You won't need to retake this one; I'm going to let you use the score you made last summer."

"Why is that?" I asked.

"Because it's the highest anybody has ever made on it."

Years later I happened onto the chief in a foreign port, and got the opportunity to thank him for telling me to finish high school—an invaluable piece of advice selflessly given to a confused boy in a confusing time.

So finally I had finished high school, and when I decided to bear down and study, that final year hadn't been difficult. One would think that, having gone back and finished, I'd have rid myself of any stigma associated with schooling. Not so. The experience would cling to me like a plague—a fear of academic failure that would tie me in emotional knots for years thereafter.

The Great Lakes Naval Training Center was huge. Its walls housed a boot camp for thousands of recruits as well as a great number of navy schools, both for beginners, like us, and advanced courses for petty officers.

Engineman "A" School, the one I had been promised at enlistment, scared me. The fact that I had done fine on the weekly tests in boot camp was little consolation; I'd met a lot of sailors who made it through boot camp and didn't appear to possess the mental prowess to master potty training.

There were twenty guys in the class, four of us who had known each other since boot camp and spent nine months together at Keyport. Strangely, we were all from the mid-continent— Colorado, Kansas, and Missouri. Jim Pickett, my buddy from Ohio, went to Boilerman School—just like Engineman School, only different, as Jim astutely described it.

The school lasted three months—eight hours a day, five days a week, with a test each Friday. We studied diesel engines, air compressors, oil purifiers, air conditioning, fresh water distilling plants, and all sorts of hand tools—everything one would find in the engine room of a diesel-powered vessel.

I neither liked nor disliked the base, and I felt mostly neutral about the school curriculum as well. But not about my grades. I studied harder than I ever had, and I found that the school was not as difficult as I had envisioned. About halfway through the course I was number one in the class, and I got to feeling a bit cocky—to my own demise. When it came down to the final test, a comprehensive that covered everything we had studied, three of us were so close that the final exam would determine which of us graduated number one. Certain that I could ace out the competition with ease, I neglected to go back and review all the material we had covered before taking the final.

Although I wouldn't admit it to myself at the time, something in me was afraid to go back and review the entire course, afraid it would somehow overwhelm me, so I convinced myself I didn't need to. Shortly after taking the final, I learned that the other two, Flowers and Coulter, had beaten me out.

I graduated number three and promptly got mad about it. After steaming in silence for the rest of the day and avoiding my friends—especially the two traitors who had the audacity to make higher grades than me—I looked them up and, along with several other classmates, accompanied them to the Enlisted Men's Club. After telling them what a bunch of lowlifes they were, I apologized for my childish reaction earlier in the day. They raised their glasses in a touching tribute, deeming me the best bad loser in the class.

Near the end of school, we all got orders, a few to shore stations, but most to various kinds of ships. In a classic military SNAFU (Situation Normal: All F_____ Up), my orders failed to tell me where I was going. The thick stack of papers, many of which were full of code and virtually unintelligible, said that after taking leave at home I was to report to the Naval Transit Station at Treasure Island, San Francisco Bay, and from there to proceed to the USS *San Joaquin County* (LST 1122), a World War II vessel called a landing ship tank.

One small problem: my orders didn't state where the ship was located. Several code words, numbers, etc., appeared on the orders, which I was sure the instructors at the school could easily interpret for me. Wrong. The cryptic codes meant no more to them than they did to me.

As it turned out, no one on the base could tell me what the codes meant or where in the world my ship might be located. I graduated and left for Colorado without learning what seemed to me a significant bit of information: my ultimate destination.

In my hometown, I went to the recruiting office and asked the chief if he could, *please,* interpret my orders for me. He could not, but after making a couple of phone calls, he told me that the codes meant "West Coast South."

"So," the recruiter said, "looks like you'll be going down the coast somewhere south of San Francisco—Long Beach, San Diego, somewhere like that."

"Ah, that sounds good," I said, relieved to finally have some idea of where I was going. Unfortunately, I was still green enough to believe the mystery had been solved. I didn't yet realize that SNAFUs had a long life expectancy. Just when you thought a SNAFU had run its course and you had found the answer, it turned out to be some sort of fake lead, a demonic ploy to make fools of the young and naïve.

Back on the train—boring hours steaming from Colorado to San Francisco, this time with neither buddies nor whiskey to shorten the miles, and a nagging worry that still wouldn't leave me: just where in the world was this mystery ship I was supposed to report to? Finally, Treasure Island, a lonely rock sitting out in San Francisco Bay and my first experience in the chaotic traveling life of a sailor: the transit station.

Transit stations are temporary quarters, staging areas for sailors en route from one duty station to another—a crowded, impersonal environment filled with strangers coming and going every day. This quick turnaround being a perfect setup for thieves, one had to be ever watchful of personal belongings, practically sitting on top of them at all times.

A good percentage of sailors possess terrible money-handling abilities. If one of these types gets the idea that another sailor has some cash, he'll hound him to death's door to try and borrow five, fifteen, or thirty dollars, promising to pay the very next payday, or, in the case of a transit station, to mail it to him from his final destination. This payback never happens, a lesson I had learned the hard way at Keyport.

In a transit station, one is assigned to a temporary bunk in a temporary barracks. At Treasure Island, no lockers were available for storing valuables—or anything else for that matter—so every sailor had to live out of his seabag.

As soon as I arrived and was assigned a bunk, I noticed an older petty officer lying in the next bunk over, reading a paperback novel. The guy was big and rough-looking with the physique of a professional wrestler, his face more scarred than I had ever seen on a man.

First impressions often being wrong, however, the scarred sailor looked at me, grinned a crooked grin, and spoke in a raspy voice, "How you doin', buddy?"

Taken aback by his unexpected greeting, I said, "I'm . . . uh, doing okay, I guess. Can't figure out what to do with my stuff since I don't have a locker to put it in."

"This your first transit barracks?" he asked.

"Afraid it is," I said.

"Here let me show you a couple of tricks," the big man said, rolling out of his bunk and shaking my hand. His hand felt powerful and rough as sandpaper, and his eyes looked like he could kill in an instant. He scared me just looking at him, but he set about showing me the ropes of living in a transit station.

"This place is a den of thieves," he said, "so don't ever leave a thing layin' on your bunk. There's lowlifes here that'll steal your socks if they get a chance."

He then showed me how to wrap the shoulder strap of my seabag around the frame of my metal bunk and fasten the padlock so that the bag could neither be opened nor removed without taking the bunk along with it. "And some of these characters have even been known to cut the strap and steal the whole bag, so keep all your money, your watch, and anything else that's valuable on you all the time. Don't leave those things in your seabag even when it's locked up."

He was gone the next morning, and I didn't even get his name.

Life in the transit station consisted of trudging to the mess hall three times a day and, in between meals, lying on your bunk listening for your name to be called over the loudspeakers, or squawk boxes, that blared out at each end of the barracks. When your name was called, you would quickly throw on your dress uniform, unfasten your seabag from the bunk, throw it over your shoulder, and hurry off to the headquarters building. For to hear your name on the squawk box meant that you were leaving.

Still not knowing exactly where I was headed to catch my ship, I dawdled around that boring place day after day, reading everything I could put my hands on and going to the Enlisted Men's Club in the evening to drink beer and watch the sailors fight. I had learned to avoid fights myself for a number of reasons. One, I wasn't very good at it; two, there was usually nothing to be gained except bruises, welts, and lacerations; and three, the shore patrol, who inevitably broke up the fights, carried heavy clubs with which they often beat knots upon the heads of the young pugilists.

To me, fighting was much more enjoyable as a spectator sport, and there always seemed to be plenty of young sailors willing to sacrifice their hard heads and soft bodies for the entertainment of those of us who didn't care to participate.

Finally, after an entire week of living in the transit barracks and chewing my fingernails to the quick, I heard my name blasted over the squawk box. I already had my dress blues on, more than ready to go. Throwing my seabag over my shoulder, I literally ran to the headquarters building.

Behind a desk at headquarters sat a chief hospital corpsman, idly thumbing through my orders—the first person I had seen who appeared to know what the cryptic papers actually said. "Are you Gary Penley?" the chief asked gruffly.

"I am," I answered.

"Well, you won't be leaving for a while," he said. "You've got to take a series of shots, and the shots are timed. You're going to be here two more weeks."

He couldn't have said what I thought I heard. "Two more weeks!" I wailed. "Why is that?"

"Because you're going to Japan."

Another two weeks in the pirate's den, sleeping with one arm hooked in the strap of my locked seabag, and finally my name was called again. Although by now, I had no faith that the SNAFU had actually ended, this time it turned out to be for real.

From San Francisco to Tokyo, across the endless Pacific in a MATS (Military Air Transport Service) prop-driven plane. In the interests of safety in case of a crash, the seats were all mounted backwards—a feature that somehow failed to make me feel any safer while flying across thousands of miles of deep water. Plus, in order to save government money, MATS planes were built with a minimum of insulation. All this causing one to not only feel the weird sensation of flying backwards halfway around the globe, but also seated inside the noisiest machine that ever took to the sky. After more than twenty-four hours of looking down at nothing but water miles below and listening to the drone of those four engines, which sounded like they were mounted in the seat beside me, I began to wonder if Charles Lindbergh had been certifiably sane.

When crossing the International Date Line going east, one loses a full day. It was December, and the day we lost was Christmas Day. We flew from December 24 into December 26. My thoughts, which I expressed to all within earshot, were that we didn't miss being home for Christmas; we simply didn't have a Christmas. Somehow that seemed better to me, but I'm not sure everyone on the plane agreed.

At long last, after landing in Tokyo and spending another couple of nights in a transit barracks, I boarded a two-engine plane—one of those with tons of cargo stacked in a heap down the center, all held down by heavy netting stretched across it and fastened to the floor. A string of web seats down each side rocked back and forth and side to side in a lopsided figure-eight motion, giving one the sensation of being suspended inside a burlap bag in a high wind. The clattery craft smelled of oil and had little or no insulation. I wondered if somehow I'd got caught up in another SNAFU and been mistakenly billeted as a paratrooper, without a parachute or any knowledge of how to use one. By now such a scenario would have made perfect sense.

Chapter Six

Japan

Iwakuni, Japan, a small city on the southern end of the large island of Honshu. Only a few miles south of Hiroshima, Iwakuni supported a sizable U.S. Marine air base and one small ship, the USS *San Joaquin County* (LST 1122). The ship was not in sight as we crossed the base and traversed a long causeway that led to a lonely pier. The marine driver pointed at a dot far out in the bay. My ship, at last, tethered to a buoy three miles from shore.

A landing boat, which for our use was referred to as a liberty boat, picked me up at the pier to take me out to the ship. Constructed of heavy steel, the WWII vintage boat was rectangular and deep with a flat bottom, cleats welded to the deck to provide traction for carrying tanks or trucks when it wasn't loaded with troops. Its straight sides were nearly as high as my head, as was a single door in front that could be dropped on a beach to unload men or machinery. I was reminded of many such boats I had seen in pictures of the landings at Normandy and on Japanese-held islands such as Iwo Jima during the big war.

As we approached the LST, I was again reminded of the same landings. The ship was built high and wide, boxy, broad-beamed with two big doors on the front that opened outward to reveal a large space—the tank deck—which could hold a number of tanks, trucks, artillery pieces, and troops. And like the landing boat I was riding in, the ship was designed to run up on the beach, open its doors, and empty out its cargo of fighting men and machinery of war.

The LST was anything but sleek, but—a tough old brute

nevertheless—a broad-shouldered juggernaut that, when churning toward a fortified beach, could not be stopped except by a direct hit from heavy artillery. These workhorses had landed on many a beach under heavy fire, and a number of them paid the ultimate price to expel their precious cargo in the face of a determined enemy.

A gangway with steps nearly as steep as a ladder led from the pitching liberty boat up to the main deck. There I saluted the flag and the officer of the deck (OOD), and I soon found myself at the door to the captain's quarters.

After being introduced to the captain, he asked me into his spartan quarters and invited me to sit down. Such an invitation surprised me, leading me to believe that the commander must be a chatty, friendly fellow. I couldn't have been more wrong. It soon became obvious that the captain felt as uncomfortable with the situation as I. I wondered why the conversation—the first and last I would ever have with the commanding officer—was even taking place.

The skipper was a tall, graying man of medium build. A square jaw, strong countenance, and eyes that bothered me. His rank was lieutenant commander, and I guessed from his age that he was a mustang, having come up through the enlisted ranks. In that I was correct. I couldn't take my eyes off of his; something about them gave me the disquieting feeling that he had personally looked into hell, and in that I was also correct.

I said very little, and during our strained, one-sided conversation, I heard things about being careful in town because of Communist influences and consequently off-limits businesses, being a good representative of the United States, and keeping myself out of trouble. I heard nothing about being a good guest in a foreign country or about treating the Japanese people with respect. In fact, I didn't hear the word Japan at all or anything directly concerning Japan or its citizens. The captain simply referred to "this country" and "these people."

The skipper never smiled during our short conversation, nor was I to see him smile more than two or three times during my tour of duty on his ship. He was known to be sultry and moody, at times storming past members of his crew without even acknowledging their presence.

The strange captain made complete sense as soon as I learned about his past. He had been a POW in a Japanese prison camp in the Philippines during World War II. The man had been beaten, tortured, and nearly starved to death by guards reputed to have been the cruelest on Earth.

After his release, the captain was decorated for bravery and commissioned to officer's rank. Why the navy, in its wisdom, had stationed him in Japan after such an ordeal is a mystery I would never understand.

The skipper was not the only mystery aboard the *San Joaquin County.* The ship sat out there three miles from shore, tied to a buoy six days out of seven, getting underway one day each week and running around the bay conducting drills and maneuvers for a few hours, then returning to the buoy before sunset.

The ship no longer operated as an LST; in fact, it was physically incapable of doing so. A steel bulkhead had been constructed just inside the large doors in the bow, rendering it impossible for anything to be moved in or out of the tank deck through the front.

The only sizable access to the tank deck was from above. A large rectangular hatch, approximately fifteen by twenty feet, allowed access through the main deck. This loading hatch remained sealed and locked during daylight hours and most nights as well. A few other hatches, just big enough for a man, allowed access to the tank deck from passageways below. The watertight doors covering these hatches also remained locked day and night, and only the officers and the few enlisted men who worked in the tank deck had keys to them. When they moved in or out of the secret space, they locked the heavy door behind them, and I suspected these men carried concealed arms.

Occasionally, at night, the topside hatch was unlocked and opened, and presumably some type of equipment, or armament, or something, was moved in or out of the tank deck. All the regular sailors on board were ordered to stay below decks during these operations, and the hatches leading to the main deck were closely watched by guards armed with machine guns.

The enlisted men who worked in the tank deck were friendly

but distant. They didn't fraternize with the rest of the crew, and when they went on liberty, they never came back drunk. They wore different insignia on their uniforms at different times, a smile being the only answer I ever got when I pointed this out to one of them. For all I knew—which was virtually nothing—they could have been officers dressed as enlisted men.

The tank deck, originally designed to haul troops, tanks, and artillery, comprised the largest portion of the ship, probably two-thirds of its total volume, the remainder of the vessel acting as a hull that enclosed the large space. Providing minimal living quarters for the crew, a mess hall, and an engine room, the sole purpose of the rest of the ship was to deliver the contents of the tank deck onto an enemy-held beach.

Most station ships such as ours utilized three watch sections; that is, each sailor had to stay on board—which was known as having "the duty"—one night out of three. Not ours. For reasons unknown and unexplained, we had the duty every other night, so that at any given time at least half the crew remained on board. This tight rotation, commonly known as "port and starboard" liberty, was extremely unpopular, lending a negative aspect to morale.

In my opinion, if someone in command had simply told the crew that, even though they might not understand why, the job they were doing was vital, making the tight security and watch sections a necessity, it would have helped immensely. No one bothered to do that, however, and the consequent low morale led to a large percentage of sailors getting into trouble, being sent to captain's mast, and court-martialed.

None of the men who worked in the tank deck ever got in trouble. They were fully aware of the ship's role and its importance in the bay of Iwakuni, lending their lives and their jobs a sense of purpose that the rest of us did not share.

I served aboard the USS *San Joaquin County* for nearly a year, and to this day, I haven't the slightest idea what lay concealed within the tank deck.

To hell with whatever secret occupied the tank deck and with whatever the ship's mission was in Iwakuni. I didn't know, and I didn't want to know. I kept my head down and concentrated on learning to be an engineman.

The engine room—the first ship-sized power plant I had ever seen—took my breath away. Located in the lowest reaches of the vessel, it was nearly as wide as the ship itself. Permeated with the smell of diesel fuel and oil, the space was dominated by the two biggest engines I had ever seen—giant diesels approximately fifteen feet long, seven or eight feet wide, and taller than a man. A maze of piping, pumps, and machinery seemed to fill every available square inch. A metal walkway passed between the engines and all the way around each one, and even though the walkway was wide enough to allow two people to pass one another, albeit closely, to me the entire space felt crowded and tight—somewhat claustrophobic but not uncomfortable.

I had never known how tight a ship's engine room could feel and, being unable to predict the future—which at that point would probably have scared the hell out of me—I couldn't imagine ever working in a space any smaller.

I worked for a chief engineman named Roberts and a first-class named Sessions. The chief was a fine guy to work for, but he practically had no job himself. Sessions, a tall, blond fellow with the face of a male model, knew everything there was to know about the engine room and didn't really need the chief's help for anything.

The first time we untied from the buoy and got underway, I stood back and watched Sessions start up the engines. I was fascinated as the big monsters roared to life, and I guess it showed; Sessions looked over at me and winked.

After everything was running smoothly and the ship was underway, we received a "bell" from the bridge, an order to bring the vessel to flank speed, the maximum knots the LST could make. The big engines screamed as Sessions pushed the throttles to the forward stops, and I envisioned the ship's reaction—its bow raised, its stern hunkered down, its twin propellers throwing a tremendous wake as it sliced through the sea like a racing craft.

After running at flank speed for some time, Sessions asked me to go topside and get something for him. That sounded exciting;

I couldn't wait to see what it looked like from the main deck with the ship making full speed! I raced up the ladder.

The ship was doing full speed, all right, but the spectacle fell somewhat short of what I had envisioned. Full speed happened to be ten knots—about eleven miles per hour. The bow was not raised and the sea was not churning from our passage. Standing on the main deck, I could barely sense that we were moving through the water.

A boatswain's mate who spent most of his time topside, sensed my surprise. "Pretty slow, isn't it?" he said with a grin.

"Sure is," I replied. "Down in the engine room it sounded like we were doing a hundred miles an hour."

"I know," he said. "You'll be better off just staying down there and pretending like we're going fast."

"Thanks, Boats," I told him. Boatswain's mate was the oldest rank in the navy, dating to the days of sailing vessels, and boatswain's were always called "Boats." They had what they considered to be a "real" sailor's job—tying up and untying the ship, dropping the anchor and reeling it in, winding up great coils of heavy rope—and for the ones below petty officer rank, chipping off old paint and reapplying new to the ship's hull. The petty officers, the "Boats," considered their jobs to be the finest in the world; the others chipped paint.

Discovering how slow the LST moved, even at flank speed, gave me a greater respect for my World War II forebears who attacked heavily armed beaches in such craft. And from that day on, I took the boatswain's advice; whenever the ship was underway I stayed in the engine room and tried to put out of my mind the fact that we were trundling around the bay like something adrift.

Under Sessions's patient tutelage I soon learned to start up the engine room by myself, get the ship underway, and answer command bells from the bridge. And when we got a flank bell, I threw the throttles forward as if we were manning a battleship, smiled as the big engines screamed, and envisioned the bow up, stern low, and plowing through the water like a seagoing locomotive.

Sailors being sailors, there was always something to break the monotony aboard the all but stationary LST.

Since my bunk was located on the first deck below the main deck, the underside of the main deck comprised my ceiling. I slept on the bottom tier, at floor-level, and directly over the aisle that bordered my bunk was a man-sized hatch with a watertight door that opened upward—a round hatch that normally stayed closed but could be opened in case of emergency. Up topside, this hatch lay only a few feet from the gangway, so that sailors returning from liberty practically had to step around it as they walked aboard the ship.

One night as I lay sleeping peacefully, several guys carried a young fellow named Jennings up the gangway. In true sailor-like fashion, Jennings had gotten drunk and passed out. His carriers, being only slightly less inebriated than the unconscious Jennings, dropped his body near the closed hatch and left him there under the stars.

One hour later, when the next liberty party arrived, the passed-out sailor still lay beside the hatch. Several of the new arrivals, being more than a little intoxicated themselves, figured out how to quickly get their unconscious shipmate below decks. While one of them unlatched the hatch door and held it open, the others picked Jennings up by his feet, dangled him headfirst over the opening, and dropped him straight down through it.

What good Samaritans. Jennings was below decks in an instant, and almost in a bed—mine. In this case, however, the status of being in bed versus almost being in bed comprised a huge difference.

The deck of the sleeping quarters, right beside my lower-level bunk, consisted of heavy steel plating—a rather hard surface for a landing. But then sailors normally made contact with the deck via their feet rather than their heads. When the top of Jennings's head rammed the deck plates like a pile driver, I nearly jumped out of bed. Switching on my reading light, I observed the young sailor in a crumpled heap beside me. At first I couldn't tell who it was, or whether or not the twisted mass of flesh was actually alive.

I must have heard the hatch slam shut as I awoke because I had the feeling that the knotted-up sailor, whom I could now see was Jennings, had come from above. I could also see that Jennings was alive, for the moment at least. However, unaware that he had been unconscious before taking flight, I assumed he had knocked himself out on the deck plates. *What a strange way to enter the sleeping quarters,* I thought.

Then, as I fought the last cobwebs of sleep from my head, it occurred to me that I should probably go get the chief corpsman if Jennings was going to have any chance of living through the night. I did, and Jennings did.

A chief boatswain's mate named Roland was the chief-master-at-arms—the equivalent of chief of police aboard a ship. Chief Roland looked like he had been born in the navy. A tight, wiry man with a taut face, a buzz cut that would have made a marine smile, and eyes that cast suspicion on everyone but the captain, Roland stalked around the ship like a badge-happy prison guard, his fisted hands close by his sides, his arms slightly bent and stiff as iron rods, as if prepared for a fist fight at any moment.

Chief Roland seemed to make Mother Teresa necessary to even out the human race.

Roland was determined to catch the culprits who had dumped the unconscious Jennings down the hatch beside my bunk. And in his quest to capture these renegades, he questioned me endlessly. I explained to him, endlessly, that I had no way of knowing who had dumped the passed-out sailor down the hatch because I'd been asleep when the unfortunate lad's head hit the deck.

I don't believe Chief Roland was particularly concerned about the welfare of Jennings; it was the breach of naval regulations that incensed the man. "I can't believe they did that," he said to me. "They could've killed the guy." I nodded in agreement and fought to hide any trace of the considerable humor I saw in the situation.

"I'm gonna find them guys," Roland said, his eyes blazing, "and hang their butts from the yardarm!" *My God,* I thought, *he really did say that.* By now every enlisted man below the rank of chief knew who had done it—probably even Jennings knew—but I nodded again as if I believed it to have been a most heinous act, and for the hundredth time, I denied any knowledge of the guilty parties.

As Chief Roland obsessed on the mystery and questioned a number of sailors besides myself, his investigation dragged on for days. Virtually all of those he interrogated knew the names of the guilty, and some had actually helped dump Jennings down the hatch. But nobody knew nothin', and ruthless Roland, not being the shrewdest swabbie who ever sailed the seas, never solved the case.

Japan was a poor country in 1962—poor, defeated, and occupied. Only sixteen years had passed since the armistice, and the Japanese economy, as well as their national conscience, still reeled from the impact of war.

Whole families—a man, his wife, and two or three children—could be seen riding on a single bicycle, their only transportation. If they were fortunate, the bicycle might have a tiny gasoline engine mounted beside the front wheel to propel it. A farmer would ride into town on a bicycle with a crate fastened on a carrier behind him. In the crate might be two or three chickens, maybe a stack of vegetables, or a small pig or two. A few, and only a few, rode small motorcycles. I never once saw a Japanese citizen driving a car.

Having been born in 1941, just prior to the attack on Pearl Harbor, and grown up during the war and its aftermath, I had become accustomed to the sadistic, maniacal image of the Japanese that had been portrayed in American movies, magazines, and even cartoons and comic books. The centuries-old human characteristic—the psychological need to demonize the enemy in order to justify killing him.

Being young, impressionable, and far less knowledgeable about the ways of the world than I considered myself, I expected to find the Japanese people much like the portrayals I had seen growing up. I was wrong—terribly wrong.

When I knew them in their home country in the early 1960s, the Japanese people were the most honest I had ever met. They possessed a work ethic, integrity, and a determination to right themselves in the eyes of the world that would rival any race on Earth. For a while, I tried to cling to my long-held bias—actually worked at holding to it—but I could not. I found that I respected them, and nothing I saw ever made me feel otherwise.

Dad wouldn't have agreed with my feelings toward the

Japanese. He hadn't even forgiven the British for opposing us in the American Revolution. But Dad was gone, and though I revered his memory, I was not him. Mom's bias didn't go back as far as the Revolution, but having lived through WWII and had friends and family killed in battle, she would never forgive any country that had fired on the U.S. in her lifetime. I did my best to avoid the subject with Mom.

What I learned of the Japanese, and from them, astounded me. It shocked me that such a country could ever have loosed an army and tried to take over a large portion of the world. I'll never fully understand that particular aspect of human nature, but the lesson I learned from the Japanese people, plus other experiences along the way, convinced me that any army, navy, police force, or government—any organization in authority— that is not somehow kept in check will become enamored of its own power and run out of control, regardless of its nationality.

Nissan, Mitsubishi, Suzuki—none of those names were even vaguely familiar at the time. Only one company, soon to become world famous, had begun making motorcycles. Mr. Honda's name was already becoming known, and Honda products along with others that followed would be instrumental in changing the connotation of "Made in Japan" from a term that depicted poor workmanship to one whose quality rivaled any in the world.

Except for the one day a week we got underway, life aboard a ship tied to a buoy could be pretty dull: cleaning the engine room every day whether it needed it or not, fixing things that didn't need fixing, and standing excessive security watches for reasons that most of us didn't understand. So I bought myself a motorcycle, a midsize Honda suitable for both highway use and running on backroads to tour the countryside.

Enlisted men were required to wear dress uniforms when leaving or boarding the ship, but since we were allowed to keep a locker on the base, we could quickly change into civvies before going into town—much more comfortable attire for riding motorcycles.

And what great weekends I had on my Honda—after nearly being killed a couple of times getting used to riding on the left-hand side of the street, that is. Japanese children, all dressed alike in school uniforms and smiling happily, would line up beside the road, wave, and gaily say "Hello" as I passed. They were studying English in school and proud to show off their speaking skills. Their adult chaperones waved a cheery greeting as well.

Some of my shipmates also had motorcycles, and we traveled Japan together at times. They mostly preferred to stay on paved roads, however, and not wander off into the countryside, as I was prone to do. I suppose my having grown up in the wilds made the difference in my taste for exploration. Several of us might start out together on a Saturday morning, but within an hour or two, I'd spot some narrow dirt path that divided a pair of rice paddies and take off for parts unknown. The others would stop on the highway, shake their heads, and yell, "You're crazy, Penley. See you back at the ship." Although I didn't agree with their assessment of my mental state, as I rode off into God only knew where, I suppose they at least deserved the benefit of the doubt.

Actually, I couldn't imagine why my friends chose not to follow me. I think they were afraid of getting lost, which I sometimes did. But then, one is never really lost, just temporarily in unfamiliar territory and not knowing how to get out. To me it was exciting, and I always found my way back, sometimes by holding ridiculous conversations with Japanese farmers working in their fields—exchanges that consisted of me saying "Iwakuni?" while holding out my hands in frustration and shrugging my shoulders to indicate that I was lost. Then the farmer would do his best to point the way for me, sometimes indicating twists and turns by drawing a map in the dirt. This worked much of the time, or at least led to more such exchanges with other farmers—usually closer to Iwakuni each time I stopped to inquire—until eventually I found my way back.

The country was breathtaking and unlike anything a boy from the Colorado plains had ever seen or even imagined. Hills, the greenest of green, rounded and flowing, terraced with the ever-present rice paddies that perched one upon another, climbing higher and higher with a beauty of their own. Arched foot bridges, gaily painted, were a trademark of Japan. And the cherry blossoms—I was fortunate enough to be there for one season. A peaceful, undulating countryside, its flowing greens accented in dazzling pink.

And every farmer in every field that I passed would straighten from his labors and wave. To me, it seemed as though I should have represented the enemy, but none of them appeared to feel that way.

One weekend in late spring, I kept to the highway with my buddies, and four of us rode to a famous place—or perhaps infamous would be the more proper term. Hiroshima.

Crossing a small bridge on the way into town, we were unaware that on that very bridge, seventeen years before, a dozen or so pedestrians had been walking across when the heat blast—the first visible stage in the detonation of a nuclear weapon—hit the city. The bridge was burned white and the pedestrians vaporized, a dozen dark shadows across the bridge the only trace left of them—shadows where their bodies had absorbed the white-hot blast.

Ground Zero—the point directly below which the first atomic bomb had detonated in the air. A small, featureless building had been erected on that spot—a museum—surrounded by bare ground that extended a block or more on all sides. Barren, as if to symbolize the totality of the devastation the bomb had wreaked from that point outward.

Inside the museum, I was glad to be wearing civvies instead of my uniform. Not that it made a lot of difference—we were the only Americans in the museum; in fact, we were the only Caucasians.

The museum was filled with remnants of the bombing as well as graphic photographs taken that fateful day in August 1945. Mannequins dressed in badly burned clothing had been designed to show the effects of the heat blast, but they could not adequately depict the true horror shown in the photographs. I remember a stack of heavy ceramic bowls, four or five of them, that had been sitting in someone's cupboard when the bomb hit. Burned hotter than the kiln in which they had been made, the bowls were misshapen and melted together into one single piece.

Standing there at Ground Zero, I avoided the eyes of the Japanese people who were visiting the museum, and they avoided mine.

The bay at Iwakuni was roughly bowl-shaped, several miles in diameter, and could be accessed only by one narrow inlet directly across the water from the marine base. Most of the time our LST was the only thing visible in the bay, except when the fleet came in. On occasion our little ship would be visited by an aircraft carrier, two or three heavy cruisers, and a pack of destroyers. During those times, the quiet little town would be visited—or invaded—by thousands of sailors. I never knew what the ships were doing there, and the sailors sure didn't know what they were doing.

The fleet would be there for only a few days, and most of the guys on the *San Joaquin County* chose to stay aboard while the fleet sailors overran the town. Not me. It was an amazing thing to see—a spectacle that no observer of life would want to miss.

In the small, quiet town that embodied the quaint beauty of an ancient culture, the streets appeared more gaily lit than usual, the merchants and bar owners having dressed up their store fronts to attract the sailors—as if they needed attracting.

Thousands of American sailors, all in dress uniform, streamed off row upon row of liberty boats and hit the town in waves, many walking down the streets drinking beer and others lined up twenty deep, trying to force their way into bars so packed that not another body could fit through the door. Scores of stern shore patrol stalked the streets, black "SP" bands on their arms and heavy clubs swinging at their hips—petty officers from the big ships who had drawn the dubious assignment of trying to keep the hordes of young savages in line.

Unlike soldiers and marines, sailors were not taught hand-to-hand combat in basic training. However, instead of considering this lack of training a liability, many swabbies believed themselves to be naturals at the martial arts. And despite centuries of historical evidence to the contrary, sailors continued to believe that their fighting prowess improved exponentially with the consumption of alcohol. Following this belief, it made sense not to get into a fight until after one had consumed copious amounts of the Herculean potion.

Fights broke out all over town, the reasoning behind them generally senseless and insignificant—the ensuing conflict being tantamount to two young bulls vying for position in the herd. And, as in nature, the duel was usually ended by the king bull— the oldest one with the biggest horns—the shore patrol.

The fight would begin with two of the young bulls circling each other in the street, mostly in faltering, irregular circles due to their state of insobriety. Poorly aimed fists would swing wildly, and the bout would invariably end with the bulls becoming sailors again, often pathetically so, being led or carried away by the shore patrol with pitiful rivulets of blood running down their foreheads from whatever amount of clubbing had been required to take the bull out of them. Generally, a couple of sharp whacks was adequate.

The fleet sailors were restricted to what was known as "Cinderella liberty," meaning they had to be back by midnight—not back to their ships, but back to the dock where they caught the liberty boats that returned them to their ships. This was an even better show than the one they put on in town.

One pier and one boat dock, generally used by our single liberty boat, now had to serve as a landing for scores of boats to pick up hundreds of sailors. The boats lined up ten or twelve deep, moving up a single boat length each time one was loaded with breathing bodies and cast off. In theory this sounds like a controlled, organized operation, and probably could have been, had it not been midnight and the sailors not have been drinking steadily for the past six or seven hours.

And it would have helped if the swabbies had been attentive enough to know when a certain liberty boat was heading back for a certain ship—theirs, to be exact. But who wanted to keep track of such minor details when there was arguing, posturing, and fighting to be done? The shore patrol—they had to sort it all out. After policing the streets for as long as the sailors had been drinking, the beleaguered shore patrol was now charged with creating some sort of order out of total chaos.

As the line of boats slowly moved up, where were these hordes of sailors waiting to board them? They were at the top of a seawall from which a ramp sloped down to a floating pier next to which the liberty boats docked. The end of a street that led to the docks, an area about twenty yards wide and half a block long, seethed with sailors.

The shore patrol had beefed up its ranks for this portion of the day's fun. A number of chiefs, armed with bullhorns designed to rattle eardrums in the manner of heavy artillery, had joined the others. As a crowd of sailors continually tried to force its way down the ramp to the boat dock, the chiefs would blast their bullhorns in their faces to hold them back—this in order to allow a loading boat to fill up before casting off and to ensure that the wrong sailors didn't jump onto the wrong boat, thus ending up on the wrong ship, a not uncommon occurrence.

After a boat was filled and cast off, hopefully with the right group of sailors on board, the chiefs would line up across the top of the ramp and begin to trumpet the name of the ship for which the next liberty boat was bound. As a wave of sailors crushed toward them, the chiefs, as well as the other shore patrolmen, would stop each one and holler the ship's name into his ear, not allowing him to pass until he had confirmed that he was indeed heading for that particular ship. When a boatload had thus been herded down the ramp, the chiefs would again stop the moving horde and signal to the shore patrol below to begin loading the boat.

On command, the sailors would begin loading themselves into the deep landing boat—a stream of humanity, stumbling, falling, and pushing one another down a single ladder, many landing in heaps on the steel bottom of the boat. The ones who fell had to quickly scramble to their feet or risk being trampled by the others.

All this pushing, shoving, and trampling had the potential to cause further dissention among the troops. One night the chaotic procedure managed to enrage an entire boatload—the incident occurring while the boat was still tied beside the pier.

Although I had secured a good vantage point near the top of the ramp, I didn't see who started the altercation—it would have been impossible to tell even close up—but when the boat, which was as deep as a man's head, was packed tightly with sailors jammed shoulder to shoulder, a fight broke out. As soon as a few guys slugged each other and knocked their opponent into another sailor, the sailor would then take offense and join in the fray. With a domino effect, the fight rapidly spread throughout the boat, soon involving every sailor on board. The boatload of tightly jammed sailors was akin to a box filled with upright bowling pins, the slugging swabbies having the same effect as trying to knock over the pins. A solid punch, difficult to accomplish under such conditions, would only cause the recipient's head to bob backward before another struggling body was encountered.

How to stop a free-for-all such as this? The chiefs knew better than to climb down into the boat and try to stop it—only an insane person would have tried that. They did, however, find a method that worked. After ordering the other shore patrol to shine huge flashlights down into the eyes of the fighters, the chiefs stationed themselves at intervals around the gunwales, which placed them above the melee. They then turned up the volume on their bullhorns, aimed them at the scrapping sailors, and screamed into them until it seemed their lungs would burst.

At first the chiefs' screaming had no effect—in their drunken rage the sailors kept slugging it out. But then the blinding lights in their eyes and the overwhelming volume from half a dozen bullhorns began to take its toll.

When the wild swinging, stumbling, and head-bobbing finally stopped, the sailors all looked up, blinking into the bright lights and trying to shade their eyes. I had seen a lot of beat-up sailors, but never so many at one time. Many of them had lost their hats, some had their jumpers half torn off, and nearly every one had at least a little blood on him; some were covered in it.

The chiefs, squatting on the gunwales with bullhorns in hand, looked beyond fatigue, beyond frustration, beyond anger; they looked murderous. Then one of them held up a hand to quiet the others. Everyone grew still—the chiefs, the other shore patrolmen, and the ragtag crowd of fighters in the boat. After a long pause, the lead chief keyed his bullhorn and spoke.

"Don't even move," the chief growled. "If one more of you so much as blinks, we're gonna start whacking heads—*all* heads. We're gonna start from the outside in and swing till there's not a one of you left standing. Then we're gonna pile you up and haul you back to the ship, dead or alive. Understand?"

Silence.

"Do you *understand*?" the chief bellowed into the bullhorn.

"Yes, sir," the sailors stammered.

"I couldn't hear that," the chief yelled.

"Yes, sir!" the sailors answered with all the volume they could muster.

With that, the chiefs walked around the gunwales and jumped off the boat onto the pier. The lead chief looked at the coxswain and said, still into his bullhorn so that all could hear, "Cast off. Take this bunch of *tough* bastards back to the ship, and tell the OOD I think every one of them ought to be put on report!"

The crew untied the boat, turned, and headed out into the bay, its pugilistic passengers having had all the fun they could handle. I'd love to have been standing on their ship when that sad lot came aboard.

Soon after the bloodied boatload left, my own ship's liberty boat moved into place next to the dock and, after undergoing scrutiny by a chief whose reddened eyes had the look of a madman, I was allowed to board.

It was fun when the fleet came in.

Although our captain seemed anything but a partygoer, once a year the USS *San Joaquin County* put on a party. The ship's party was the biggest social event of the year, and the only one that included both officers and enlisted men. A well-appointed nightclub, located on the main street of Iwakuni and reputed to be the classiest place in town, was rented for the occasion. All hands wore dress uniforms, including the officers, and wives and dates turned out in their finest.

The captain was a handsome officer, striking in his gold lieutenant commander stripes, but even when he laughed, his eyes were stone. He sat at the head of the officer's table, which dominated one side of the room, his wife seated to the right of him, the executive officer to his left, and the rest of the officers and their ladies down the table. The chiefs and their companions sat at a table of their own, and the other petty officers were spread throughout the room. I had passed the third-class engineman test and so was now a petty officer, albeit a junior one. Several of us third- and second-class took over a large table along with our wives and dates.

Our table sat beside a long wall opposite the captain's table. A lengthy food buffet, situated between our table and the captain's, dominated the center of the room. A live band, with just the right volume to create a pleasant atmosphere, occupied the back wall.

Roland, the chief-master-at-arms, being single and possessing the social skills of a pit bull, didn't have a date for the ship's party. Considering himself in charge of security, keeping the peace, and whatever else his Napoleonic mind might conjure, he had wrangled a seat as close to the captain's table as possible. There he smiled along with their conversation as if he were in fact a part of the captain's group.

The food was good, the music fine, and the drinks plentiful, but as the evening wore on, the party began to feel as boring as a ship tied to a buoy. Something or somebody needed to liven it up.

While watching Chief Roland put on his cheerful act for the benefit of the captain's table and trying not to wretch at the sight, an idea occurred to me—a masterful idea, I thought. I shared it with Mike Fox and Jack Swinney, two other young petty officers at the table. They loved the idea. It would have been impossible not to.

Leaving our dates at the table, one by one the three of us quietly made our way out the front door and gathered in front of the club. Then, quickly heading for one of the seamier parts of town, we rounded up half a dozen prostitutes—the best looking and most scantily clad we could find—and told them they were invited to a party. Just follow us, we said, and they could go to this really nice place and eat and drink all they wanted. The six prostitutes beamed at the invitation.

All were good-looking girls, a couple of them even striking. And though they were clean and expensively dressed, the revealing nature of their clothing left little to the imagination and little doubt as to their profession.

As we neared the club, we stopped and had a talk with the

girls. We explained to them that since we had dates, we would go in first and rejoin our ladies, then in a few minutes they could come in and get plates of food, find seats, and eat all they wanted. They were visibly impressed with being invited into such a fancy place, and I'm sure they thought they might drum up a little business as well.

The three of us eased back into the club and rejoined our dates. A few minutes later, the prostitutes came in, looked around, and headed for the buffet line. They saw me sitting at the table and smiled and waved. Uh-oh. Why me? Why did the girls have to spot me?

The women started making their way through the buffet line and filling their plates to the brim, and for awhile, they didn't attract any special attention. Several of them even found seats and started eating before men off the ship and their wives began to take notice. When the crowd spotted them, however, they took notice in a hurry. The wives audibly sucked in their breath at sight of the scantily clad women, and the staring men were mostly laughing or trying not to.

Then it happened: Chief Roland saw the girls. His reaction alone made the endeavor worthwhile. I thought I had seen the chief-master-at-arms mad before, but nothing could compare with this precious moment.

The chief cop was out of his chair in a flash—wildly swinging his arms, hollering in the faces of the prostitutes, and asking what the *hell* they thought they were doing in there. I thought he might have a heart attack, an event that would *really* have topped off the evening.

As Chief Roland rushed the girls toward the door, trying to control his own screaming, two or three of them turned and pointed at me—not at either of the other guys involved—just me. They were trying to tell Roland that I had invited them in. The last one out, as she was being given a not-so-gentle heave-ho by the chief, pointed directly at me and hollered, "B.S. Boy-san!"

When the door closed and the girls were gone, Roland looked at me with eyes that could have burned a hole in a steel bulkhead. I shrugged, shook my head, and held out my hands as if I knew nothing. The chief didn't believe me. He started for our table, but then apparently wanting to let things settle down as quickly as possible, he decided against it and returned to his own. I saw him look at the captain and shrug, and then he looked back at me again. I turned away and tried to involve myself in conversation as if nothing had happened. It didn't help that several people at our table couldn't keep a straight face.

The very next morning, back on the ship, Chief Roland caught me before I had a chance to drop down to the engine room and hide. I was hurriedly dressing beside my bunk, and all the other guys in the compartment scooted out when Roland appeared.

The chief looked like a Rottweiler, ready to grab me and rip my throat out. "Penley," he said, "what's the hell's the idea of bringing them women into the ship's party?"

"Women?" I said. "What women?"

"You know damn good and well what women," he barked. "Them . . . whores!"

"Why, I don't know anything about that, Chief."

"You're fulla crap, Penley. They even pointed at you as I was runnin' them out the door."

"I know they did," I said. "And that puzzles me. Maybe they mistook me for somebody else they knew."

"How dumb do you think I am?" Roland roared.

Lord, hold my tongue, I thought.

Chief Roland stood silent for a moment, his teeth clenched, seething. "I *know* you brought them women in there, Penley, and it was a damn lousy trick to pull. If I could prove it, I'd hang you for it. I'd hang you so high you'd wish you never met me."

Actually, I already wished I'd never met him. I chose not to point that out, however.

The chief started to leave, then stopped and looked back. "You better watch your rear, Penley—*real* careful—because I'll have it if I can get it." Then he stomped out. I suppose I should have been worried, but I was having too much fun.

Down in the engine room, Sessions greeted me with a huge smile. "Penley, I about laughed myself to death when you brought those women in last night."

"Women?" I said.

"Yes," Sessions said, "those *ladies of the night.*"

"I don't know what you're talking about," I answered, unable to say it with a straight face.

"The hell you don't, *B.S. Boy-san,*" Sessions said. "I think the captain even got a kick out of it when Roland got so mad."

"Speaking of Roland," I said, "the chief already caught me this morning and told me he was going to hang me if he could get anything on me."

Sessions grinned. "Oh, so that's what the *chief-master-at-arms* told you, huh? Well, to hell with that strutting old rooster. He doesn't know how to have any fun, anyway. Don't worry, if he tries to hang you I won't let it happen."

"Thanks," I said, and we both burst into laughter.

Later that day, Lieutenant Heredia, the chief engineer, came down to visit the engine room. The lieutenant gave me a strange look when he stepped into the room.

"Hello, Mr. Heredia," I said.

He nodded. "Hello, Penley. How are you doing today?"

"Very well, sir," I replied. For a moment, I thought the lieutenant was going to laugh, but he turned and quickly left the engine room, only a minute or so after he had arrived.

Summer was ending, the chill of fall cutting across the bay. Sessions had taught me well, and I knew nearly everything there was to know about the engine room. I could run it by myself, which I greatly enjoyed, but I never liked repairing broken equipment. "You're an operator, Penley, not a fixer," Sessions told me, and he was right. Unfortunately, getting underway only once a week didn't give me much opportunity to be an operator.

One afternoon while I was working on some boring job in the engine room, Chief Roberts came down and said, "Penley, Mr. Heredia wants to see you in his quarters."

"Mr. Heredia," I said, startled. "What does he want to see me for?"

The chief shrugged. "I don't know," he said, "but you'd better hurry and get up there."

I rushed toward the engine room hatch, concerned as to why the chief engineer, wanted to see me. Was I in some sort of trouble, was someone in my family sick, or maybe dead? When I looked back and saw both Chief Roberts and Sessions grinning, I began to wonder if this was some kind of joke.

Hurrying up to the berthing level, I quickly brushed off my dungarees, washed my face and hands, and checked my hair in a mirror. Then I walked to Officers' Country, found Mr. Heredia's quarters, and knocked on the door. The lieutenant opened the door and motioned me in.

Mr. Heredia was a tall Hispanic officer with an easy manner and a quiet voice. Having never before been ordered to his quarters, I wondered, for a moment, if the incident at the ship's party had finally caught up with me. Then I saw the lieutenant smile and knew I wasn't in trouble. He took a seat behind his desk and invited me to sit as well.

"I have some great news for you, Penley," Mr. Heredia said. "At least *I* believe it's great news."

"Great news? What's that, sir?"

"A while back the captain received a fleet wide notice that the navy is badly in need of power plant operators for nuclear submarines. The captain passed the notice on to me and asked if I had anyone that would qualify for Nuclear Power School and that I could recommend for it.

"I checked your records, and as I suspected, your test scores from boot camp are high enough to get you into the school. When I asked Chief Roberts and Sessions their opinions concerning your work and dedication, they both recommended you, and I did too. Today we received the word that you've been accepted into the school—if you want it, that is."

"Wow!" I said, too overwhelmed to say anything else.

Mr. Heredia laughed. "As I said, it's up to you, Penley. Have you heard of Nuclear Power School?"

"Yes, sir, I have," I said nervously.

"Then you probably know that it's one of the best schools the navy has to offer and one of the hardest."

"Yes, I know, sir."

"The school is a full year long, and it's an accelerated course. It'll be a tough year. As I said, you're qualified for it, and you've already been accepted. There is a catch, though; you'll have to extend your enlistment for three years, for a total of seven, in order to get the school."

"What if I don't make it through the school?" I asked. "Do I still have to do the extra three years?"

The lieutenant smiled. "I'm afraid so. Once you sign on the dotted line, you have to stay in for seven years no matter what happens. But don't be thinking negative, Penley. I have every confidence that you can get through the school with flying colors." At the moment, I was wishing I felt the same confidence.

Mr. Heredia continued, "I've heard things about the school too, Penley, and I won't kid you, it'll probably be the toughest thing you ever did. But, on the positive side, I imagine this is the best opportunity you've ever had in your life. Correct?"

I nodded. "Yes, sir. It certainly is."

"You don't have to make up your mind right now," he said. "Take your time. Take a few days if you need to, then let me know your decision."

He shook my hand as I was leaving and repeated, "It's a great opportunity, Penley."

Chief Roberts and Sessions were still in the engine room when I went back down. Both were grinning. "Well, what do you think?" the chief asked.

"I don't know," I said. "It's . . . kind of overwhelming."

"Think it over well," Roberts said. "It'll change your life."

Sessions, the tall, handsome, quintessential sailor, chimed in. "That's right, Penley. That school will put you in a different navy. You'll be where we'd all like to be. Take that school; I sure would if I was qualified for it."

I hardly closed my eyes that night. Once more I was the country boy from Colorado, the one who almost flunked out of high school. Nuclear Power School and submarines would be a different navy all right, and it scared the hell out of me.

I remembered what Chief Loibl had told me in boot camp. "If you ever get a chance at one of the navy's high-powered schools, jump at it," the chief had said.

But what hit my mind the hardest, and finally made the decision for me, was a vivid memory of Dad. Two days before he died, so weak that I thought he would never again raise a hand, that tough old man sat up in bed, clenched his fists, and said, "Gary, when you see an opportunity, grab it!"

And something else occurred to me that I had learned from Dad, not from anything he said, but by watching the way he lived his life. I had noticed that many people lived their lives in a certain manner because they had more or less drifted into it, and even though they might not necessarily be happy with their plight, they had grown accustomed to it and become afraid of change—afraid of trying to live any other way. Dad had not lived his life like that; he had made choices and taken risks, many that scared him, I'm sure.

I vowed not to live my life in a certain way simply because I was afraid to try something else. And I *was* afraid.

The next morning, dressed in freshly pressed dungarees and, bright-eyed in spite of a night with little sleep, I walked into the engine room and looked at Chief Roberts and Sessions. They both smiled, and spoke in unison. "You're going to do it, aren't you?"

I took a deep breath. "Yep, I'm going to do it."

They both pumped my hand, and then the chief said, "Well, get up to Mr. Heredia's quarters and tell him what you decided."

"Just go up to his room, this early, without an appointment or anything?" I said.

"Sure," the chief said. "He'll be happy to see you."

I ran up to Officers' Country and knocked on Lieutenant Heredia's door. He opened it, regarded me with a grin, and repeated exactly what the chief and Sessions had said, "You're going to do it, aren't you?"

"Yes, sir. I'm scared to death, but I'm going to do it."

The news traveled quickly through the little ship. Everyone seemed happy for me except Chief Roland. He looked at me like a prosecutor eying a criminal who had escaped justice.

A few days later, I saluted the flag on the forecastle of the USS *San Joaquin County* and, seabag in hand, boarded the liberty boat for Iwakuni. Crossing the bay, I looked back at the LST and wondered one last time what lay hidden in the tank deck. Then I turned my gaze away from the last surface ship I would ever ride and sailed into another life.

Chapter Seven

School and More School

The trip from the states to Japan had seemed exciting, but much of that feeling had been due to my inexperience with military travel. The return trip turned out to be eventful in its own right.

Same hop to Tokyo on what felt like the same small, loud, twin-engine plane with a pile of cargo lashed down the middle of the craft. Same seating arrangement—web seats strung down each side that rocked and rolled and gave me the distinct feeling that someone had forgotten to issue me a parachute.

As we lifted off the runway at Iwakuni, I looked out the window and saw a speck far out in the bay—the *San Joaquin County,* with its great secret intact. As we gained altitude, I was on a high of my own. Off to school, and neither Japan, its people, nor the tough old LST that introduced me to engine rooms had left me with anything other than good feelings.

We landed on the northern outskirts of Tokyo and boarded a bus for a transit barracks that lay near the southern end—a slow trip through a giant city. Much of what I saw consisted of mile after mile of closely crowded shacks with no electricity or indoor plumbing. How did so many people, packed so closely together, manage to make a living? Occasionally one could see torn ruins and timeworn craters, remnants of the blanket bombing raids that Tokyo endured during the war—raids that killed more people in one day, through the use of multiple planes and hundreds of conventional bombs—than the single atomic bombs had done at Hiroshima and Nagasaki.

I had figured that all transit barracks were basically the same, but the one in Tokyo actually had a personality—far from endearing, but a personality nonetheless—given to it by the second-class boatswain's mate, "Boats," who was the man in charge. In his own words, made raspy by an excess of cigarettes and daily practice at sounding gruff: "I'm the skipper of this here land vessel, and don't none of ya ferget it."

Boats thought the use of the word "vessel" made him sound erudite. A sour, skinny runt with more lines in his face than an octogenarian, none of which were laugh lines, Boats was the antithesis of a class act. In the several days that I spent bunking on the second floor of his land vessel, I grew so weary of listening to Boats's rude voice on the squawk box—the microphone in his office being his favorite instrument—that I actually spent time contemplating ways in which I could destroy his mic without getting caught. And I could probably have pulled it off if I'd really set my mind to it, Boats's mental prowess being approximately on par with that of a paramecium.

Being a fairly new third-class petty officer, and on my way to Nuclear Power School, I suppose I was feeling a bit cockier than my status warranted. I was also bored and decided to have some fun with Boats.

Boats's official title was master-at-arms of the barracks. He had an office on the first floor, and every day he would put together work details to clean the sleeping quarters, clean the heads, clean his office, and various other tasks that occurred to his fuzzy mind—a mind that had, without fail, been thoroughly drenched in alcohol the night before.

The manner in which Boats put his work parties together was particularly loathsome. He would first make himself a list of names, rear back in his gray metal chair, pick up the microphone as if he were the CEO of a large corporation preparing to address his staff, and key the mic. Then he'd begin to rasp out the names.

"Johnson, master-at-arms office."

"Harlan, master-at-arms office."

"Hernandez, master-at-arms office," and so on until he had finished the list.

When one heard his name growled over the squawk box, he was to quickly get dressed in dungarees and rush to Boats's office to receive orders—in the same runty growl—as to which work party he had been assigned.

I escaped work parties for the first couple of days after I reported to Boats's land vessel, then one afternoon as I lay in my bunk, dressed only in skivvies and reading a book, the squawk box screeched, "Penley, master-at-arms office."

I didn't even look up when I heard my name, just went on reading. Within ten minutes, a young sailor who worked for Boats showed up at my bunk. "Are you Penley?" the nervous kid asked.

"Yes, I'm Penley," I answered.

"You better get down to Boats's office," he said. "And you better hurry, too. Boats is really mad."

"Okay," I told him. "I'll be down."

I took my time dressing, then meandered down the stairs and made my way to the master-at-arms office. Boats was boiling.

"Are you Penley?" he barked, jumping out of his chair like a bantam rooster who'd been goosed.

"I am."

"Did you hear me call you down here?"

"No," I said.

"You didn't hear me call ya down here for a work party, on the squawk box?"

"No, I didn't hear that," I answered. Then, doing my best to mimic Boats's exaggerated rasp, I said, "What I heard was 'Penley, master-at-arms office.' That doesn't mean anything. Hell, that's not even a sentence."

Boats's face went through myriad changes in a very short time—anger, confusion, hatred, maybe even insanity—some that seemed to incorporate a number of emotions all at once. In his fury, the man could not speak.

I could speak, but I didn't. I could also smirk, and that I did.

At that point, I thought Boats could not possibly look any madder, but when I smirked, he proved me wrong. He stepped close, trying his best to look menacing. We stood toe to toe and would have been nose to nose if his hadn't been several inches below mine—a nice thing in itself, because the man's breath would have turned a grizzly away.

He looked up at me, so enraged I thought he was going to slug me. I was hoping he would, because in self-defense, I planned to clean the little rooster's office with him.

The kid who had been sent to fetch me was standing to the side during all this. The look on his face alone made it worthwhile.

Boats didn't hit me, causing me to wonder if he might be smarter than I gave him credit for. He plopped down in his chair, gripping the arms until his knuckles turned white, and it was a long time before he spoke. When he did, the words came out slowly. "Listen, sailor, I don't know who you think you are, but I'm the skipper of this here land vessel, and don't you forget it."

He waited for a reply. I said nothing.

"Did you hear me?" he roared.

"Yes," I said wearily. "It would be pretty hard not to."

A wry smile creased Boats's face. For a moment, he seemed to consider my reply a compliment, but then his expression turned to puzzlement and back to anger.

"Now," he said, jabbing a finger in my direction, "I'm *ordering* you, to get up to the second level and clean every head on that floor, *by yourself*. Understand?"

Again he waited for a reply, but I refused to accommodate him. I walked away, up the stairs, and spent the rest of the afternoon cleaning bathrooms.

I stayed in Boats's land vessel several more days, and expected to find myself assigned to every lousy work party the skipper could think of. To my surprise, however, Boats never again called my name. I guess he thought it wasn't worth the trouble.

When finally I heard my name growled over the squawk box again, it was my cue to leave for the States. A happy day, both for me and for Boats.

As before, I would be flying on a large four-engine prop plane, but instead of it being a military air transport craft with no insulation and the seats mounted backwards, the U.S. military chartered a commercial airliner. Friendly stewardesses, drinks, and leg room that didn't bring on an attack of claustrophobia before one even tried to sit down. Sailors, marines, soldiers, and air force—all enlisted men—shared the plane, and we rejoiced at not having to ride across the endless Pacific in one of those loud, vibrating MATS monsters that would have given the Wright brothers a chuckle.

We were young though and early in the lessons of life—blissfully unconcerned, as well as unaware, that not all things that seem great in the beginning prove so in the end.

I looked out the window, with fondness, at the shoreline of Japan as it faded into the mist, then I leaned back to enjoy the long, comfortable ride across the Pacific—on to new adventures and home.

The adventures began sooner than I had anticipated. Way, way out over the wide Pacific, as I was relaxing in an aisle seat, reading a book and enjoying an occasional drink, I began to notice something different in the sound of the engines—not a great difference—but with my engine room experience the change in sound caught my attention. None of the other passengers appeared to notice, and when I asked one of the stewardesses, quietly, if the plane was experiencing engine trouble, she quietly told me nothing was wrong. I sat back in my seat and listened, knowing that she had quietly lied to me.

The aberrant engine noise grew slightly worse, but still no other passengers seemed to notice. Not caring to cause panic throughout the plane—the same reason the stewardess had told me everything was fine—I kept quiet about what I was hearing.

Finally, the captain's voice came over the intercom. "We appear to be having a bit of trouble with engine number three, folks. Now there's no reason for alarm; everyone please remain calm. As a precaution, we've radioed ahead for clearance to land on Wake Island. Please fasten your seat belts, as we'll be landing there shortly. We'll deplane as soon as the craft is safely parked on Wake. Thank you."

Now everybody knew.

Although I didn't fully appreciate it at the time, I was developing a keen sense for the sound of machinery, a sense that would become second nature to me in submarines. The stewardess whom I had asked about the engine noise stopped by my seat, leaned over, and whispered, "I don't know how you heard that; I could hardly hear it myself." I laughed.

Several of the passengers gave me a strange look, wondering what could be funny at a time like this, and I felt a bit smug about my ability to laugh in the face of danger. I might not have felt so cocksure if I could have seen into the future and known what awaited me in the years ahead.

Wake Island, a pinpoint in the middle of the Pacific, did not top the list of places I had longed to see, especially out the window of a crippled plane.

We landed, quickly deplaned, and were directed into a small terminal to wait while some airport flunkies, none of whom appeared to be mechanical wizards, checked out the engine. After the would-be mechanics finished their checking, the man in charge of the little airport came into the terminal and told us the engine was in bad shape and that it was beyond their capabilities to repair.

When some of the disgruntled passengers complained of the inconvenience, the man reiterated, vehemently, that the plane was unsafe to fly and that they had neither the parts nor the expertise needed to repair the engine. Looking at the flunky mechanics standing around him as he spoke made his analysis easy to believe.

We had no other choice but to wait until parts and technicians arrived from Hawaii to repair the engine. According to the head man, everything we needed was on the way, but he had no idea when it might arrive.

After being put up in a makeshift barracks, we found ourselves in an unusual situation—the United States Navy, Marines, Army, and Air Force all crammed together, with no one in charge. And a strange phenomenon occurred: since we were all in the same predicament, the normal interservice animosity never reared its ugly head. We each found a bunk to our liking, with no bickering over who got which one, and then we all agreed on one universal military necessity—beer. A group of us, with representatives from each branch of the service, went to the terminal and asked the man behind the desk where we could find beer. He calmly told us, as if it were a matter of little significance, that there was no beer.

After looking at one another and passing a long moment of collective incredulity, we all turned as one and explained two things to the man behind the desk: 1) We weren't stupid enough to believe that a group of people living in isolation on Wake

Island did so without the benefit of beer. 2) He was out of his mind if he thought he was going to deny us access to said beer.

We had plenty of beer that night, compliments of the airline, I guess.

The following morning, with our lame craft sitting on the same spot where the pilot had taxied to a stop, we learned that neither the parts nor the technicians had arrived from Hawaii. We hadn't seen any of the airline crew since shortly after we landed, but soon the pilot, copilot, and stewardesses showed up at the terminal, looking as impatient as the rest of us.

We all watched the sky as nothing, and nobody, arrived from anywhere.

Later that morning, three or four of the Wake Island flunkies— the ones whom we had been doubly assured *could not* fix the engine—carried a ladder and a toolbox out to the plane, climbed up to the broken engine, and banged around on it for an hour or so. Minutes after they finished whatever they were doing, the pilot and the man in charge came out and announced that the engine was fixed—ready to go.

Most of the guys broke into smiles, grabbed up their bags, and ran for the plane. I did not. With two or three young fellows following me, I walked over to the two men. "Ready to go?" I asked. "Yesterday you told us . . ."

The head man interrupted me. "I know," he said, impatiently waving us toward the plane. "I was wrong yesterday. Didn't turn out to be as bad as we thought." The pilot wouldn't look at me.

I picked up my bag and headed for the plane, not in any particular rush to get back aboard. The other doubtfuls continued to follow me. "Do you think they really got it fixed?" a young soldier asked.

I didn't believe for a second that the engine had actually been repaired, but I couldn't tell them that. "We'll be okay," I said. "That plane will fly on just one engine if it has to." That seemed to satisfy them more than it satisfied me.

After the pilot got on the intercom and again assured everyone that the problem was history and the plane fit to fly, he started the engines. They sounded all right to me, until we were racing down the runway and about to take to the air. Then I heard the same noise as before.

The stewardess with whom I had had the discussion the day before came by, smiled noncommittally, and asked, "Would you like something to drink, sir?"

I smiled back. "Yes," I said. "You'd better bring me a double."

The engine noise remained the same, and my eyes never closed. I memorized every emergency procedure and mapped the quickest way to an emergency exit in my mind. Most of the passengers acted as if nothing was wrong. Perhaps, like me, they were simply acting, but I didn't think so.

Most were shocked when, after we finally touched down in Honolulu, on the farthest landing strip from the terminal, the air controllers directed us to taxi to a far corner of the field, shut down the engines, deplane, grab our own baggage, hurry to a waiting bus, and leave the vicinity of the aircraft as quickly as possible.

Smiling at my stewardess friend as I passed her on the way out, I said, "Well, we made it, didn't we?"

She grinned. "Yep, we made it."

Another plane took us on to the mainland, thank God.

The first half of Nuclear Power School—"Nuke School"—was located in Vallejo, California. Reporting there in the fall of 1962, I could not fully appreciate the life-changing experience on which I was embarking or the mountain of work that lay ahead. And if I had any vestiges of cockiness left from having been accepted to the school, my new division officer laid them to rest in a few tense minutes.

Lieutenant Samson was the first submariner officer I had ever met. Broad-chested, cool-eyed, and squared away as a warship ready for action, he was seated behind a desk that was as neatly arranged as himself. When the lieutenant called me into his office, the first thing I noticed were the dolphins—the mark of a submariner—on his chest.

"Engineman Third-Class Penley reporting, sir," I said, snapping to attention in front of his desk.

"At ease," he said, his eyes probing mine for a long moment. Then he looked down at a stack of papers that lay in front of him. In a decidedly dissatisfied manner, Lieutenant Samson began slowly turning the pages over one at a time. To my horror, I saw that they were copies of my high-school transcripts. The look on his face told me that those abominable grades had returned to plague me once more.

After turning several pages and shaking his head each time he scanned one, he looked up. "Do you know what kind of school this is?" the lieutenant asked.

"Yes, sir," I answered smartly.

"Do you really think you can get through a school like this?" he said, sarcasm tainting his voice.

"Yes, sir. I do," I replied.

The lieutenant thumbed through another page or two, disgustedly, then looked me hard in the eye. "You've got a damn poor background for this school, sailor. I think you'll have a hell of a time getting through it."

His words tried my patience and prodded my determination. "I'll make it through, sir. Guaranteed."

He regarded me thoughtfully, waved his hand, and said, "Dismissed."

I left Lieutenant Samson's office, mad—steaming mad—and determined to get through that school just to prove him wrong. *Telling me he thinks I can't do it. How dare he!*

The officer said exactly the right thing to motivate me. I suspect he knew that when he said it.

Since the navy had only one nuclear-powered surface vessel at the time, the giant aircraft carrier *Enterprise,* the lion's share of men in the nuclear navy were submariners. I hadn't seen more than a handful of sub sailors in my previous two years in the military; now they were everywhere. Unlike myself, most of the enlisted students had previous underwater duty, some on nuclear subs and some on diesels—many of the old WWII boats still in commission at the time. And virtually every instructor, all of whom were officers, were career submariners.

Lieutenant Samson didn't exaggerate when he told me the school would be tough. The curriculum, personally designed by Adm. Hyman Rickover—a relentless genius who earned the title "Father of the Nuclear Navy"—entailed eight full hours of class work each day. Monday through Friday, we studied mechanical and electrical theory, electronics, steam plant technology, reactor technology, nuclear physics, geometry, algebra, advanced algebra, and calculus. Everyone was tested weekly, and if a student fell 1 percent behind, he was assigned one night of mandatory study per week—four hours of it. If one fell 2 percent behind, he had two nights of mandatory study, and so on up to a maximum of six nights per week. Even with such stringent requirements, the school had a 50 percent attrition rate, many of whom flunked out academically and others who simply gave up and threw in the towel because they couldn't stand the stress.

I never allowed myself to fall behind, because I was right there in the study room five or six nights a week to ensure that I didn't, remembering the terrible feeling of coming so close to flunking out of high school and vowing never to feel that way again.

The stress of day and night study took its toll, and I went back to fighting on Friday and Saturday nights when I went into town on liberty—the fisticuffs generally following the consumption of a considerable amount of beer. Some of my classmates thought I'd gone crazy, and maybe for a while I did. However, after once again proving to be a poor student of the martial arts, I gave that up and searched for less painful methods of stress management. Reading, for pleasure rather than study, became a lifelong refuge from the inevitable storms of living.

I managed to pass the second-class engineman test during the long six months—a little extra study seeming like nothing in that pressure-cooker environment—and was promoted to E-5.

Near the end of the school, I passed Lieutenant Samson in the hall one day. "How's it going for you, Penley?" Mr. Samson asked. He already knew the answer, of course. He was my division officer.

"Very well, sir," I said. "I'm doing it."

The lieutenant smiled. "Good for you," he said. The man was a born leader, and I was ten feet tall.

Two hundred and eighty students graduated from the school. I was number eighteen, the top six percentile—a record for me. Lieutenant Samson shook my hand and smiled a second time—perhaps a record for him as well.

Most people, sailors and civilians alike, would never guess where the second half of Nuke School was located—in Idaho—an experience that generated a lifetime of questions. What was a sailor doing stationed in Idaho? At times I questioned it myself.

The purpose of Nuke School II (as we affectionately dubbed the second half of Admiral Rickover's endurance test) was to teach us, hands-on, how to operate a power plant and to qualify us as certified operators. The public had a great fear of nuclear plants in those days, a fear that even extended to the energy they generated. This is why the two working prototypes—one of the submarine *Nautilus* and the other of the aircraft carrier *Enterprise*—were located far out in the Idaho desert, an arid land of tumbleweeds, yucca, and cactus inhabited by coyotes, jack rabbits, snakes, horned toads, lizards, and tarantulas. And the tremendous amount of electrical energy the reactors generated was wasted, dissipated in giant cooling towers instead of being put to some practical use.

Although security was extremely high, in order to minimize military exposure to the civilian populace, the isolated facility did not look like a naval base per se and we weren't allowed to wear uniforms except on the bus that carried us to and from the location.

Students and instructors alike lived in town, either Idaho Falls or Pocatello, and we were paid per diem to rent apartments or houses. A friend of mine and I rented a mobile home in Idaho Falls—a sixty-mile bus ride from the reactor facility.

A paradox existed in the nuclear training program. More operators were needed for submarines than surface ships, but the *Enterprise* prototype, being much the larger of the two, could handle more trainees than the mock-up of the *Nautilus*. Many of the students, including myself, who were slated for nuclear sub duty ended up assigned to the huge *Enterprise* plant for training. The principles of operation being the same, I didn't particularly care which plant I trained on.

And what a power plant it was. When I walked into *that* engine room, I knew I had found my niche.

The carrier *Enterprise* boasted eight reactors and four engine rooms, one to power each of its four giant screws. The working prototype in Idaho, an exact replica of one of the engine rooms on the ship, was fed steam by two large reactors that together generated more than 100,000 shaft horsepower—the most powerful land-based nuclear plant in existence at the time. I loved it.

Adm. Hyman Rickover, who reputedly possessed the mind of a genius and the disposition of a wolverine, was small in stature but projected the presence of a giant. Short and coyote-thin with a sharp-edged face, eyes that neither smiled nor blinked, and a strange nose that could have been grafted from a koala bear, the admiral cared not a whit what anyone else thought of him or their personal opinion on any subject it seemed. I'm sure that none of his subordinates or superiors ever mentioned these particular attributes in the admiral's presence, however.

The admiral disliked wearing uniforms, and so when he showed up in civilian clothes, either on a land base or on a nuclear submarine, he would borrow a set of khakis from one of the young officers to wear during his time aboard. It was said that when he left he never returned the uniforms nor did any of the young officers ever dare ask for them.

Admiral Rickover visited the plant in Idaho one day, unannounced, as was often his way. Shiley, a humorous second-class and a friend of mine, happened to be recording readings from gauges in the plant that day. One pressure gauge that was known to sometimes give erratic readings needed to be shaken in order to ensure its accuracy.

Holding his clipboard in one hand, Shiley reached up and shook the gauge with the other. Then, as he proceeded to write down the pressure, a voice behind him said, "Why did you shake that gauge?"

"Aw, the damn thing don't work some of the time," Shiley said, "and you gotta shake the hell out of it to make sure it's right." After this raw explanation, Shiley turned around and looked directly into the unblinking eyes of the admiral. Rickover stood and stared at him for an endless moment, then walked away.

The errant gauge was magically replaced that very day, probably after the chief engineer received a personal butt chewing from the admiral—the greatest dread of all officers in the nuclear program and enlisted men as well. Shiley told me that he had nearly filled his pants when he realized who he was talking to.

Our work schedule, a diabolical scheme designed by Rickover, of course, defied logic. Working a six-day week, we alternated between eight- and twelve-hour days. We got to go home in the evening on the eight-hour days; on the twelve-hour drags—which we endured every other day—we had to sleep at the facility. And to top that off, we changed shifts weekly. One week we worked days, the next week we worked the swing shift, then graveyard for a week, and then back to days. Simply keeping up with one's schedule was a challenge, let alone working such hours without falling asleep on your feet. It must have been another of the admiral's weird tests: to see how long we could go without becoming disoriented or falling stone dead from exhaustion.

The scenery on the bus ride to and from the arid location was bleak, but that didn't matter. The only person who ever stayed awake was the driver.

Only the young, hearty, and half-crazy could have done it. And even after finishing the high-pressure six months of classroom work in California, the stress of the second half still overwhelmed some. One fellow, a second-class petty officer who was supposed to be on the bus, just stood on a downtown street one morning and waved at us as we went by, so drunk he could barely stand. The man didn't have to worry about riding the bus again; he lost a stripe and got thrown out of the nuclear program the following day. I talked to him just before he shipped out, and he told me he was greatly relieved. He simply couldn't stand it any more.

The school may have been tough going, but sailors being sailors, even working that insane schedule we often managed to put together parties on our one day off. And wild parties they could be, the likes of which astounded the quiet populace. The good civilians, however, many of whom were Mormons—a religion that does not believe in drinking—were far more understanding and patient than we would ever have expected. In fact, many Mormon girls, although they did not drink, ended up marrying sailors they met at these parties. Perhaps the girls hoped to change the sailors' habits, an ambitious goal indeed.

I had already seen too many failed marriages in the navy, and would see even more on submarines. There were exceptions, of course, and I witnessed some loving, understanding partnerships that weathered it all. For myself, still clinging to the dream of returning to the old ranch in Colorado after the navy, I decided that the military, my future plans, and marriage would not jibe. I would continue the adventure single, and I did.

Finally, the long, high-pressure year was over. I had made it, the biggest achievement of my life. And just a few days after officially becoming a qualified nuclear power plant operator, I almost screwed it up. Sitting at home one evening, with the tremendous pressure off, I hardly knew what to do with myself. I figured it out, though, and the solution I came up with does not rank high in the annals of good judgment. In true sailor-like fashion, I went downtown and drank and drank and drank. I then was arrested, incarcerated (thrown into the drunk tank), and kept until morning. I had to be bailed out of jail and I missed the bus, the one and only time in my military career that I was AWOL—late reporting for duty.

It was a grim scene when I arrived at the facility. Lieutenant Gardiner, my normally polite, soft-spoken division officer, was anything but soft-spoken when I reported to him. The man shamed me, telling me how upset, disappointed, and just plain mad he was that I chose to be out drinking instead of preparing to come to the site and work, as I had always done and done well. Everything he said was correct, and everything he said pained my soul. I thought I was finished, and I should have been.

Mr. Gardiner relieved me of all duties, restricted me to the facility, and let me sweat it out for two weeks. Nothing to do but wonder what was going to happen to me. Scared, ashamed, and physically sick with worry, I had no one to blame but myself. I had just finished a grueling year of school, with grades to be proud of, and now I felt sure I'd be washed out of the nuclear program. And probably busted in rank as well.

Despair had never been a part of my makeup, but now the shame overwhelmed me, both for what I had done to myself and the thought that I had failed my country, and Dad.

At long last, Mr. Gardiner sent for me. Standing at attention in his office, I waited for the words that would ruin my life. Seated behind his desk, the tall lieutenant looked at me angrily, then motioned me to sit down. "I was going to send you to captain's mast, Penley—recommend that you be busted and thrown out of this program—and you certainly deserved it for pulling that stunt."

"I know, sir," I said. My heart was racing; he sounded as if he might have changed his mind.

Continuing to frown and stare holes through me, the lieutenant went on. "More than half the instructors on this site came to my office to plead your case, and a lot of your fellow students did the same. Did you know that?"

"No, I wasn't aware of that, sir."

"You'd better say a big 'Thank you' to most of the men in this plant, sailor. They saved you."

I couldn't speak.

"What have you got to say for yourself?" Mr. Gardiner asked.

"I'm . . . thankful, sir," I stammered. "Very thankful. I overreacted to finishing the school, and I thought I'd blown it. This school means more to me than anything I've done in my life."

"Well, you came within a hair's breadth of messing up your life," he said. "You're a smart sailor, Penley. Now get yourself off to sub school, and don't be pulling any more crap like this."

We stood up. "Thank you, sir," I said. "I won't let you down again."

"See that you don't," he said, and shook my hand. "Good luck, Penley."

I found a secluded corner in an empty barracks, sat down, and cried.

New London, Connecticut, home of the submarine service.

Sub school, the one all would-be submariners attended. Cooks, stewards, torpedo men, electricians, machinist mates, electronics technicians, quartermasters, fire control technicians, and enginemen—from seamen and firemen to first-class petty officers—all in the same class for three months. Some in the technical rates, such as myself, were nuclear trained; others were not.

We "nukes," having completed Rickover's stringent program, tended to be treated with suspicion by the others. They suspected we might be arrogant asses due to our advanced training, and in some cases, they were correct. Since I considered it stupid to deprive myself of potential friends for such a senseless reason, after the first week or so, I felt accepted by both nukes and non-nukes.

The U.S. Naval Submarine School is a place of tradition—a proud, violent tradition of danger and daring that gripped me and took me under the sea as I moved slowly down its hallowed halls. It was impossible to simply walk down one of the halls. They were lined with hundreds of arresting pictures, many of which were photos of torpedo-blasted ships taken through the periscopes of World War II boats—enemy vessels ablaze and going down, many broken into halves, each ragged piece beginning to tip toward the depths as crowded lifeboats and men in the water fought to get away from the shattered wreckage before it pulled them down.

There were also portraits of heroes of the Silent Service such as the daring Richard O'Kane and "Mush" Morton, skippers of the USS *Tang* and USS *Wahoo,* two of the most famous and deadly submarines in the war. And Commander Howard Gilmore who, trapped topside and too badly wounded to crawl to the hatch, ordered his sub to dive to escape lethal fire from attacking aircraft, posthumously receiving the Congressional Medal of Honor for sacrificing himself while saving his ship to fight again. And Capt. Edward Beach, survivor of a dozen war patrols, author of *Run Silent, Run Deep,* and skipper of the USS *Triton,* the first nuclear submarine to circumnavigate the globe without surfacing.

I had already studied much of the history of submarine warfare. Most civilians, and many in other branches of the military, thought sinking a ship with a submarine to be a simple task—just find an enemy ship, shoot your torpedoes, watch her sink, and go on your merry way, seeking other sitting ducks to blast apart and send to the bottom.

Nothing could be farther from reality.

In World War II, submarine warfare was one of the most dangerous forms of battle, confirmed by the fact that more submariners were killed, per capita, than any branch of any military service. The United States lost more than 30 percent of her submarines, Germany lost 75 percent of her U-boats, and Japan had only one sub left when she surrendered. Submarines on both sides exacted a tremendous toll on enemy shipping, but they paid a terrible price for their efforts.

All the instructors at sub school, whether enlisted or commissioned, wore dolphins on their chests—the mark of a qualified submariner. And a few of the old-timers wore war patrol medals, an insignia so revered among sub sailors that the sight of one on a man's chest would bring a hush to the room.

Some might argue that this proud heritage was carried a bit too far, but I would disagree. A diesel submarine that had gone down years before with all hands aboard had been recorded on sonar by another sub—every grim sound captured as the vessel broke apart on its way to the bottom. Our lead instructor, a chief petty officer, played this audio tape in class about every week. You could hear the whine of the steel boat as it picked up speed on its way to the bottom, and every now and then, a muffled boom as another compartment imploded from the pressure of the sea.

The chief knew the tape by heart. "Listen, now," he would say as the sounds of the sinking submarine filled the room. "Another compartment is getting ready to blow; this one sounds like a big one, probably the After Battery."

It was a scary recording, but after so much repetition, many of us began to laugh and make jokes about it. The chief didn't appreciate our irreverence, but after hearing it over and over, we tired of that garbage, which is how we referred to the tape. That is, some of us referred to it that way, others became more frightened every time they heard it. They didn't make it through sub school.

Because it's impossible to force someone who is claustrophobic to enter an airtight tube and ride it into the depths, the submarine service is manned by volunteers only, and in sub school a student who couldn't take the training was not disciplined for giving up. The sub service didn't want men who were afraid and prone to panic; if one expressed a strong desire to get out of the school, he was sent back to surface ships with few questions asked.

At the beginning of the school, we all took a series of psychological tests that weeded out most of the men who were unfit for sub duty. A few—very few—slipped by the initial tests but not for long.

Many WWII diesel subs were still in commission in the 1960s, and several were tied up at the pier in New London. Fearless warships that had fought countless battles, often limping back to base after surviving depth-charge attacks that all but tore them apart, these aging subs were now used for training—school boats, they were called—an innocuous connotation that seemed beneath the dignity of these brave old warriors.

Sometime during the second week our lead instructor began coming into the classroom and calling out the names of four or five students. The named sailors were told to go down to a certain school boat that evening and eat dinner with the crew. That seemed a strange practice, so I asked the chief the purpose of it. He told me it was simply for an initial orientation, an answer that sounded shallow, and it was. A few days later, when my name came up, I learned the real reason why new students were ordered to eat a meal on one of the boats.

Three other guys and I were told to go to the USS *Cavalla* (SS-244) that evening and have dinner with the crew. The chief explained that the forward hatch, which led down into the forward torpedo room, would be left open for us. After climbing down the ladder into the torpedo room, we were to proceed aft to the crew's mess, which was located amidships.

The four of us met in the barracks that evening, walked to the pier, and found the *Cavalla*. Sure enough, the forward hatch was open, a welcoming beacon of light pouring out of it from inside the dark hull.

After crossing the gangway and explaining our mission to the topside watch, I quickly walked to the forward hatch and hurried down the ladder, eager to see the inside of my first submarine. The other three moved slower, the last one, a seaman named Bringer, tentatively making his way down the ladder as if he thought he might fall at any moment.

What a wonderland—albeit more than a little cramped. Levers, gauges, valves, and piping: more than the eye could take in all at once. There were even bunks scattered about the torpedo room, and I found myself standing on a narrow steel walkway directly between a pair of long torpedoes.

"Wow," I said, "would you look at this!" The others were looking around as well, the last one down the hatch, Bringer, staring at the compartment with a wary eye. He hadn't let go of the ladder.

I pointed forward. "Well, I guess that's the way to the crew's mess. It's not like there's a lot of other directions to go." Two of the other guys chuckled at my little attempt at humor. Bringer did not. We all started forward, except for him.

"Aren't you coming, Bringer?" I said, thinking I was being facetious.

The seaman shook his head. "Nope. You guys can go on back there if you want to, but I'm not taking one more step into this thing."

In the next second, Bringer was back up the ladder and gone, and gone from sub school the following day. Now I knew why students were sent to eat aboard a submarine before going to sea in one.

The three of us walked aft, ducking through rounded hatches that appeared to have been made for dwarfs, banging our heads, shoulders, arms, and knees on protruding equipment until we reached the crew's mess. A tiny galley adjoined the dining space, which itself was cramped by any standards other than the sub service. The food, however, tasted like we had sat down in a five-star restaurant.

I soon learned that submarine cooks were handpicked, and if their meals didn't turn out to be among the finest in the navy, they didn't make it in the sub service. There was no written procedure for getting rid of bad cooks; if it became known that the crew didn't like the meals a cook put out—and it *would* become known—the cook was gone.

A couple of weeks later, portions of the class began going to sea for one day at a time on one of the school boats. I was lucky enough to be assigned to the same boat on which I'd eaten my first delicious meal: the old *Cavalla,* a sub that had actually sunk a Japanese aircraft carrier during the war. To attack an aircraft carrier was a near suicidal endeavor, but the *Cavalla* succeeded in sinking the mighty ship and paid a high price for her audacity. The carrier's escorts quickly located the submerged sub and dealt her a devastating depth-charge attack that reportedly lasted for twenty-four hours—an unimaginable horror to endure, and the reason the men with war patrol medals rated such respect.

Studying the tight spaces in that sub, I couldn't imagine the terror that those men had undergone during the depth-charge attacks. Again, thank God I couldn't see into my own future.

Submarines are pure fighting machines, and the more I learned about them the more my fascination grew. The first and most interesting thing we learned is what allows a submarine to do what it does: dive, operate as a submerged vessel, and return to the surface.

The enclosure in which the crew lives is the pressure hull—a watertight cylinder of thick steel designed to withstand tons of pressure exerted by the heavy column of water bearing down on it when submerged. The deeper the sub dives, the greater the pressure the hull must withstand. Surrounding the outside of the pressure hull are a series of tanks—ballast tanks—which have openings in their bottoms to allow the inflow and outflow of sea water. Large valves in the tops of the ballast tanks are opened and shut hydraulically, these valves being the key to submerging and surfacing the boat.

When the submarine is running on the surface, the valves are shut and the ballast tanks are filled with air. This keeps the sub afloat, not unlike riding on great balloons. When the valves are opened, the air rushes out the top of the tanks, allowing seawater to flood in through the open ports in the bottom, and the boat quickly submerges; in effect, it sinks. In order to surface again, the valves are closed and high-pressure air is introduced into the tanks, blowing the water out the bottom ports and forcing the boat back to the surface, where it again rides on cushions of air.

When running submerged and being pushed by the stern-mounted propeller, the boat literally flies through the water, movable diving planes driving it upward or downward in the same manner as flaps on airplane wings. After we had been to sea a couple of times, listened to the A-ooo-ga!, A-ooo-ga! of the diving alarm, submerging and surfacing a number of times each day, we began to think of ourselves as sub sailors. We didn't dare utter such blasphemy to the instructors, who were all seasoned submariners, but we privately considered ourselves at least a little bit salty.

Submariners are a difficult lot to scare, even novice almost-submariners. Once we got the jumpy ones weeded out, neither the horror stories from the salty instructors nor recordings of sinking submarines seemed to bother us at all. When such things began to draw chuckles and wise remarks from the class, the instructors gave up trying to maintain a stern countenance and joined in the laughter, for they, of all people, knew the nature of submariners.

One trial scared most of us, however—the escape tower. A one-hundred-foot steel structure about thirty feet in diameter, the columnar tower was filled to the top with water, a man-made ocean from whose depths we had to escape, simulating ascension from a sunken submarine.

The eight-story tank rose from the submarine base like a giant pipe standing on end. It could be entered at ground level, with a hundred feet of water above, or one could ride an elevator to the fifty-foot level, the escape depth required of sub school students.

A round, blister-like room extended from the side of the tank at the fifty-foot level. Approximately twelve feet in diameter and constructed of thick steel, the arc-shaped room had a flat bottom, a rounded ceiling, and an iron bench that extended all the way around the arc. At the break in the arc, where the room met the side of the tank, was a small watertight hatch that allowed entry from the room into the tank, a frightful move that suddenly placed one at the bottom of a fifty-foot column of water.

The blister room was entered from the outside through another watertight door, the smaller door to the huge tank being dogged shut at the time to allow students to walk into the room and sit down on the bench. It felt like being seated around the inner periphery of a flying saucer—a saucer that had landed in fifty feet of water and settled to the bottom.

Dressed only in swim trunks, a deflated Mae West life jacket around our necks, and led by a giant navy diver, a dozen of us ducked through the hatch, padded through several inches of water that covered the bottom, and sat down on the narrow bench. We clung to the life jackets as if our lives depended on them, because they did.

Thus seated and jammed together in a tight circle, the metal ceiling six inches above our heads, we watched the big diver close and dog the thick steel door to the hatch we had just entered. Then slowly he began to open a valve, and water came rushing into the room from beneath our feet. The diver didn't look scared, but eleven other faces did, and if I'd had a mirror, it would have made an even dozen.

The bubbling water rose around our legs, reached our knees, and began to cover our thighs. As the water filled the tiny compartment, the increasing pressure on our ears forced us to equalize them every few seconds. The diver, a Southerner, drawled, "Water's right chilly, ain't it?" Except for chattering of teeth and spasms of shivers, no one responded.

As the water continued to rise, beginning to lap up to our waists, our escort diver turned off the valve and stopped the flow. It felt like taking a break in the middle of the Battle of the Bulge. "How's everybody doin'?" he asked jovially.

Attempting my normal response to fear or discomfort, I said, "This is j-j-just great, s-s-sir. Doing j-just fine."

The diver smiled wryly, while the others looked at me as if I might be deranged, a conclusion difficult to refute given the circumstances.

After we all got our breath—I didn't realize I'd been holding mine—and equalized our ears, the diver opened the valve again. Once more, the cold water began to rise. When the water reached chest level, we had only about a foot and a half of air space left between it and the ceiling.

The tiny room took on a demonic aspect, a wet torture chamber that closed in on us, threatening to kill us all. We stretched our necks and turned our faces upward, placing our noses as close to the ceiling as possible; a few tall men could actually touch the steel with their faces. When the water reached the chin of the shortest guy, the diver turned off the valve. We settled in our seats, just a bit, and found that we didn't have to stretch quite as high as we had been in order to breathe.

There we sat, under water except for our noses, our eyes, and the tops of our heads. That much space and a miniscule amount between our heads and the ceiling held all the air that existed in our tight, scary world. And that air was pressurized to nearly twenty-five pounds per square inch (psi): the same pressure as the fifty-foot column of water right outside the hatch that led into the tank.

The diver, who had shut off the valve just short of drowning us all, asked cheerily, "Everybody okay?"

"Hell, no," I said, and I wasn't joking this time. The diver got a good laugh out of that one.

We had been through the drill in a classroom, and so we weren't surprised—nervous, but not surprised—when the diver ducked his head underwater, undogged the submerged door leading into the tank, pushed it open, and swung it outward until it latched in that position.

We knew that nothing was supposed to happen when he opened the steel door, but still we were surprised, maybe even shocked, when nothing did. It seemed that the fifty feet of water above us, to which we were now exposed, should have rushed in, filled the little room to the top, and drowned us in our seats. But the bubble of air we were breathing remained in place, just as we had been assured.

I was not without a certain amount of claustrophobia, and I had long known that. It showed up only in very tight places, and this was a very tight place. There appeared to be thirteen people in the watery little room that frightful day, but I know there were fourteen. Dad was in there with me.

I could hardly wait to get out the hatch and up through that fifty feet of water to freedom, but it had to be done in a certain manner, if one wanted to reach the surface alive. Our lungs were charged with pressurized air, the same twenty-five psi that the column of water was exerting on us. One had to exhale, strongly, all the way up to the surface; otherwise your lungs would burst from the rapidly expanding air. If fear overtook a man and induced him to hold his breath, he was dead.

When the diver tapped a man on the shoulder, that was his cue to pull the cords and inflate his life jacket. Then he would duck his head underwater, step through the hatch, and hold tightly to the top of the hatch as the life jacket fought to shoot him to the surface. In that crucial moment he had to straighten his body, turn his face upward, begin exhaling with all the force he could muster, and let go.

I'd been wondering how one could exhale all the way to the surface without taking a breath. When the life jacket rocketed me upward, I learned the answer: there was plenty to exhale. As the air in my lungs continued to expand, it just kept coming. When I broke the surface—or when Dad and I broke the surface—I felt I had been reborn.

The guys who had already completed the ascent and climbed out of the tank clapped and cheered each time another made it.

Submarine School, class 292, graduation photo, January 16, 1964.

Everyone had been warned that, if their performance in the tank proved unsatisfactory, they would have to repeat the ascent. Morgan, an outsized first-class with one eye that wandered, looked like a man who could hunt bears with a stick. Climbing out of the tank, he scowled at one of the diving instructors. "I hope you ain't plannin' to make me do that again," he said.

The instructor grinned. "I'd hate to be the one who tried to make you do it again, Morgan."

Morgan laughed.

I didn't have to repeat the ascent either, thank God. Some did, however, and I felt for them. In the end, we all made it.

The divers who ran the escape tank assured us that no one had ever died in it. I didn't believe them.

Shortly after qualifying in the escape tank and taking a few more dives on the diesel boats, we graduated from sub school. Though we were far from being qualified submariners, we cocked our white hats, swaggered, and felt more than a little salty.

I received orders to a fleet ballistic missile nuclear submarine, commonly known as an FBM, or even more commonly—a Boomer. Boarding the USS *Alexander Hamilton* (SSBN 617), the most powerful warship of its day, I began a thrilling chapter in my life.

Part Two

The Boomer Boys

Over the course of three and one-half years, I made six submerged patrols on the USS *Alexander Hamilton,* a fleet ballistic missile submarine. This section chronicles the events of two of these patrols, as well as an interim period between patrols.

Chapter Eight

Shipping Out

All in dress uniforms—our best—we filled the terminal. Pacing, sitting, joking, exchanging shallow insults that held more affection than rancor, some holding hands with wives or girlfriends, others clutching teary children who didn't want Daddy to leave again. I sat in a chair off to the side, watching them, studying them, perhaps closer than even I knew.

The men ranged in age from eighteen to a few crowding forty, roughly half were career navy men. Some of the other half were too; they just didn't know it yet. The lion's share of them hailed from the South and various New England states. The rest, like me, had wended their way from the West, the Midwest, and places as remote from a sailor's world as Montana and North Dakota.

Whitey, a short, blond radioman with a Charlie Brown head who looked more like a towheaded boy than a submarine sailor, had a face that could have been described as cherubic had he not unequivocally qualified as the wildest man I had ever known. His constant sidekick, Donny Skelton, another short radioman with bowed legs and a round belly, looked for all the world like a leprechaun. The two of them, Whitey and Skelton, could create more havoc and generate more laughs than any pair in the navy.

Whitey caught me watching the pair of them and looked at me with an impish grin. "Go to hell, nuke," he said aloud.

I laughed. "I love you too, Whitey."

Bob Lee and I, the odd couple, were seated together. Looking up momentarily from the book he was absorbed in, Bob shook his head and grinned at my exchange with Whitey. While I tended to be gregarious, Bob was the quiet one. The two of us were inseparable, especially on liberty.

We were young, some of us little more than boys, but we didn't see ourselves as such. In our minds, we were invulnerable, and despite our care-less postures and joking manners, terribly focused on the jobs we were trained to do.

We moved—sitting down in a chair for a moment, standing up and walking around the next, punching one another on the shoulder, ducking and feigning karate blows, flipping the bird, sticking our tongues out at each other as we passed, then falling into a seat again. The very young—the ones for which this would be their first patrol—did their best to look cool. They were scared to death.

Capt. Norman "Buzz" Bessac, a stern man with a square jaw and touches of gray about the temples, stood six-foot-two and rigid as a bridge beam. His athletic build and commanding presence made him appear even taller—the quintessential sea captain.

The skipper entered the terminal, his gold-striped uniform and gold-leafed hat impeccable, his strong wife holding his arm.

Lieutenant Commander Rawlins, Bessac's second in command, walked beside the captain. The fiery executive officer had been transferred off the USS *Thresher* just one year before the sub went down with all hands aboard.

Mr. Green, chief engineer of the *Hamilton* and third in command, walked a step behind the captain and the exec. A quiet man of detached mannerisms and unpredictable aloofness, Lieutenant Commander Green's competence was questioned by some of the crew, but they were wrong.

Captain Bessac and the executive officer strode into the terminal like MacArthur wading ashore at Manila Bay. While the captain looked straight ahead as if he were focused on an enemy target, Rawlins smiled grimly and nodded at several men. Mr. Green looked around and tried to smile at the crew as he passed, but like most of his attempts at personal connection, it didn't work well.

A number of junior officers, seated around the terminal in small groups or standing among the men, hungered for a crumb of recognition from their passing superiors. Few received it. Several of the chief petty officers and other senior enlisted men were given knowing nods and smiles—more respect than the young officers could hope for. I was a second-class engineman, two steps below chief, and young for my rank. The exec glanced over and winked at me as they passed.

Senior Chief Kennedy, the senior enlisted man on the *Hamilton* and head nuke—the Teddy Roosevelt of the engine room—even rated a nod from the captain.

The terminal grew quiet as the commanders passed. DeWayne Catron, a movie-star-handsome sailor, held his pregnant wife's hand—it would be their first—as the officers drew near. Catron maintained a respectful demeanor, but deep within those eyes one could see that DeWayne knew he was as smart as any of them. Something else in Catron's eyes warned against turning one's back on him, an act that could easily trigger some sort of outrageous practical joke.

Danny Dawson, a devil-may-care quartermaster whose face was sculpted in laugh lines, grinned as if he considered the command parade some sort of humorous spectacle put on specifically for his entertainment.

"Rusty" Romer, a husky nuke engineman and an inveterate loner, stood by himself at slack attention, his demeanor reflecting a half-hidden attitude of insubordination. His expression as the commanders passed was one of feigned respect—more a sneer than a smile.

Jim Nelson, a cocky, talkative sailor with years of submarining under his belt, sat on the other side of me, opposite Bob Lee. Although he was loath to admit it, Nelson didn't like to fly. He always sat next to me when we crossed the Atlantic, because, he said, "Penley ain't afraid of anything." Little did he know.

Tall, slender, dark-haired and dark-eyed, Nelson considered himself a ladies' man. And, like many submariners, Nelson had a nickname. He was known as Motor Mouth. And though everyone knew about it, few dared use the name to his face.

The diminutive Whitey didn't fear Nelson, however, or anyone else for that matter. "Hey, Motor Mouth," Whitey hollered across the terminal. "Where's your girlfriend?"

"She had to work," replied Nelson. "Where's yours?"

"She's out gettin' laid," answered Whitey, "bringing in some extra cash." Then Whitey turned to me. "Watch out for Motor Mouth, Penley. Don't let him fall out of the sky."

I smiled at Whitey as Nelson shook his head in disgust, but the look that he and Whitey exchanged held no malice. Around the room, a number of sailors laughed.

The year was 1964. The Cold War was raging, and we comprised one crew of a fleet ballistic missile submarine (FBM), one of the greatest deterrents to a first strike against the United States. The USS *Alexander Hamilton* carried sixteen Polaris missiles, all of which could be fired from underwater or on the surface, each missile capable of delivering a nuclear warhead to a target nearly two thousand miles away, and each holding the destiny of an enemy city or military base in its sights.

From the earliest days of sea-going submersibles, submarines had been called boats instead of ships. Even now, when they had grown huge compared to their historic counterparts, we who rode them still fondly referred to them as boats.

Our big boat's nuclear plant could propel the cigar-shaped craft in excess of twenty knots submerged, it could dive deeper than one thousand feet, and even its torpedoes carried atomic warheads.

Every FBM submarine had two crews, the Blue and the Gold. They alternated taking the boat to sea on two- to three-month patrols. Our crew, the Blue, was preparing to fly out of Charleston, South Carolina, where we had spent our off period. Our destination was Rota, Spain, a coastal base where we would relieve the Gold Crew. We'd land in Rota that night and watch the Gold Crew bring the boat in the following morning.

Members of the Blue Crew smirked and made derogatory remarks at mention of the Gold, confident that we were far superior to the Gold boys. The Gold Crew felt the same about us, but they were wrong, of course.

Doug Dunn, chief of the boat and official top cop among the enlisted men, held a position comparable to chief-master-at-arms on a surface ship. A popular authority among the men, Dunn received the nod from the gatekeeper that the time had come to board the plane. Chief Dunn stood up and looked over the crew. "All right," he announced loudly. "Let's do it." Somehow Dunn's raspy voice always managed to sound a bit boozy and his knowing eyes perpetually tickled at something, even when we'd been at sea for a month or more.

Senior Chief Kennedy, a square man with gun-barrel eyes, stood up and looked at his men, the nukes. Though they were scattered throughout the crowd, each one felt that Kennedy's eyes fell directly on him. There was an order in those eyes, a silent command that came through louder than the one the chief of the boat had hollered across the room. Chief Kennedy had sailed around the world submerged on the USS *Triton* under command of the famous Capt. Edward Beach. The nukes would have followed Kennedy to hell if he had ordered them to, and he would have if the need arose.

A big nuke machinist mate named Bob Cantley, a roly-poly guy who was loved by all but Chief Kennedy, came hustling into the terminal—late, as usual. Immediately catching Kennedy's eyes, Cantley grinned a weak apology at his boss. The chief just shook his head, then turned smartly toward the gate.

We boarded two planes, the rosters designed to split the crew exactly in half—this in case one plane went down while crossing the Atlantic. In that event, half of the crew, and therefore half the expertise in each department, would be preserved. The captain boarded one plane, the exec the other. Half of the enginemen, machinist mates, and electronics technicians boarded the first plane, the other half boarded the second. Half of the radiomen went on one, half on the other, and so on. Along with our seabags, a few of the guys carried cases containing musical instruments: guitars, violins, mandolins, and even a steel guitar would make the patrol with us.

We normally flew on air force planes, though occasionally civilian airlines were contracted. The civilian stewardesses received a lifetime's worth of flirting on the long flight to Spain. Air force planes had young enlisted men as stewards. They received a lifetime's worth of goading on the trip. Feigned flirting, winks, and a planeload of constant smirks made the flight a long one for those boys, but they had been handpicked and trained well. They served our every need on the flight, and usually gained the submariners' respect before we landed.

It was late when we landed in Rota, and by then even the wise comments had slowed down considerably. Two planeloads of tired sailors were bussed to the pier where the USS *Holland* was docked. *Holland* (AS-32) was a submarine tender, the ship to which the *Hamilton* would fasten itself for the next twenty-eight days, an upkeep period during which the crews of both the tender and the sub would ready the big boat to go to sea again.

The night the Blue Crew arrived in Rota we were assigned berthing quarters on the *Holland*. We'd live on the tender during crew change—a four-day period in which the Blue and Gold Crews worked together on the boat, each man conferring with his counterpart concerning routine maintenance, equipment condition, and major repairs needed during the upkeep.

The cooks on the *Holland* always had a hot meal waiting for the crew when we arrived from the States, no matter what time of night it might be. Though the *Holland* cooks worked hard and late preparing the meal, many of the sub sailors failed to show proper appreciation for their efforts.

Food is an important morale factor when men are subjected to isolation, a fact the navy discovered early in the history of submarining. As a result, not only were submarine cooks specially selected, subs were allocated more money for food than surface vessels. Thick steaks, home-cooked vegetables with a Southern flair, gourmet pasta dishes, asian food, and even an occasional lobster dinner appeared on the mess hall tables during the prolonged patrols.

Roy Scott was head cook of the *Hamilton* Blue Crew—a quiet, polite first-class, and one of the finest chefs in the navy. As Scott sat eating the *Holland*-prepared meal without comment, Motor Mouth Nelson walked across the mess hall, looking with disdain at the tray of food he was carrying. Nelson looked around until his eyes found Scott, then he hollered out loudly: "Hey, cookie, you ever fix anything like this on patrol, we'll blow ya out the torpedo tube."

Half the guys in the mess hall grinned, while a few laughed out loud. Scott just smiled and went on eating. The weary *Holland* cooks who were serving us turned away in disgust, their every assumption about those crazy submariners confirmed once more.

I slept fitfully that night; I always did when the boat was due the next morning. I had to grin at the snoring of my buddy, Bob Lee. In a bunk directly across the aisle from mine, the unshakable Bob slept like the dead.

The *Holland,* a tall, multitiered ship, was designed not for seaworthiness, but to remain in port for years at a time repairing submarines. The following morning, the crew lined up against the rail on the highest deck, watching for our boat to come in.

The 425-foot *Hamilton*—nearly a football field and a half in length—carried a crew of 130 men. With a submerged displacement of more than eight thousand tons and carrying more firepower than any warship in history, it was one of the largest submarines of its day, and the single most dangerous machine on Earth.

The boat surfaced far out in the bay, hidden in the fog. We waited tensely, and then through the mist we spotted her, miles away, plowing through the sea. Proud smiles, pointing fingers, and a great cheer: "There she is!"

She rode low in the water, dark, her nose plunging through the choppy seas like a great leviathan, her shadowy silhouette redolent of the machine of destruction that she was. After the initial cheer, we all grew quiet, gazing at the deep-diving warship that would be our home for the next three months.

Regarding the happy, determined faces of my shipmates and feeling an overwhelming pride to be a part of all this, I shared in their glee—a glee that few men would ever experience. Deep inside, however, in a place that I kept secret, lay a suppressed dread, a fear that I hardly dared admit even to myself. I wondered if any of the others felt the same dread, but I would never know. It wasn't something one could ask.

Benjamin Sherman, captain of the Gold Crew, stood on the bridge, the command station atop the *Hamilton*'s tall sail. Accompanied by his exec and several junior officers, Sherman watched intently as the long sub approached her berth next to the *Holland*.

Line handlers—select enlisted men who would tie up the boat when it reached the *Holland*—lined up smartly on the rounded deck forward of the sail and on the flat deck aft of it. Despite the rocking of the boat, the line handlers stood at parade rest, their dungaree uniforms fresh, their white hats squared away, their chins held high. In a tradition that had persisted nearly as long as submarines themselves, the proud manner of the men returning from patrol signified that they had swept the seas clean of enemies. During World War II, returning subs had tied a broom to the top of the sail, symbolizing the sweeping in a more literal manner.

Captain Sherman, a thin man with a kindly face, looked more like a poet than the commander of a warship, but he had a commanding name, and standing atop that big submarine, with his gold braid glistening in the sun and his jaw firmly set, the Gold Crew skipper appeared very much in charge.

Sherman looked over at his Blue Crew counterpart, Captain Bessac, waiting stiffly on the deck of the *Holland*. Captain Sherman waved from the top of the sail, then snapped Bessac a respectful salute. Bessac smiled and returned the salute.

From our perches on the upper decks, we watched the Gold Crew unwind heavy hawsers and tie the *Hamilton* alongside the *Holland*. As always, we marveled at the pale faces on the men of the Gold Crew. They looked like albinos—the same ghostly pallor that we ourselves displayed when we returned from months without a ray of sunshine touching our skin.

After the boat was tied, we all went back down to our temporary quarters aboard the tender. Captain Bessac and his team of officers would cross over to the *Hamilton* as soon as the gangway was in place, but because of the time required to shut down the engine room, cool down the reactor, and bring logs up to date, it would be several long hours before Blue Crew enlisted men could step aboard the boat.

Sometime in mid-afternoon the call came: the Blue Crew

could board the *Hamilton*. Faces lit up as if we had received surprise invitations to the Olympic Games. We jumped from our bunks, threw down paperback novels, or quickly abandoned poker games at the mess hall tables. Hurriedly buttoning our shirts, fastening our belts, or trying to tie our shoes on the run, we raced for the gangway.

Most of the guys ran across the gangway and quickly disappeared down the ladder to the inside. I slowed when I reached the deck of the boat, however, and hung back, stopping a moment before walking to the open hatch.

Although I knew that every compartment in the boat would be bright with electric lighting, as I entered the hatch and stepped onto the top rung of the ladder that would take me below, I felt a hard knot in the pit of my stomach, a fear that somehow a darkness awaited me—haunting, foreboding—a shadowy cave that would return in nightmares years after my discharge.

But the dark cave existed only in my mind. Down below, the boat was well lit, familiar, and small. Despite the fact that I had spent countless months inside her airtight hull on previous patrols, each time I stepped back aboard after an off period I was accosted by a feeling of confinement, an iron world where everything was too close, too tight.

The tight feeling persisted as I made my way down narrow passageways and steep stairs to the crew's berthing area and found my bunk. After the Gold Crew, left I would store my gear, neatly and carefully, in a small locker that would barely contain it. The bunks were stacked in threes: one at floor level, one at waist level, and one near shoulder height. Each bunk had a reading light at one end and a small metal shoe locker at the other. At the moment, the bunks seemed small, the headroom inadequate, the passageway between them impossibly narrow. But that feeling would leave—or at least lay dormant—as I accustomed myself once more to the closed environment that would house me and protect me for the next three months.

Inside, the 425-foot sub consisted of seven compartments of varying sizes. Although I worked in the engine room, the farthest aft compartment, when I first entered the boat I always went to the forward compartment and slowly worked my way back through the boat, carefully inspecting each space. I knew every valve, every pipe, and every electrical switch on the entire boat. Every sailor was supposed to know these things, but I prided myself in knowing them better than most, and I reviewed their locations regularly. If this habit indicated a bit of obsessive-compulsive behavior—which I knew it did—I didn't worry about it. I considered it a beneficial trait on a submarine.

The torpedo room, located in the nose of the sub, was a relatively small compartment, cone-shaped and filled with torpedoes, firing equipment, and the butt ends of four large tubes that faced the front of the boat—tubes from which the big fish were fired. Lashed down with iron straps to prevent movement in heavy seas, the torpedoes were the most powerful on the planet. I always patted them as I walked by, like a gunfighter stroking his six-shooter.

Directly behind the torpedo room lay the forward battery. The second largest compartment on the boat, the forward battery comprised three levels. The highest level, directly beneath the sail, housed the control room. Control—the heart of the boat. A raised platform directly beneath the periscopes dominated the center of control. On this dais, the captain or the conning officer stood and drove the sub.

The diving officer, the man in charge of the depth, trim, and speed of the boat, sat on the forward port side directly behind two planesmen, enlisted men who operated the diving planes and the rudder through the use of heavy levers that were each fitted with a steering wheel. The levers controlled the diving planes while the wheels controlled the rudder. The diving officer took his orders from the con.

A conspicuous tongue-in-cheek sign hung in the control room: "Evil, Evil. Man was not meant to fly."

Forward of control lay the captain's cabin, the exec's stateroom, the radio room, ship's office, and sonar. The next level down, the middle level, contained the chiefs' quarters, officers' quarters, wardroom, crew's mess, galley, walk-in freezers, trash compactor, and so forth. The lowest level housed the crew's berthing area, enlisted men's lounge, a small library, and the missile control center. In the very bottom of the forward battery, beneath the lowest deck, rested a huge electric battery. Reminiscent of the old conventional submarines, the battery, along with an emergency diesel engine located farther aft, was capable of propelling the boat in case the reactor failed.

And the smells. Whereas the old diesel subs I had trained on were permeated with the smell of diesel fuel from one end to the other, the nuclear boat had a variety of odors throughout, none of which were as overwhelming as diesel. Forward of the engineering spaces, which comprised about one-third of the boat, the compartments had little smell at all; the air was clean, almost sanitary—except for the mess hall and galley, that is. From them wafted the most pleasant aromas on the boat—food—twenty-four hours a day. The only restaurant in town, and it was a fine one.

The mess hall was one of the few places that showed a bit of color. As opposed to most of the rest of the boat—which varied from stark white to drab gray—the booths in the mess hall were covered in green vinyl. A few seats and benches throughout the boat were also green vinyl, Captain Bessac's choice of color, chosen in the shipyard during construction.

Aft of the forward battery, amidships, was the largest space in the boat—the missile compartment. Also comprised of three levels, the missile compartment housed sixteen Polaris missile tubes. The seagoing silos, standing upright with a diameter of four and one-half feet and a height of thirty-one feet, penetrated every level. Since I worked farther aft, in the engine room, I passed through the missile compartment several times a day. Knowing that each of the three-story silos contained a multistage rocket with a warhead more powerful than the ones dropped on Hiroshima and Nagasaki combined, walking through the forest of tubes gave me a sense of awe every time I saw them.

Continuing aft from the missile compartment, I passed through auxiliary machinery room #1, known simply as AMR1. AMR1 contained a supply room filled with spare parts bins, a number of pumps, the ever-present piping in both the overhead and the bilges, and two oxygen generators. A wonderful machine—and more than a little dangerous—the oxygen generator took in seawater, H_2O with a dash of salt, and separated the oxygen from the hydrogen. Following the separation process, the highly flammable hydrogen was injected back into the sea, while the oxygen was slowly bled into the boat to give breath to the crew.

Another necessary component of atmospheric control, carbon dioxide removal, was accomplished by charcoal-filled CO_2 scrubbers located throughout the boat.

This combination—being powered by a nuclear plant that required no air to generate heat, along with the ability to make its own oxygen for the crew to breathe and the ability to remove CO_2—is what allowed the boat to remain submerged for months at a time. Admiral Rickover may have been a tough taskmaster, but his genius cannot be overstated.

Running through the overhead in every compartment were large ventilation ducts, approximately one foot in diameter. And in every compartment were outlets that branched off of this piping system, open extensions from which clean air was pumped through the boat. These short extensions ended in "spot coolers," tuba-like terminations that were covered with heavy wire mesh and could be adjusted to direct air to different areas of the compartment. Our clean, man-made atmosphere flowed to us every minute, whether submerged or on the surface.

As my self-guided tour proceeded through the boat, once again familiarizing myself with every single thing that surrounded me, my feelings of confinement and tightness began to dissipate—being shed like an old skin, and replaced with a new one more suited to the environment. As these uncomfortable sensations left me, compartment by compartment, I marveled at the changes that simple conditioning can achieve in the human mind.

After AMR1 came the reactor compartment, AMR2, and the engine room, in that order. Nuke country, where we propelled the boat through the sea.

The reactor compartment, which housed the nuclear engine that drove the sub, was locked tight when the boat was underway. A narrow passageway through the top of the compartment allowed men to pass through, its heavily shielded walls and lead-glass windows protecting us from the deadly radiation generated by the reactor.

The clean, sanitary smell continued until I reached the second auxiliary machinery room, AMR2, a compartment comprised of two levels that housed myriad electrical panels, switches, chemical testing stations, the emergency diesel engine, miles of electrical cable, and hundreds of feet of piping that snaked fore to aft and top to bottom. Here the atmosphere became tainted with the odor of fluids—various kinds of oils, special lubricants, chemicals, even a slight tinge of fuel from the emergency diesel—the smell of working machinery. Still not overpowering or unpleasant. We joked that uranium smelled a lot nicer than diesel.

The farthest aft compartment was the engine room. With two spacious levels that housed tons of heavy machinery—main propulsion turbines, reduction gears, turbine generators, air-conditioning units, air compressors, lube oil purifiers, and the like—the engine room may have been situated in the very back of the sub, but it was the center of my world.

Near the front of the engine room on the starboard side sat a small box-like compartment that housed the primary controls for the nuclear plant—the maneuvering room. Simply known as maneuvering, the room contained control panels for the reactor, the electrical system, and the main propulsion turbines. When the boat was underway, an operator sat at each of the three panels, and seated behind them was the man in charge of the power plant, the engineering officer of the watch, or EOOW as the position was known.

The top man outside maneuvering—the one who continually roamed the plant—was the machinery watch supervisor. And the one in charge of the engine room was the engine room supervisor. Along with these positions, there were four other men on watch: one in the upper level and one in the lower level of AMR2, and one in each level of the engine room.

My world—the reactor compartment, AMR2, and the engine room—back where submicroscopic particles called neutrons caused atoms of uranium to blow apart, releasing tremendous amounts of energy when they split, and ultimately pushing us through the sea.

I knew everything in these compartments—every electrical switch, pipe, valve, nut, bolt, and screw. Everything. It was my job to know.

In my memory, the engine room looms large, with plenty of room to move around, but that's just the years playing tricks on me. Everywhere I walked I had to duck, step to the side, or lean one way or the other to avoid touching a valve, a gauge, or a pipe hot enough to fry my skin. At the time, I was conditioned to the tight environment, but having since toured several submarines over the years, I've come to realize that not only the engine room, but the entire interior of the boat appears larger in my memory than it was in reality.

Chapter Nine

Upkeep

Ridiculous hours and hard work, prompted, of course, by Admiral Rickover's insistence that every last piece of equipment be in top condition before the sub left on patrol. And all repairs and scheduled maintenance *would* be accomplished in twenty-eight days, *not* twenty-eight days and one minute. Occasionally Rickover sent a group of his henchmen to look over our shoulders—surprise us with operational drills and generally breathe down our necks for a couple of fun-filled days.

The admiral must have abhorred rest. Some of the guys postulated that Rickover was sleeping long hours in his comfortable bed in Washington while we worked our butts off. I doubted that. From what I'd heard, the man didn't know the meaning of relaxation.

We alternated between twelve-hour and eight-hour days, and we were only allowed to go on liberty every other evening—at the end of the eight-hour day. Sometimes we were too tired to change into our dress uniforms and hit the beach; but, sailors being sailors, on most liberty nights we made the best of the time we had.

Chief Kennedy—*Senior* Chief Kennedy, that is—had a metal stand-up desk near the front of the engine room, a desk that was never to be touched by anyone but the chief of chiefs. Beside the desk stood a restaurant-size coffee pot that was never allowed to run dry, and God help the sailor who spilled a single drop of coffee on Kennedy's hallowed desk.

Senior Chief Ralph Kennedy, the quintessential submariner—tough but fair.

Senior Chief Kennedy at this engine room desk, looking at his infamous worklist.

Above his desk, Chief Kennedy posted a list of jobs to be done in the nuclear plant. The larger jobs, ones that required several men, were assigned to certain groups with a senior petty officer in charge of each one. Other tasks, smaller ones that could be done by one or two guys, were up for grabs. Anyone who wanted to volunteer for one of these could simply write his name beside the job and go to work.

A young second-class engine man named Paul Ashford, a walking smirk known as "Small Paul," showed up in the engine room one morning with all the signs of having spent a very long night somewhere. From the looks of him, I doubt even he could remember where he had actually spent it.

Not only were Small Paul's eyes road-map red and his face the color of a stagnant pond, he was hanging onto rails, pipes, and valves to keep from falling down. Of course, Paul wasn't the first sailor to ever show up in the engine room with a hangover, but this was a severe case. In fact, he didn't appear to have yet reached the hangover stage.

Fortunately, there were no chiefs or officers present when Small Paul made his reeling entry. As he peered at the rest of us and made a weak attempt to smile, we watched him painfully make his way to Chief Kennedy's job list. Weaving on his feet, our young hero squinted at the paper in a valiant effort to focus his bleeding eyes, then scratched his name beside the dirtiest task there: clean the lube oil settling tank.

A small tank nestled deep in the recesses of the lower-level engine room, the lube oil settling tank was used for storing dirty oil to allow accumulated grime to settle out of it. The tank had already been drained, and a small round plate that allowed access into the tight, filthy space had been unbolted and removed. A large man could not have squeezed through the opening or moved around inside the tank enough to clean it.

With slow, deliberate movements, Small Paul gathered up several buckets of water, an armload of cleaning rags, and a bottle of strong detergent with which to clean the settling tank. He also took a strong flashlight to enable him to see inside the dark space.

A nasty smell emanated from the opening as he approached the unlit cave. Since Small Paul was a friend of mine—and an interesting fellow to watch as well—I kept an eye on this procedure, both for his own safety and a heightened sense of curiosity on my part. I wasn't sure how long one could breathe inside that tank and remain alive, especially a guy who looked half dead already.

The opening into the tank was near floor level. Dropping to his hands and knees on the steel deck plates, Paul carefully lifted the buckets and the rest of his cleaning gear and sat them inside the tank. Then, still on his hands and knees, he dropped his head and slowly swung it from side to side, staring at the deck plates as if mesmerized. I thought he might be getting ready to pass out. He didn't though; in a moment he looked up, stuck his head through the little hatch, and disappeared into the darkness.

Unaware that I'd been watching him, Small Paul was surprised when I walked over to the tank and bent down to the hatch. "You okay, buddy?" I asked.

"Yes, I'm okay!" his defiant voice echoed out of the tank. He obviously wanted to be left alone, but I decided to keep checking on him throughout the day.

When I returned to the tank a while later, another smell attacked me—at least as rotten as that of the old oil. Small Paul was cleaning the filthy tank, as he had vowed to do, but releasing copious amounts of his own bodily gases during the process. The olfactory assault was too much. I left.

Sometime around noon, a young chief named Don Durham took a walk through the lower-level engine room. Durham was so personable that most of us called him Don instead of chief. When the airborne concoction hit Don's nostrils, he charged back up the ladder and asked me what was going on in the lube oil settling tank. When I told him that Paul was in there cleaning it, he grimaced. "What the hell is that God-awful stink coming out of it?"

"Well, the tank itself smells bad enough, Don, but Paul seems to be emitting a large amount of his own gas," I said. Durham asked me to follow him back down to the lower level. Standing near the odoriferous hatch, the chief held his nose and said, "Tell him to come out of there."

I leaned down and hollered, "Paul, Chief Durham said for you to come out of there."

Paul hollered back. "Tell him I'm not gonna do it. I'm cleaning this tank, and I'm not coming out till I'm done."

I looked at the chief and shrugged. Durham looked thoughtful for a moment, then chuckled and walked away.

The saga continued. An hour or so later, a young lieutenant named Mr. Stubbs, who happened to be the division officer over both Paul and me, also made a tour through the lower level. Just as Chief Durham had done, Mr. Stubbs found me and asked what was going on in the settling tank. I explained that Small Paul was cleaning it. This time I was ordered to follow Mr. Stubbs back down to the tank.

As the division officer and I stood in front of the tank, doing our best to fan the nauseating air away from our faces, Mr. Stubbs asked, "Does the settling tank always smell that bad, Penley?"

"Not necessarily," I replied. "I believe Ashford is . . . passing gas in there, sir."

With a touch of humor dancing about his eyes, Mr. Stubbs said, "Tell him I want him to come out of there."

Again I bent down to the open hatch, this time trying to impart the graveness of the situation to Paul. "Paul," I pleaded, "Mr. Stubbs is out here now, and he said for you to come out of that tank."

A roar blasted out of the hatch. "Tell him I said to stick it!" Small Paul yelled. "I'm not coming out till I'm finished cleaning this thing."

All I could do was shake my head. Lieutenant Stubbs, a soft-spoken gentleman who smoked a Meerschaum, pulled the pipe from his mouth and thoughtfully tamped it a few times. The officer looked back down at the hatch and, without expression, turned and walked away. I would have given odds that Small Paul's naval career had just ended.

Later that afternoon, I heard Paul hollering for me. I quickly made my way to the settling tank where I found him with his head sticking out of the hatch. I guess by then he had to be sober, but he actually looked worse than when he had entered the tank that morning.

Paul asked me to take his gear from him as he handed it out. I agreed, and out came bucket after bucket of filthy water, greasy rags, and thick, oily sludge. He had indeed cleaned the space, but an indescribable smell lingered, probably having permeated the very metal of the tank. I took the horrid buckets from him and quickly set them on the deck plates. I wouldn't have done that for many people.

Paul crawled out of the tiny hatch and stiffly pulled himself to his feet, so filthy I couldn't understand how he'd gotten the cleaning rags so dirty. He looked like he had simply rolled around inside the tank until all the muck was transferred to him. I took his flashlight—an instrument so slimy I could barely hold onto it—and shined it inside the tank. Unbelievably clean. I looked back at Paul again. His face appeared to be darkly camouflaged—a greasy blob—and the condition of his head could only be described as nasty. He must have done the final polish job with his hair.

I helped Paul carry the refuse and gunk from his cleaning fiasco up to the trash, gently hinting that his day might have gone a bit easier had he started it out sober. He didn't answer, the concept seeming too complex for him to grasp at the moment.

I don't think Small Paul remembered his insubordinate retorts to Chief Durham and Lieutenant Stubbs that day, and God bless them, they acted as though they didn't either.

Chief Kennedy called me over to the job list one afternoon and pointed at an item that no one wanted to touch: "Replace Hull Valve, Starboard Side Engineroom." The valve was basketball-shaped and large, about a foot and a half in diameter, its body made of steel two inches thick. It weighed five hundred pounds. The good news: since it was located above water line when the boat was on the surface there was no danger of flooding when we removed it. The bad news: this meant that the valve was mounted high on the side of the rounded pressure hull where the hull began to roll inward, positioning it about shoulder height as one stood on the deck plates in front of it. To unbolt the valve, take it down, and mount a new one in its place would be a complicated and dangerous job.

Kennedy spoke with a hard New England accent, and he sounded tough whether he was saying good morning or chewing someone out—a skill at which he excelled.

"You're going to be in charge of this job, Penley," the chief said. "And you're going to do it tonight, when everybody else is out of your way." At the time, I was a second-class engine man with less submarine experience than many of the other petty officers in my group. I wasn't sure I felt qualified to supervise such a job, but when Chief Kennedy told you to do something, that's what you did.

"Who else will be working with me?" I asked.

"Pick three guys," Kennedy said, "any three you want. But you're in charge. Period." That meant I had to choose men who were junior in rank to me.

I picked my unflappable friend, Bob Lee, and two other fellows whom I trusted. When I told them what we'd be doing that night they didn't look particularly happy to find themselves among the chosen, but none of them complained.

*Bob Lee, on patrol in the North Atlantic, 1965. He is the calmest man
I ever knew—nerves of steel.*

I spent the rest of the afternoon studying the awkward position
of the big valve and trying to figure the best way to haul it down
and replace it with the new one. After dinner, when half of the
crew had finished working—either gone on liberty, gone to bed,
or joined in a poker game in the crew's lounge—the four of us
headed back to the engine room.

The valve, which pointed downward at a forty-five degree
angle due to its position on the concave pressure hull, was held
in place by a dozen heavy bolts—much the same as lug bolts on
a vehicle, only larger. If we simply removed the nuts from the
bolts, the valve would fall. Maintaining control of the heavy piece
at all times was key to the project. We went to work rigging up a
number of chain falls that would suspend the valve in the air like
a spider web after we removed the nuts, hopefully preventing its
fall.

It was midnight by the time we got our web of chains rigged
up and began to unscrew the big nuts. When the last nut came

off, the five-hundred-pound valve fell away from the bolts. We all jumped back, in case our rigging didn't work as planned.

The valve swung out a few inches and caught on the maze of chains, suspended in midair five feet above the walkway. After sharing a collective sigh of relief, we began lowering the valve, loosening first one chain and then the other. Within a few minutes, we had lowered it to the steel deck plates and unfastened it from the chains.

After rolling the valve out of our way—its five hundred pounds fighting all four of us—we shoved the new one into place and fastened the web of chains around it. Then, in a reverse procedure of the way we had lowered the old valve, we began methodically raising the new one into the air.

All went fine until we got the valve positioned close to its final location—hanging in the air just inches from the circle of bolts that it would fasten to. We had to swing it in by hand those last few inches, at the same time turning it a few degrees to the right to line it up with the bolts.

The four of us took hold of the valve, turned it slightly to line it up, and shoved it onto the bolts. It slid all the way on, and then something snapped. A chain popped loose, a crucial link that would allow the valve to drop all the way to the deck plates unless we could somehow hold it in place.

I moved quickly. Wisely or unwisely, I dove under the valve. Landing directly under the massive piece of steel, I leaned back against the pressure hull, reached up over my head, and grabbed the valve. The other guys were still holding the valve onto the bolts to keep it from falling, but their strained faces told me they couldn't keep it in that position for long. The valve being far too heavy for me to hold in place, I pulled downward on it with all my weight, lifting myself off the deck plates as I pulled. This downward pressure forced the threads into a bind and briefly kept the valve from sliding off the bolts.

I looked into Bob Lee's eyes and screamed, "Get a nut on one of those bolts; I can't last much longer!" Cool Bob let go of the valve, swept up a nut, and spun it onto one of the top bolts with his fingers. Securing the heavy hunk of metal in place, Bob saved the valve and me.

It was 5:00 a.m. when we finished. I told the guys to go to bed and not to worry about getting up until they were rested. Quiet Bob didn't say a word, just gave me a half grin as if I might be insane—a look he tended to give me often.

I left a note on Chief Kennedy's desk: "We finished the job, and we'll be sleeping in this morning."

Later that afternoon, when I woke up and walked back to the engine room, Kennedy looked at me and said, "You guys did a good job."

"Thanks, Chief," I said, feeling as if I had won the world championship of valve replacement. "Good job" was the best you could get from Senior Chief Kennedy.

In order to move up in enlisted ranks, navy men and women were required to spend a given number of years in each rank (E-3, E-4, E-5, etc.), then complete a correspondence course for the next level. Following completion of the course, one had to pass a fleetwide competitive test. Why was the test competitive? Because simply passing it didn't ensure promotion. The navy needed only a certain number of petty officers in each rank, and only the highest scorers got the promotions.

For eons, chief petty officer, grade E-7, had been the highest enlisted rank in the navy. Chief petty officers wore khakis, much like officer uniforms, and rated the respected title "Chief." Shortly after I joined the navy, in 1960, two higher ranks were instituted: senior chief (grade E-8) and master chief (E-9). These levels were especially competitive and difficult to achieve.

Chief petty officers had always belonged to a special fraternity, and having achieved this high level, they enjoyed special privileges. Even on submarines chiefs had separate berthing areas from the rest of the crew, and on many surface vessels, they even had their own mess hall.

Since chief petty officers had long shared this lofty brotherhood, in the new organization, which included grades E-8 and E-9, when one became a senior chief or a master chief they were still simply called "Chief," and the others generally considered them to be the same as they had always been: chiefs. And most of those who made E-8 and E-9 considered themselves the same and changed little as far as command went. There were still E-1 through E-6 levels, and then there was chief, whether the chief be E-7, E-8, or E-9.

Not *Senior* Chief Kennedy. Chief Kennedy was the highest-ranking enlisted man on the *Hamilton*—the only E-8, and there were no E-9s. Kennedy never let anyone forget it. Several other chiefs, E-7s, worked in the engine room, and Kennedy even made them join in the regular weekly cleanup, a job from which chiefs had traditionally been exempted.

Chief Durham, an easygoing fellow and the junior chief in the nuke gang, didn't seem to mind working for Kennedy. Neither did Chief Turner, a smart young engine man who accepted his place and quietly went about his work.

Chief Hoople, an older, slow-moving chief who was overweight and balding, didn't care either. In fact, the incompetent Hoople seemed to care little about anything. And Chief Kennedy didn't help his self-confidence by exclaiming for all to hear, "When Hoople walks into the engine room, watch to see if he takes his hands out of his pockets; when he does, everything goes to hell."

Hoople would smile philosophically and try to engage someone in an off-the-wall conversation that had nothing to do with the engine room, or even with submarines for that matter. Kennedy would just shake his head and mentally prepare to write Hoople another scathing fitness report.

Another older chief, T. K. Russell, cared greatly about his position, and was visibly bothered at having his authority usurped by Senior Chief Kennedy. Russell had been around for a long time, long enough to wear the revered War Patrol Medal on his chest. Having fought in numerous WWII battles in which enemy ships were blown apart and sent to the bottom, Chief Russell had undergone devastating depth-charge attacks for having engaged the enemy from a sealed submersible tube barely wide enough to walk through—an experience so terrifying it drove many wartime submariners out of their minds.

Chief Russell was tall, lean, and leathery with a deeply lined face—the look of the fighter he was. He might have appeared mean but for one small giveaway: his eyes. Although he spent much of his time trying to look stern, something in his eyes led one to suspect that his bark was worse than his bite. And it was. Everyone in the nuke gang liked Chief Russell, and most were aware of his true colors, but they went along with his tough act anyway.

Not me. After I figured Chief Russell out, I couldn't resist messing with his mind.

Submariners are required to "qualify" on every submarine to which they're assigned; that is, they have to study the workings of all the main systems on the boat, get signed off on each system by a qualified operator, and then pass a comprehensive exam. On his first boat, this is how the novice submariner earns the dolphins he'll wear on his chest for the rest of his career.

As power plant operators, we nukes had to do more. Besides studying the major boat systems like everyone else, we also had to study every system in the reactor compartment, AMR2, and the engine room in minute detail and pass comprehensive tests on the entire plant.

Being a relatively new submariner, and the *Hamilton* my first boat, besides my regular work during upkeep I had to put in extra hours studying for qualifications, something that Chief T. K. Russell bugged me about daily. Although the chief was a good guy, he could be a pain in the butt. Every time he saw me, anywhere in the power plant, he'd stop me and ask, "Where you going? What you working on? How you doing on qualifications?"

Tired of the chief's endless questioning, one morning I hung a large piece of cardboard around my neck on which was written with a permanent marker: "Chief Russell, I am going _____; I am working on _____; I am _____ on my qualifications." I then filled in the blanks with a pencil, which dangled from the sign by a short length of string.

The first time I ran into Chief Russell that morning, I stopped directly in front of him and stuck out my chest, pushing the sign in his face. He read it, nodded, smiled narrowly, and walked away. I updated the sign as I changed where I was going or what I happened to be working on, and I stopped Chief Russell and forced him to read it at every opportunity. Of course, everyone in the aft part of the boat saw the sign and quickly figured out what I was doing to the chief. Russell quit smiling about the third time I stopped him and made him read it, although everyone else was doing their best to keep from laughing out loud. I continued this routine all day, even wearing the sign in the mess hall, to the chagrin of Chief Russell and the delight of the rest of the crew. Even Chief Kennedy got a laugh out of it.

Chief Russell stopped bombarding me with questions after that. Although this was far from the only incident in which I gave Russell a bad time, in actuality we got along well and enjoyed a mutual respect. Despite all of my kidding, however, some of which bordered on insubordination, when the chief told me to "Shut up," which he did more than once, I shut up.

A strange phenomenon occurred among the crew: dreams. Many of the men experienced disquietingly similar dreams, all involving an escape from a sunken submarine. We would dream of sinking and sitting on the bottom, and in our dreams we'd invent complex, and usually impossible, ways of escaping from the sunken sub and making our way back to the surface. Not all of the guys talked about these dreams, but a lot of them did. I suspect that a large percentage, maybe everyone in the crew, had them. I certainly did. They began shortly after the upkeep period started and continued when we went to sea and all through the patrol.

Claustrophobia: the first word that comes to mind when one hears the word "submarine." And a little-known fact is that many submariners, myself included, are not totally free of the fear. Very tight spaces bothered us—places where the body felt extremely confined. Some of us reacted to this worse than others.

The heaviest pieces of equipment in the engine room—main propulsion turbines, reduction gears, and turbine generators—were mounted on a floating bedplate, a steel platform that spanned the width of the engine room and most of its length. This bedplate rested on giant shock absorbers that allowed it to shake when the boat fired a missile. The terrific concussion from the firing required that the heavy equipment be allowed to move in reaction to the recoil. And when we fired test missiles, which we did on occasion, all that monster equipment jumping up and down several inches was a scary thing to watch. No one ever stood on the bedplate during a firing, because it would have thrown you high into the air, connecting your body with overhead equipment that would have been tough on the cranium.

The floating bedplate, along with the heavy equipment it supported, rested on a frame that consisted of two square tubes called box girders. Shaped like giant packages of saltine crackers, the box girders lay horizontal, running forward to aft in the overhead of the lower-level engine room, one on each side. Each about thirty feet long, two feet wide, and hollow, the girders had an opening at one end only, forming a dark tunnel that appeared tight and foreboding from the open end. Some of my shipmates didn't seem to mind crawling into the box girders, but even though I was inside a submarine, I suffered an overwhelming fear the first time I tried to enter one of the dark tubes.

There was really no reason to go inside the box girders. However, some of the guys thought it cute, and macho, to store a number of portable tools at the far end of one of them. When the tools were needed, retrieving them required crawling to the very back of the tunnel. Then, with tools in hand, one had to back out of the thirty-foot support, the tightness of the black space making it impossible to turn around and crawl out forward. A spelunker's delight.

I had looked down into the girders, but had never been inside one of them. And I could see no reason whatsoever to store tools at the deepest end of such a space. Why not store them near the open end, where they would be easily accessible?

Leroy Lavender, a tall, blond machinist mate who outranked me, insisted on keeping the tools at the back of the starboard box girder. Lavender was a gentle-seeming fellow who neither acted nor appeared tough; perhaps that's why he backed away from nothing, constantly volunteering for the hardest and most dangerous jobs, or volunteering me for such jobs. I think I was supposed to appreciate being selected for these tasks; sometimes I did, and sometimes I didn't.

One day Lavender told me to go crawl into the starboard box girder and retrieve a set of hydraulic jacks that were needed to move the main shaft. Frowning my displeasure at the order, I climbed down the ladder into the lower-level engine room, and then up into the entrance to the deep girder. I had absolutely no desire to enter the dark tube, but I'd been ordered to. I started in. About ten or twelve feet inside the thing, I stopped. I could not go on. Nothing short of a hydraulic ram could have forced me to the back of that tight tunnel.

I backed out in a rush, into the light and the comforting space of the engine room. Climbing the ladder to the upper level, I told Lavender that I refused to crawl to the back of the box girder. Leroy gave me a bad time. "Are you a submariner?" he said. "What do you mean you can't crawl to the back of that girder?"

"Yes, I'm a submariner," I replied testily, "and I can ride this boat anywhere, and as deep as the skipper wants to take it, but I am *not* going to crawl into that damn tube. There's no reason to keep those tools at the back of it, anyway. Put me on report if you want to, but I'm not going in there."

Leroy and I were more than just shipmates; we were friends. He knew my refusal was not a bluff, and I knew he wouldn't put me on report. He shook his head in disgust, went down the ladder, and retrieved the jacks himself. When we finished with them, he returned the jacks to the far end of the tunnel, where they continued to be stored. I never once crawled in after them.

Dan Trent, a young machinist mate who was smaller than me, was also once ordered to crawl into the box girder and retrieve the hydraulic jacks. Unlike me, Trent made it to the far end of the tunnel and got the jacks in hand. On the way out—backing out, that is—Trent tried to turn himself around inside the tube so that he could crawl forward instead of backward. Halfway through his turnaround attempt, the young sailor got stuck.

One is never far from the onset of panic in extremely tight spaces, and when the body gets stuck, the panic rushes to the surface. In the middle of that dark box girder, fifteen feet from the closed end and fifteen from the opening, Dan Trent panicked.

Seized by the terror of confinement, Trent began to breathe hard, his body swelling against the sides of the girder, trapping him tighter and tighter in his contorted prison. And no one in the engine room remembered where he was—that he had gone down to get the hydraulic jacks from the back of the box girder. Trent remained alone, in the dark, painfully trapped in a fetal position, for an hour and a half. After crying, screaming, and thinking he might die from fright alone, he finally managed to get hold of his emotions enough to straighten his aching limbs. Terrified that his every move might get him stuck again, he crawled out of the tube, backwards.

Lavender stubbornly continued to store the jacks at the deep end of the box girder, but like me, Dan Trent never crawled into it again.

In a later incident that the devil on my shoulder considered a bit of poetic justice, Lavender would find himself in a tight spot—a very tight spot.

An old adage says that all work and no play makes for dull boys. This does not apply to sub sailors. Whether at work or at play, we were never dull boys.

Up front, where Whitey and Skelton worked, there wasn't as much to do during upkeep. And if ever a pair existed who did not need time on their hands, it was our two short radiomen.

In a moment of madness, Doug Dunn, the chief of the boat, assigned Whitey and Skelton to the trash detail, a lengthy job that entailed carrying large plastic bags of trash across the *Hamilton*'s gangway to the *Holland*'s gangway, up to the main deck of the *Holland,* aft to the poop deck of the tender, down another gangway that led to terra firma, and then twenty or thirty yards along the beach to a group of dumpsters.

Whitey and Skelton lugged the bags of trash, a mountain of them, topside and stacked them forward of the sail. Contemplating the long, tortuous path to the dumpsters and the many trips the pile of bags would require, they noted that, as the crow flies, the dumpsters were actually located quite near the *Hamilton.* The big trash receptacles sat just across a small neck of the bay. Noting that only a narrow body of water about forty feet wide separated them from the dumpsters, the two sailors crafted a plan—unorthodox and against regulations—but a plan nevertheless.

Whitey and Skelton were both first-class petty officers with top-secret clearances, and it took only a moment for them to exhibit their brilliance and problem-solving abilities. One by one, they threw the entire pile of trash bags into the bay, in the direction of the dumpsters. Then, when all the bags were bobbing in the water, our two heroes removed their shoes, jumped in, and began to swim. Gathering the trash bags together in a floating mass that resembled some sort of large, lumpy raft, they swam them to shore, pushed them up onto the beach, and heaved them into the dumpsters.

Then, with their dungaree uniforms already soaked, Whitey and Skelton dove into the water once more, swam back to the *Hamilton,* put on their shoes, and disappeared down the hatch. The impromptu procedure had been executed flawlessly except for one small detail: the officer of the deck on the *Holland,* standing several tiers above the water, had witnessed it all. And despite the resourcefulness demonstrated by the two sub sailors, the OOD was not happy with what he had seen. In fact, the man was livid.

The *Holland* officer immediately phoned the *Hamilton* and reported the incident to our OOD, who in turn reported it to Mr. Rawlins, the executive officer. All this reporting went up the chain of command in a flash. Before Whitey and Skelton even had a chance to change into dry uniforms, they were ordered to report to the executive officer's quarters.

The scene would be told and retold, not only aboard the *Hamilton*, but on virtually every submarine in the Atlantic fleet. Soaked and dripping water on the exec's carpet, Whitey and Skelton stood in puddles that steadily grew, holding their soggy white hats in their hands as the fiery Rawlins asked them what the hell they thought they were doing jumping overboard in uniform and pushing loads of trash across the bay.

Tales of Whitey's and Skelton's antics had spread farther than just the *Hamilton*. Their reputation was known by virtually every submariner up and down the East Coast, so Commander Rawlins knew what he was up against. When the mischievous radiomen, looking like little boys who had been caught swimming in a forbidden creek, explained that they had considered their plan innovative and timesaving, even the stern exec had difficulty keeping a straight face. Before Rawlins lost his composure completely, he said, "All right you two, get out of here and stop dripping on my carpet, and no more swimming in the bay! Understand?"

"Yes, sir!" the wet sailors said as they scurried away, leaving watery tracks down the passageway of officers' country. Whitey and Skelton swore they could hear the exec laughing aloud before they were out of earshot.

A large nightclub in Rota added a pleasant touch to the evening skyline—a stately white building dedicated to professional entertainment, fine Spanish food, and peaceful evenings. The Flamenco Club, a place for lovers.

The Flamenco Club consisted primarily of one gigantic room with live Spanish music, the most beautiful I had ever heard, enhancing the ambiance of the tastefully appointed space. Indirect lighting accentuated the fine art that adorned the high walls, faint murals looked down from two-story ceilings. The periphery of the great dance floor was lined with hand-carved tables and chairs complete with bouquets of red roses, their sweet scent permeating the club.

The Flamenco Club, a place so nice that submarine sailors should not have been allowed inside. Alas, we were.

Danny Dawson, a second-class quartermaster from Lubbock, Texas, and an inveterate prankster, knew a bit of Spanish—a crude facsimile that he termed "border Mexican." Since Danny was the only one of us who knew any Spanish, we were foolish enough to appoint him our native guide.

The dubious value of being accompanied by a joker who spoke the native tongue became apparent one awful night at the Flamenco Club. As Danny and I entered the front door, we saw half a dozen stunning young women standing in a circle talking—in Spanish, of course. Without thinking, I turned to my Texas friend and said, "Danny, look at those beautiful girls! Quick, tell me a nice greeting in Spanish so I start a conversation with them—get to meet them."

Danny complied, whispering a sentence in Spanish that ended as if it were a question; I imagined it to be something like "Beautiful evening, isn't it, ladies?" After I repeated the line back to him to ensure that I had it right, Danny nodded and said, "You got it. Go over there and tell 'em that."

It was one of those times when one looks back over his life and says, "Should have known better."

I sauntered over to the circle of luscious young ladies, flashing my best Don Juan smile, and greeted them with the unknown Spanish phrase that Danny had whispered to me. The girls had all smiled at my approach, now they grabbed their mouths, gasping in shock and horror. Turning to look back at Dawson with a huge question on my face, I couldn't find him. Then I spied him far across the room, bent double in laughter.

The irate girls began waving their arms and verbally flailing me in Spanish, looking at me as if I might be a serial rapist covered in animal dung. Retreating like a homeless dog kicked from a stranger's doorway, I walked over to Dawson and asked him what the hell he had told me to say to them. He was unable to talk at that point, but when he finally caught his breath and wiped the tears from his eyes, he explained that I had coolly eased over to that bevy of gorgeous females, smiled, and inquired as to their availability for a round of unnatural acts.

So much for my native guide.

Even Whitey and Skelton were allowed into the Flamenco Club, resulting in a spectacle that, had I not personally witnessed it, would have left my entire life incomplete.

Each night, around 8:30 or 9:00, the club put on a tremendous floor show—an extravaganza of Spanish dancing, music, and costumed fanfare. Floor-length curtains parted on one side of the great room, revealing an open archway. The music would begin, guitars only at first, and out of the archway would pour a line of flamenco dancers—tall ladies in flowing black and white dresses trimmed in flaming red, their male partners in wide, flat-crowned hats and tight formal wear with great red sashes flying from their waists. The dancers would whirl, snap their fingers, and clap their hands as the long dresses and flaming sashes whipped the air.

As the music picked up, it seemed to fill the room, the smiling dancers followed onto the floor by a full mariachi band. Trumpets, violins, guitars, castanets, snapping fingers, clapping hands, and whirling dancers, the entire troupe flowing in a serpentine succession across the floor, the undulating dancers leading them around the room.

Enter our heroes. Whitey and Skelton, seated at a table in white uniforms, looked at the bouquet between them and, without exchanging a word, became possessed by the same demon. Simultaneously picking red roses from the vase and clenching the long stems in their teeth, they rose as one, charged to the front of the dancers, and began leading the troupe with their own version of flamenco—an awkward, flailing thing that would have made a donkey look graceful, even a donkey with a rose in its teeth.

The other submariners whooped and clapped their hands, considering Whitey and Skelton to be a great addition to the show. The Spaniards did not.

The club manager, a thick, mustachioed man with a voice to match his girth, strode onto the floor, threw up his hands, and put a stop to everything. Puffing himself up in a pompous show of anger, the man pointed at Whitey and Skelton, swept his arms about the room to encompass all their irreverent mates, and fairly shouted his indignation in Spanish. The dancers and the mariachis backed away as if being blown by the wind of his tirade. Whitey and Skelton, their white hats askew, the sad roses drooping from their mouths, held their tenuous ground.

When the manager finished whatever he was saying, the entire troupe left the floor, closing the curtain behind them with an angry flourish. After making it clear that we seagoing barbarians were not worthy of watching such a show, the big man himself stomped off the floor.

Whitey and Skelton, discovering to their utter surprise that they were not being thrown out of the club, gripped the drooping roses in their teeth and continued their donkey dance all the way back to their table.

Strangely, Whitey and Skelton were not barred from the Flamenco Club. The dancers and mariachis never again performed when the two were present, however, a wise decision on the part of the management.

DeWayne Catron should not have been turned loose in public. A nuke electronics technician with remarkable intelligence, DeWayne was an amazing piece of work. A trim physique, dark wavy hair enhanced by a dashing mustache and goatee, bright eyes that accentuated a perfectly proportioned face and reflected not only intelligence, but an unshakable self-confidence. Not all of these attributes, however, were as obvious as his description might lead one to believe. The devilishness behind those eyes tended to override much of the rest and to keep one on his toes if DeWayne happened to be in the vicinity.

Generalissimo Francisco Franco was the undisputed ruler of Spain at the time, and General Franco, who had led the successful Spanish Revolution in the 1930s, employed harsh methods of ensuring civil obedience after his takeover.

Besides having regular police forces in every city, the country was permeated with paramilitary police called the Guardia Seville (civil guard). The Guardia Seville were Franco's elite, possessing more authority than the regular Spanish police and having virtually free rein to wield it at any time or any place. Walking in teams of two, each armed with a .45 automatic on his hip and one with a Thompson sub-machine gun slung over his shoulder, the fearsome pairs wore starched green uniforms, high black boots, and distinctive black hats—the trademark of the Guardia Seville. The wide-brimmed hats were constructed of patent leather that shone brightly in the sun, the front turned straight up against the crown as if the wearer had run directly into a wall and put a ninety-degree upward bend in the brim.

The description of such headwear may sound ridiculous, but sitting squarely atop the heads of men armed with machine guns who moved with the easy confidence of legal assassins, the shiny upturned hats appeared ominous, a symbol not to be taken in jest. Saluting one another like soldiers and talking only to their partners, the Guardia Seville never so much as acknowledged the presence of Spanish civilians, or American sailors, as they walked among the populace—coiled violence ready to strike in a moment.

To the utter shock of everyone aboard the *Hamilton,* DeWayne Catron walked into the mess hall one morning with a genuine Guardia Seville hat perched foolishly on his head. On DeWayne, the shiny leather hat with the turned-up brim did look ridiculous and silly and unbelievable. We couldn't imagine that even *he* was capable of attempting such high-wire larceny, and getting away with it, for God's sake.

No one knew where Catron had obtained such a prize, and no one even dared sit in the same booth with him. When I walked in, looked aghast at the hat and sized up the situation, I sat down across the table from him. "All right, stupid, where'd you get that hat?" I asked. DeWayne did his best to look stern—playing the role of a Guardia Seville—and didn't answer me. In fact, he said nothing through the entire meal.

After eating breakfast with the glistening black hat on—an act akin to dining in a stolen garment of Al Capone's—DeWayne put the hat in his locker and went back to the engine room to work. Within minutes, he was ordered forward to report to the executive officer, immediately.

The poor exec, second in command of the greatest warship on Earth, and we, his highly trained crew reputed to be among the navy's finest, kept him busy dealing with boyish pranks.

The moment DeWayne knocked on his door, Lieutenant Commander Rawlins threw it open and thrust his face directly into Catron's. "I *know* you had a Guardia Seville hat on this morning, Catron—a real one!"

DeWayne later confided that he had felt *kind of uneasy* in the face of the exec's fiery blast. "Yes, sir," he admitted, "I did."

The exec shook his head, hissing through clenched teeth. "Listen, sailor, I don't want to know anything about that hat. I don't want to know where you got it, or how you got it—and I'd better *never* lay eyes on the damn thing again."

Catron answered sharply, "I understand, sir."

"Good," said the exec. "Now get out of here."

We seemed to spread good will among Spanish citizens of all ages. One evening Danny Dawson, Catron, and I were walking in downtown Rota when a small boy of about six or seven fell in behind us. We couldn't figure out what the little guy wanted, but after he had followed us for several blocks, we knew he could speak at least three words of English: "You on ship? You on ship?"

It was not against naval regulations to tell the boy that we were on a ship, but we were conditioned not to talk about our submarine with any civilians, even children. He seemed to be a nice little fellow and was reasonably clean, but we became annoyed with his constant question, which we refused to answer. As he continued to ask, "You on ship?" we started trying to figure out how we might get rid of him. Danny spotted an open-air ice cream parlor and suggested we stop in there, figuring the management wouldn't allow the little boy to follow us in.

The ice cream parlor had walls that were about waist high, the area between the low walls and the roof being open to the outside. Sure enough, the waitress stopped the boy at the door and told him he couldn't come in. We thought we had won, until she seated us at a table that abutted an outside wall. As we were ordering our cups of ice cream, the little boy walked up to the outside of the low wall and leaned his elbows on it, essentially placing himself at our table. "You on ship?" he said.

Conceding that we couldn't ditch the boy, we decided to buy him a cup of ice cream. The Spanish waitress tried to nix the idea. Frowning at the three of us and the boy, she asked, "You sure you want to do that?" We nodded patiently, assuring her that we did.

He continued to ask the same question over and over until the waitress brought cups of ice cream for all of us. As I handed one across the wall to the boy, he said, "You on ship?"

Danny finally broke down. "Yes, we're on a ship," he told him.

The boy beamed. "What name ship?" he asked.

Oh, no, I thought. *He knows more English.*

The boy persisted. "What name ship? What name ship?"

After listening to this question about a dozen times, I told him. "*Alexander Hamilton.*"

He looked stumped for a moment, then he gave it a shot. "Al . . . , Al . . . , Al . . . To hell your ship," he said, and walked away.

Machinery is merciless, and danger sits on your shoulder when dealing with heavy, high-pressure equipment in confined spaces.

For certain tests of tolerance, the main propeller shaft had to be jacked forward and aft during each upkeep. A heavy shaft about three feet in diameter and weighing several tons, it ran from just behind the main propulsion turbines to the farthest aft point in the engine room where it penetrated the pressure hull.

Outside the hull, it turned the large screw that propelled our great iron fish through the water.

During this maintenance operation, the shaft was jacked back and forth by the use of a hand-operated pump, the lines running to and from the pump containing hydraulic fluid under thousands of pounds of pressure. It was a one-man job, and Melvin, a first-class engineman, volunteered to do it.

Melvin signed off on Chief Kennedy's job list and began the task, alone in the rear section of the engine room. A few minutes later, he came running forward, his head tilted to one side and a red, dripping hand covering his left ear. Melvin's face was ghostly white, as frightened as I've ever seen a man. An unstoppable stream of blood filled his hand and ran down his arm and his left side.

As he charged past me, heading forward to find the doctor, Melvin hollered over his shoulder, "Hydraulic line broke, shot through my ear!" and then he was gone.

A freak accident, unforeseeable and unavoidable, and Melvin was lucky to be alive. As he was moving the main shaft with the jack, a line burst, shooting a pencil-size stream of hydraulic fluid—a lethal shot of oil with tons of pressure behind it—at his head. Luckily, it barely missed Melvin's skull, neatly punching a quarter-inch hole through his ear. Had the stream of high-pressure fluid hit him in the head, it would have penetrated the front of his skull and probably exited out the rear—a liquid bullet that would have killed him instantly.

We shook our heads as we looked at the ruptured hydraulic line, amazed that our shipmate had not been killed on the spot.

I often worked jobs with Leroy Lavender, mostly by choice, even though the two of us had personality differences that could have precluded us working well together. I considered him a fuss budget who worried too much about memorizing detailed instructions on everything we touched, and he seemed to think I needed a lengthy lecture before we started a job. We voiced our differences with no restraint—much like an old married couple, it was said—but Leroy was a friend, and we always got the job done.

In the lower level of AMR2, situated deep in the bilges beside a narrow walkway, was a spaghetti-like array of piping associated with the emergency diesel engine that stood nearby. The job that Leroy and I had signed up for required one of us to make his way down through this twisted mess of piping, slide in flat on his stomach beneath it, and, in this trapped position, take apart a leaking pipe joint and install a new gasket. One of us would have to do the repair work in the deep space while the other stayed up on the walkway to hand him tools and parts.

Since Leroy was thinner in the waist, he opted to go down through the piping while I stayed above. I didn't argue with him. After taking his shirt off to gain every bit of clearance possible, Lavender took my hand for support and, going in feet first, began snaking his way down through the piping. Soon he let go of my hand and, looking like a contortionist, continued to force himself down through spaces that appeared too narrow for his body to fit. He made it and was soon lying in the greasy bilges on his stomach, his arms stretched out in front of him. He was now in position—albeit awkward and anything but comfortable—to take apart the leaking pipe union.

From my position up above, I could just see the top of Leroy's head and parts of his outstretched arms. "You all right, buddy?" I asked.

"Yeah, I'm okay," he answered and asked me to hand him a ratchet wrench and socket, which I did. I could tell it was difficult for Leroy to gain the leverage needed to loosen the half dozen bolts on the pipe union from his cramped position, but my friend was not a man to give up easily; in fact, he was not a man to give up at all. He took frequent breaks, stopping to rest his arms against the steel pressure hull on which he lay. Each time he stopped I'd ask him if he was all right, and each time he'd assure me he was.

After working on the pipe joint for nearly two hours, I knew Leroy had to be exhausted, especially his outstretched arms, but he continued to assure me he was okay, even beginning to sound a little annoyed at my asking. However, knowing the dangers of working under such conditions, I continued to talk to him regardless of what he thought of it. Not only did he require my help with tools and parts, I knew he needed the reassurance that someone was close by.

In order to see what he was working on, Leroy had to hold his head up in a strained position, painfully craning his neck for two and a half hours. Finally, with a gasp of relief, he dropped his head and said, "Done."

"Good job!" I said. "Now hand me those tools and get yourself out of that place."

"Give me a minute," Leroy said, breathing heavily as he rested his arms and neck.

"Take your time," I answered.

After resting for several minutes, Lavender handed up his tools. Then, with a tired but determined effort, he began to twist his body up through the maze of piping. He made progress for a few feet, but then he stopped, his head and shoulders protruding above the pipes, his lower body and legs twisted in a painful position. I could see a tautness in his face—the first hint of panic—something I had never expected to see in Leroy.

I didn't have to ask; we both knew he was stuck. From the waist down, he couldn't move. I needed to keep myself calm, and try not to show the concern that I felt.

"Can you back up?" I said. "Go back down and start over?" Appearing embarrassed and a bit confused, Leroy just shook his head. Panic began to seize him, swelling his body tighter in the twisted iron bonds and making it difficult for him to breathe. We had a problem.

I needed help, but I couldn't risk leaving Lavender alone. Panic might take him completely, and he could suffocate. When another fellow passed through the lower level I got his attention and mouthed, "Get Chief Kennedy." He took one look at Leroy and rushed to get the chief.

Kennedy charged down the ladder and ran to where Leroy was stuck, with me crouched beside him trying to keep him calm. When Leroy saw the chief, he frowned at me, perturbed that I had sent for him. I was glad to see that—better he be mad at me than panicked. The chief took one look at the situation and needed no explanation.

"How you doing, Lavender?" Kennedy asked.

"Not too good, Chief," he replied, his voice strained.

Kennedy glanced at me for an assessment, and I shook my head.

"Have you tried greasing him down?" the chief asked me.

"No I haven't, Chief. I didn't want to leave him to go get the grease."

"I'll stay with him. You get some grease, Penley."

Rushing to the engine room, I returned with a large can of bearing grease. Leroy raised his arms, and I began smearing the slick stuff all around his midsection. When he was thoroughly greased from above his waist to the top of his pants, I told him to see if he could move his body. As Chief Kennedy and I watched, Lavender made a tremendous effort to squeeze himself out. It didn't work, but painful as it was, Leroy wouldn't give up. As he strained harder, he began to breathe in great gasps, a wild, fearful look in his eyes. Chief Kennedy told him to stop, but Lavender wouldn't listen.

The chief bent down, shook Leroy's shoulders, and hollered in his face. "Lavender! Stop that. Stop it now!"

Scared, confused, and embarrassed, Leroy stopped struggling.

"All right," Kennedy said, "we're going to have to take this piping apart in order to get you out, Lavender. Penley, tell me which two guys you want me to send down to take it out."

Leroy started to voice his own preference, but the chief stopped him short. "I didn't ask you, Lavender; I asked Penley." He knew Leroy was in no condition to be making decisions.

I told the chief I wanted Bob Lee and young Dan Trent, the fellow who had gotten himself stuck in the box girder and also had helped install the big valve that almost fell on me.

"Okay," Kennedy said, "you got 'em." Then he looked at Leroy. "Lavender, you might outrank these guys, but don't be trying to tell them how to do their jobs. Just keep quiet, and they'll get you out."

The chief left, and within five minutes, Bob Lee and Dan Trent came down the ladder carrying every tool conceivable for undoing the piping. I didn't have to tell them a thing. Bob took one look at Leroy, at the twisted pipes that had him trapped, and knew exactly where to begin.

Lavender had now been down inside the piping for three hours, and trapped for over half an hour. Another hour was required to free him, during which time Chief Kennedy kept everyone but the four of us out of the lower level AMR2.

A gray, dead look began to creep into Leroy's eyes. This troubled me more than the wild desperation he had shown when trying to pry himself free.

Bob Lee and Dan Trent worked silently and fast. I squatted beside Leroy, talking to him and resting a hand on his shoulder. He tried to smile, and at one point even attempted a joke. "Your hand's greasy, Penley. Now you're getting it on my shoulder."

I laughed. "Aw, you've got grease all over you, Leroy. This is just love grease."

"Not like any love grease I ever felt," he said. Then he stopped talking, because it hurt his clamped sides when he tried to laugh. The dead look crept back into his eyes.

Finally Bob removed the last bolt from a pipe union and the two lifted out a large curved length that had been bearing against Leroy's left side. After four hours in that hellish maze, he was free. We had to help him climb out, and he was unable to stand up for several minutes. When he finally pulled himself to his feet, he looked at us all with relief on his ashen face. "Thanks, guys," he said. "Thanks for saving me."

After Leroy got his breath and began to relax a bit, I couldn't resist a jab. "Now are you going to store those hydraulic jacks somewhere besides in the depths of that box girder?" I asked.

He managed a wry smile. "No," he replied.

As we neared the end of the upkeep period and prepared to submerge for two months, we could hardly wait. Not only was everyone tired and looking forward to catching up on sleep, we were anxious to fire up the big boat, dive under the sea, and do the thing we knew best.

Of course, tired or not, such preparations called for one last fling, another thing we knew best.

There were three enlisted men's clubs at Rota, a structure common to all naval bases. The EM Club, for the youngest ones, E-1 through E-4; the "Acey-Deucey" Club, for E-5s and E-6s; and the Chiefs' Club. Since most of the nukes were first- and second-class petty officers, we frequented the Acey-Deucey Club.

Housed in a classic two-story Spanish-style building, the Acey-Deucey Club featured live music, excellent food and drinks, and fine service by formal Spanish waiters. A nice place for base personnel to take their girlfriends, wives, and even children. The manager of the club was a dapper first-class petty officer, never dressed in uniform, always a suit and tie.

Out back, behind the Acey-Deucey Club, was a fenced enclosure about fifty yards long by thirty yards wide. A cement dance floor under the stars, the perimeter ringed with tables and chairs, a large covered stage at one end. USO shows were performed there, and I happened to know that Bob Hope had appeared on that very stage more than once.

At the opposite end of the broad concrete floor stood a small building separate from the Acey-Deucey Club. The Stag Bar: the animal house where the manager strongly urged guys such as submarine sailors to drink, so as not to terrorize the nice people in the main club.

The night before we were scheduled to depart on patrol, a large group of us, including Whitey, Skelton, Paul Ashford, DeWayne Catron, Danny Dawson, Bob Lee, and the like, donned our dress uniforms and headed for the Stag Bar. Our mission: for each of us to down at least one drink of every alcoholic beverage the club served. We were big-time sailors, and as such, we felt obligated to pursue big-time goals.

The manager seemed to visit the Stag Bar often when we were there, and about halfway through the evening, we decided it was time to add champagne to our growing list of drinks downed. We told the manager on one of his visits, and soon a Spanish waiter appeared from the main club with a chilled bottle of champagne in a silver bucket of ice. As we watched, the waiter lined up a number of glasses on the bar, smiled as he spun the bottle in the ice, and deftly popped the cork. We all cheered.

Still smiling, the gracious waiter poured champagne into the glasses with a professional flair and returned the bottle to the ice. We turned up the glasses, drained them in a gulp, and began to pass the bottle around, everyone who hadn't gotten a glassful taking a big swig. The waiter looked appalled, especially when we immediately ordered a second bottle. He whirled, walked out with a frown, and returned with another bottle, already opened. He slammed it down on the bar and stomped out. That was okay; we didn't need glasses.

Sometime late that evening I decided it would be fun to stand on the same stage where Bob Hope had performed. I walked outside, leaving the door to the Stag Bar standing open. It was a beautiful starlit night, and I could see the stage in shadows at the far end of the concrete floor. Wandering down that direction, I made it to the stage, climbed up, and stood at center front for several minutes, imagining myself performing before a packed audience on the very spot where Bob Hope had stood.

When my mock performance came to a smashing end, I bowed to my silent audience, climbed down off the stage, and headed for the lighted door of the Stag Bar. Making my way down one side of the dance floor, I happened onto something that had the potential for speedier progress: a bicycle, leaning against one of the tables.

The bicycle was a nice one—a narrow-tired racing type, ready to go. I climbed on and took off. A wonderfully exhilarating ride, whizzing along under the starlit sky, so much fun that I turned and headed back up toward the stage. Really getting into it now, I executed great loops and figure eights on that wide expanse of concrete, laughing aloud, with no one to hear but myself.

In times of exhilaration, my adventuresome spirit has been known to overcome common sense. I stopped the bicycle at the far end, happily leaning against the stage, and eyed the open, lighted entrance to the Stag Bar, fifty yards away. Without a second thought I turned the bike and headed for the open door, pedaling with everything I had. I must have been doing thirty miles an hour as I neared my target.

At the last moment, an unfortunate coincidence of timing occurred. The manager, on his way back to the main club, stepped into the doorway. I didn't have time to throw on the brakes, nor did the wide-eyed manager have time to react. He just stopped, facing me, as I sped into him. A direct hit.

I collided with the manager at bicycle warp speed, ramming the front wheel between his legs. Somehow, he managed to reach out and grab a handlebar in each hand. Supported by his arms, he threw his head down into my lap and his legs straight out behind him, his feet now the leading part of this flying catastrophe. In this manner, we entered the Stag Bar.

Colliding almost instantly with the bar itself, we stopped short, turning over stools and piling up against the bar in a tangled heap. Everyone in the room was aghast, unsure as to what had just happened. To their eyes, it had been only a blur, followed by a loud noise. After the motion stopped and the noise died, the spectators began to put the scenario together. One of the guys laughed, and in moments, the Stag Bar broke into a great roar. Sailors pointing, whooping, and wiping tears from their eyes.

I climbed to my feet, shocked to discover that I wasn't hurt, and looked at the manager as he unwound himself from the downed bicycle and a couple of bar stools. Standing up, the man brushed at his clothes and looked himself up and down, as if expecting to find broken bones and gushing lacerations. He found neither. Miraculously, he had also escaped injury. The manager stood and stared at me for a long time. I'm sure I looked quite foolish, and it must have been difficult for him to maintain a serious air with my shipmates rolling on the floor and howling like lunatics.

When the manager finally spoke, he did so with a straight face. "I'm going to lock the bicycle up."

"Good idea," I said.

The following morning, the skipper made a final inspection of the boat to see that all gear was stowed properly, lashed down, and ready to withstand whatever the sea might throw at us. As he was leaving the engineering spaces, he turned and said, "Good job, men." We all smiled. Like Chief Kennedy, that was the best you could get from Captain Bessac.

The reactor was fired up, "critical" in the vernacular of nuclear energy, the turbines hot and singing their shrill song of power. Morale soared as we untied our big sub, backed away from the tender, and swung her nose toward the deep Atlantic.

Chapter Ten

On Patrol

We had to steam several miles on the surface, straight out into the Atlantic, until we reached the edge of the continental shelf, the point where the shallow bottom quickly drops off into the abyss. There we would dive.

We were greeted three miles out—the boundary where international waters begin—by a number of Russian trawlers. No surprise. These small crafts, posing as fishing boats but known by both sides to be spy ships, always awaited us exactly three miles out. As we plowed through them at high speed, the enemy vessels would try various maneuvers to get close enough to take pictures and look at us through binoculars and telescopes.

For what purpose did the Soviet sailors watch us as we passed? Simply to make an appearance, to let us know that they knew what we were up to. Big deal. We could, and did, easily outrun the trawlers, and soon they were mere specks miles behind in our wake. And from the time they lost sight of us until we surfaced again two months later, they had no idea where we were. That's why we were the greatest Cold War deterrent on Earth—a submerged launch pad that the enemy could not track.

When the double A-ooo-ga! A-ooo-ga! of the diving alarm sounded and the twin words, "Dive, dive," resounded from loudspeakers throughout the boat, we slipped beneath the waves. There we would live for eight weeks. An artificial world of steel, where there was no sun, no moon, no stars, no clouds, no ground to walk on or sand to dig your toes into, and the farthest one could see was the length of a single compartment.

The skipper had the con. Bessac was a fearless submarine pilot, and anyone who doubted that was about to get a lesson. After leveling off at periscope depth, back in the engine room we received orders to accelerate to flank speed. Soon the main turbines were howling and the *Alexander Hamilton* was flying through the sea at more than twenty knots, just beneath the surface.

When running slower, the engine room was a reasonably quiet space, but at flank speed the noise from the turbines and the reduction gears was overwhelming—a wild metallic scream that forced us to yell into each other's ears to be heard.

Normally, when we changed depth, either up or down, we did so at a low angle—something like two or three degrees. The order from the con to the diving officer would be "two-degree down bubble," "three-degree up bubble," and so on. The diving officer would repeat back the order to ensure that he had heard correctly, then he would execute it.

As we tore through the water at periscope depth, Captain Bessac gave the order, "Thirty-degree down bubble."

The diving officer, believing he had misheard the skipper's order, repeated back, "Three-degree down bubble. Aye, sir."

Bessac scowled. "Put the planes on full dive and don't take them off till I tell you to."

The faster the boat is moving, the more reactive the diving planes become. At flank speed, we quickly nosed down at a tremendous angle. I was on watch in the upper level engine room, wondering why the hell we were going so fast at periscope depth. When the nose turned down and we raced for the deep, I ran to the door of the maneuvering room and yelled at Lieutenant Commander Green, the EOOW, "What's going on, sir?"

Mr. Green looked at me and shrugged. He was on his feet, looking just as confused and concerned as I felt. The three guys at the control panels looked grim. I headed back into the engine room.

With such a great down angle on the boat, it was a steep climb from maneuvering back up to the machinery I had to monitor. I grabbed hold of a guardrail, pulling myself hand over hand until I reached a position between the twin turbine generators. There I turned around and, dangling from waist-high rails on either side, leaned with gravity toward maneuvering, a space now far below me. Directly behind me, the big propulsion turbines screamed, driving us ever deeper.

A young trainee, fresh out of nuke school, was standing in the aft end of the engine room when all this started. Terrified, he came running toward me. Hanging onto the guardrail to keep from falling forward, the kid hollered into my ear over the noise, "What's going on?"

"I don't know," I hollered back. His face lost all color.

"How deep are we?"

"I don't know that either. The depth gauge is in maneuvering."

"Oh, no!"

"Get back up where you came from," I told him, "and watch for leaks."

"*Leaks?*" His eyes looked like a man gone mad.

"That's right," I yelled. "Leaks. Now get back there."

I would hear the story over and over from the guys who were on watch up forward in the control room. The skipper stood like a stanchion, his stoic countenance revealing nothing.

Finally, Bessac spoke. "Level her off at five hundred feet," he told the diving officer.

"Five hundred feet. Aye, sir," the diving officer replied.

The planesmen heaved back on the controls with all they had. The big boat shuddered as the diving planes fought to stop its descent, but traveling at full speed, the eight thousand tons of metal didn't react as quickly as the captain would have liked. They couldn't catch her at five hundred feet or even at six. Somewhere between six and seven hundred feet, she slowly turned up her nose and leveled off.

The executive officer was standing beside the captain. Bessac looked at the diving officer and, with the steely smile of a gunfighter, gestured toward the exec. "Mr. Rawlins has the con." With that, the skipper stepped down from the platform and strode forward to his quarters.

Back in the engine room, the young trainee again ran up to me and skidded to a stop. "No leaks!" he said.

I almost laughed. "Not a single leak, huh?"

"Nope, not a one," he said proudly.

I clapped him on the shoulder. "Good man."

After the captain finished testing the integrity of the boat, along with the nerves of his crew, we reduced speed and again rose to periscope depth. After ensuring that we had no "contacts"— ships that could potentially hear us on their sonar and begin to track us—we swung the rudder hard to port, turned, and headed for the Straits of Gibraltar.

The mouth of the Mediterranean Sea exhibits a strange phenomenon long known to submariners: a natural circulation in and out of the Atlantic. Cold water flows into the smaller, shallower sea while slightly warmer water, after being heated by the Mediterranean, flows back out. The cold, inbound layer runs near the bottom, while the warmer layer flows outward above it. During World War II, submarines put these thermally induced flows to good use, quietly sneaking in and out of the Med with little chance of being detected by enemy sonar. The diesel boats shut down all power and rode the thermal currents—the only propulsion needed to carry them in either direction through the Straits of Gibraltar.

We did the same on the *Hamilton,* silently riding the inbound thermal layer without the use of propulsion turbines. It was a thrill to be using the same stealthy techniques that our WWII counterparts had perfected.

As opposed to the screaming of the engine room at flank speed, when running silent one could literally hear a pin drop. We walked in our stocking feet, and instead of speaking, we wrote notes to each other. Some of the guys delighted in referring to silent running as being "quiet as a tomb." An apt analogy, I suppose, but I preferred to think of it in more palatable terms.

Once inside the Med, where the patrol officially began, our lives settled down to a routine—at least as routine as the captain, the engineering officer, and our own devious minds would allow.

The crew was divided into three watch sections, each of which spent six hours on watch followed by twelve off. The result: we lived an eighteen-hour day instead of a twenty-four. This mattered little, however; there was no day or night beneath the sea, just the passing of time.

The only reminder of what time of day it might actually be in the real world was mealtime. With one section coming off watch and another going on every six hours, the cooks had to serve four meals a day: breakfast, at 6:00 a.m. (0600 hours); lunch, at noon (1200 hours); dinner, at 6:00 p.m. (1800 hours); and soup and sandwiches at midnight. Each ongoing watch section ate just before relieving the offgoing bunch, who then went directly to the mess hall to fill their own empty gullets.

This rotation ensured that we had a hot meal before going on watch and another six hours later when our watch was done. And in case a favorite dish was being served during one's twelve hours off, a friend could wake you in time to take advantage of it. Every meal was good, but the highlights consisted of a steak dinner once a week—as many steaks as one could eat—and lobster three or four times during the patrol.

Aside from which meal of the day we might be eating, time meant nothing. After a week or so at sea, we not only lost track of day and night, most of us didn't know the date, for weeks at a time. We had no reason to know, or care.

And most of the time the majority of us didn't know exactly where we were in the world, nor did we need to know. Every couple of weeks I'd go up to control and ask Danny Dawson where we were positioned at that particular time. Danny would point his finger at a spot on a large-scale map of the entire Mediterranean and say, "Oh, we're about here." I'd nod, thank him, and we'd both grin. I doubt he ever showed me our correct location.

Inside a submarine is an alien place, an unnatural environment for humans, and operating beneath the sea is an inherently dangerous occupation. Accidents, emergencies, and leaks are all a part of life, and the survival of a submersible vessel depends always on the training of its crew.

Drills, drills, drills. Various messages were regularly passed throughout the ship via the intercom: mealtimes, movies starting, etc. One learned to sleep right through the normal messages, but let something out of the ordinary come over the intercom and the entire crew was awake in an instant—awake, alert, and on the move.

Every man had a battle station. The Gong! Gong! Gong! of battle stations created a melee throughout the boat, a controlled melee in which every man, whether asleep, eating, watching a movie, reading a book, or playing a guitar in the crew's lounge, was on the move—grabbing pants, shirts, shoes, and running for his station. The torpedomen to the torpedo room, missile controllers to the missile compartment, planesmen to the diving plane controls, and so on. Men running hard, brushing shoulders in passageways hardly wide enough for one, and diving cleanly through iron-rimmed hatches—an exercise in which an untrained man would have broken bones or knocked himself out. Since I and every other nuke worked in the aft end, we had the longest run.

As soon as a compartment was manned for battle stations—watertight doors secured over every hatch and all hands present and ready for action—the compartment commander reported, "Battle stations manned." The captain, who had begun the drill, took over the con and closely monitored the clock to see how long it took the crew to man battle stations throughout the boat.

Incredibly, from the moment the first gong sounded over the intercom until all compartments reported battle stations manned took slightly over one minute. Within seventy to eighty seconds, the boat was ready to launch missiles, fire torpedoes, or handle any emergency in any compartment.

Before ending the drill, the captain always announced how long we had taken to man battle stations. If he was happy with the result, he sounded that way. If he was not—and the difference amounted to only a few seconds—we knew the drills would continue with maddening frequency until the old man *was* happy.

We also had drills such as "Flooding in the Torpedo Room!" or "Fire in AMR1!" Again, we were on our feet and on the run, all having specific jobs in every emergency imaginable. We didn't know if it was a drill or the real thing until the emergency team arrived on the scene. In the case of a drill, an officer would be waiting in the compartment. He would point out where the simulated flooding or fire was supposed to be and watch as the team rolled out fire hoses or shut off valves to isolate a section of piping—taking every measure as if the emergency were real.

A fire inside the boat, be it electrical or conventional, was one of our worst fears. Submarine movies always seem to feature fires—fires that burn for a long time and require extensive efforts by the crew before being extinguished. This is *not* the way it happens in real life. A submarine fire will quickly burn up all the oxygen and suffocate the crew. It must be contained quickly, at any cost. If a submariner has to run directly into a fire to get to its source, he will.

My battle station was the engine room upper level, alongside Frances Koslouski ("Ski"), a tall sailor with coarse good looks and laughing eyes whose battle station was engine room supervisor. Ski served as my main mentor, and we had a lot of fun together. Being Polish, Ski took the brunt of all the Polack jokes—jokes which I, being from the Colorado prairie, had never heard. And knowing Ski didn't help me to understand them, either, because he was one of the more intelligent sailors I had ever known. Ski was unflappable, though, and the guys hitting him with the jokes soon learned that they had such little effect that telling them wasn't worth the effort. In fact, Ski knew more Polack jokes than anyone else.

And for an incident that once occurred in Fort Lauderdale, Florida, Ski had become famous.

The lounge in Fort Lauderdale's Marlin Beach Hotel featured a long bar that swept outward in a great arc. A glass-sided swimming pool behind the bar served as a backdrop—like looking into the side of a large aquarium. Shapely girls in bikinis and snorkel masks would dive into the pool and do underwater ballets for the entertainment of customers seated at the bar. During their submerged show, the girls would teasingly motion to customers to come in and join them.

Once upon a time, when the *Hamilton* was visiting Fort Lauderdale prior to our first patrol, Koslouski had been sitting at the bar, in uniform, when one of the swimming girls gave him the come-hither motion. Without hesitation, he answered the call. Running to the end of the bar and through a door to the back, Ski eyed a set of stairs that led to the top of the pool. He charged up the stairs and, to the shock and delight of everyone out front, dove in. He still had on his shoes and his white hat.

The girls in the pool, both surprised and laughing, tried to get a snorkel mask on Ski, a flailing attempt that failed due to his being both drunk and fully clothed. After swallowing several great gulps of water, Ski swam to the surface, coughed several times, and dove back down to wave at the laughing crowd at the bar. He then surfaced again, climbed out of the pool, and returned to his seat.

Sadly, I missed the show, but I happened to walk in just as Ski regained his seat at the bar. Spotting him from the front door, I walked over and sat down beside him. Only then did I notice that he was dripping wet.

"How did you manage to get so wet?" I asked. Ski, still coughing up water, pointed at the pool behind the bar.

"You didn't!" I said.

A man seated beside me roared, "Oh, yes he did!"

At that point, several people began describing what Ski had done. And they all bought him drinks, none of which he needed, but all of which he drank. They bought me just as many.

Later, with me three sheets to the wind and Ski about six, we headed back to the boat, which was tied up only a few blocks away. Ski could barely walk, and his soaked shoes splop-splopped with every weaving step he took.

Lieutenant Commander Green, the normally solemn engineering officer, had the duty that night. And as luck would have it, Ski and I ran into him as soon as we reached the bottom of the ladder.

"What in the world happened to you, Koslouski?" Mr. Green asked, looking the soaked sailor up and down.

Ski had a tough time talking, so I took over and explained what he had done. Mr. Green wasn't even known to smile very often, but by the time I finished the story, the man was laughing and slapping his knees.

When the duty officer finally gained control of himself, he looked at me and said, "Ski looks like he might need a hand, Penley. Think you can get him into bed?"

"Yes, sir," I said, and Ski and I splop-splopped off toward the berthing area.

I was fairly new to submarines when that incident occurred. When I laid my head down that night, still laughing to myself, I knew I had found the navy I'd been looking for.

The engineering officer had his own drills, dozens of them, that he delighted in pulling on the nukes. He held them at odd times, of course, informing no one but the captain and the conning officer of his plans.

With the engine room humming along and none of us anticipating any problems, Mr. Green would wander into AMR2, where most of the major electrical panels were located. From there he could flip switches and breakers, shutting down various pieces of equipment in the engine room, which he did. This nearly always included lighting, emergencies being more fun to handle in the dark and also more realistic.

The surprise drills usually began with the loss of a major piece of equipment, such as the main air-conditioning unit. A steam plant inside an airtight tube requires a great amount of air conditioning and must be cooled at all costs. When things were running smoothly, as they were just before we were ambushed by the drills, we engine room guys often stood under one of the overhead ventilation outlets—spot coolers—and let cool, refreshing air blow over us.

Then came chaos.

Sometimes several pieces of equipment, along with the lighting, were shut down at the same time, the loss being accompanied by loud exclamations from maneuvering and various parts of the plant.

"Oh, no!"

"What the hell?"

And away we'd go. The total darkness didn't last long; emergency lighting, in the form of battery-powered flashlights called battle lanterns, switched on automatically upon loss of AC power. Although the battle lanterns provided only minimum light, they were positioned to shine on the most crucial elements of the plant—switchboards, isolation valves, steam trip valves, and the like. And even if all lighting failed, we could find every piece of equipment in the dark almost as easily as we could in the dim light of the lanterns.

First things first. Find out what equipment had been lost. Prioritize what needed to be done. Restore power. Problems included the loss of propulsion, turbine generators, hydraulic power, pumps, and so on. Several things might shut down at once, or they might do so sequentially. As we fought to correct one set of problems, another would arise.

If a trip valve had shut off the steam that powered a crucial piece of equipment, it might be a matter of simply resetting the valve. If the valve on the machine would not reset, emergency equipment had to be started and brought on line to take its place. All this at a dead run, dodging tightly spaced pipes, hundreds of valves, levers, and low-hanging spot coolers. The dim light of the battle lanterns—narrow rays here and there—left most of the engine room in dark shadows.

Finally, after everything was up and running, the lights would be restored, as would hopefully have been the case in a real emergency.

I carry lifelong burn scars on my arms from brushing against darkened steam pipes as I ran. The scars don't bother me; I earned them.

I hated the darkness. Somewhere in a secret spot in my mind, almost hidden even from myself, was the haunting knowledge that if I died in a submarine I would die in the dark, that my last vision would be an inky blackness—no vision at all. I never allowed myself to consciously think about this until after I was discharged. A submariner cannot afford such thoughts.

Despite centuries of study, much of the sea remains a mystery. And, despite our extensive training and readiness, the deep blue could deal us a surprise whenever it chose.

I was eating lunch in the mess hall when it happened. As usual, guys were chatting, joking, and laughing as they ate.

WHAM! A terrific noise from the starboard forward quarter. A great shock ran through the boat, a shudder, and we knew we had collided with something underwater.

"What the hell!" someone shouted, and men ran for their battle stations. All stations were manned within a minute, with no idea what we had hit, or what might have hit us.

Back in the engine room, we stood silent. Watching gauges, listening on emergency phones, waiting for word—any word. The main drain pump was manned and ready in case the boat flooded. Faces taut. Eyes intense. Had we ripped a hole in the pressure hull? Were we taking on water?

After what seemed an eternity, the captain's steady voice came over the intercom. "As you all know, we collided with something underwater, evidently connecting with it on our forward starboard quarter. We don't know what it was; all we know is that it was submerged and heavy enough to give us quite a jolt.

"The pressure hull has not been compromised, and all systems appear to be in working order. There may or may not be a hole in one of our forward ballast tanks, and that we have no way of knowing until we surface at the end of the patrol.

"We will continue on patrol and complete our mission. All hands stand down. Battle stations secured."

The drain pump and its controls were located in the lower-level engine room. The operator stood in front of a complex manifold—a spaghetti of heavy piping and a great number of quick-throw valves. From this position he could pump flood water from any compartment in the boat or from all compartments at once if need be, returning the water to the sea from whence it came, hopefully before its added weight took us down.

The drain pump operator had to be fast, quick thinking, and a man with rock-steady nerves. Bob Lee was a natural for the job. The drain pump and manifold remained Bob's battle station as long as he served aboard the *Hamilton,* because no one could do it better.

When Bob climbed out of the lower level after the captain secured battle stations, he was met by an anxious young trainee who was making his first patrol. "Do you think we tore a hole in a ballast tank, Bob?" the trainee asked.

Bob looked at the young fellow with a blank face and shrugged his shoulders. Without saying a word, Bob ducked through the engine-room hatch and returned to the mess hall.

I was standing near the door to the maneuvering room, talking to Lieutenant Dewhirst, a striking young officer, blond and handsome, who was engineering officer of the watch.

The young trainee, after being ignored by Bob Lee, turned to me with worried eyes. "Do you think we tore a hole in a ballast tank, Penley?"

"I don't know," I replied. "It's like the captain said; there's no way to tell until we try to surface."

"*Try* to surface?" the trainee said.

Lieutenant Dewhirst and the three other guys in maneuvering were beginning to enjoy this. "Here's the way I see it," I told the novice submariner. "If there's a hole in a forward ballast tank, the boat might do some funny things when we try to surface. If the hole is down low, near the bottom of the tank, it probably won't make much difference. That would put the hole near the normal flooding port, and some of the water in the tank would just blow out of it and we'd do a normal surface.

"On the other hand, if the hole is up high on the tank, we won't be able to blow all the water out of it. In that case, that part of the boat will try to stay under. What will likely happen is we will surface, but not all the way; the bow will be riding low in the water, and the boat might try and heave over to starboard some too, kind of lean over on one side instead of float upright. We'll probably look pretty funny coming into port if that happens."

I looked at the lieutenant. "Is that the way you see it, Mr. Dewhirst?"

The officer looked at the trainee. "Yep, I think Penley hit the nail right on the head."

My analysis did not placate the trainee. "Okay," he said, "but we were submerged when we hit whatever that was. What if we tore a hole in the top of a ballast tank, or in the top of more than one tank? What if we ripped two or three of them open?"

"Look," I said. "We have to surface. It's simple mathematics. The old one-and-one principle, just like they taught us in sub school."

The trainee looked puzzled. "The one-and-one principle?"

"Yeah, one dive and one surface. You have to surface every time you dive, or you won't make it very long in the submarine service."

Mr. Dewhirst threw back his head and laughed. The trainee did not.

Captain Bessac would tolerate no nonsense from his officers, especially in the control room. One young lieutenant junior grade (LTJG) learned this the hard way.

Mr. Dunson was a round-faced, portly young officer, friendly and rather unkempt. Uncharacteristically for the nuclear navy,

Dunson had not attended the Naval Academy. Having received his engineering degree from a civilian university, everyone wondered how Dunson had been able to get by Admiral Rickover's personal scrutiny. Captain Bessac probably lay awake in his bunk wondering this.

The skipper made Mr. Dunson stand training watches for a disproportionate amount of time before finally, reluctantly, deeming the young LTJG qualified to stand watch as conning officer.

Whenever a surface vessel, referred to as a "contact," was detected at any distance, the conning officer was required to report the contact to the captain. Whether the captain was awake or asleep, he was informed of the contact's exact position relative to the *Hamilton,* and the conning officer had standing orders to quickly move away from the other vessel, be it Soviet, American, or unidentified. And, after first reporting the contact, if the *Hamilton* moved any closer to the other vessel for any reason, the conning officer also had to report this to the captain.

During one of his first watches as conning officer, Mr. Dunson detected a surface contact approximately six thousand yards away. He immediately sent a messenger to inform the captain, who happened to be taking a shower. The messenger, a seaman, knocked on the door to the captain's private shower. The captain turned off the water and answered, "Yes?"

"Surface contact, Captain," the young fellow reported. "Six thousand yards, relative bearing two-eight-zero."

"Six thousand yards, bearing two-eight-zero," repeated the captain. "Thank you."

"You're welcome, Captain," and the messenger returned to control.

Mr. Dunson misjudged the surface vessel's heading and turned the boat the wrong direction. About five minutes after the bumbling conning officer sent his report to the captain, the *Hamilton* was closing with the contact. Again, he sent the messenger. Again, the messenger knocked on the captain's shower door and, again, the captain turned off the water. "Yes?"

"Closing with surface contact, Captain. Now 5,500 yards away."

"Five thousand, five hundred yards," growled the captain. "Thank you."

Another five minutes, and Mr. Dunson had steered the *Hamilton* even closer. The messenger went to the captain a third time.

The captain had turned off the water and was toweling himself dry when the young seaman knocked. "What is it?" asked the captain.

"Contact is closer, Captain. Now five thousand yards away."

Captain Bessac threw open the door and came boiling out of the shower, stark naked. Propelling his tall frame past the startled messenger, the naked skipper stormed down the passageway and burst into control.

Two long strides carried him to the conning platform. He jumped up on it, grabbed Mr. Dunson by the shoulders, and threw him off onto the deck. As Dunson reeled backward to catch himself against a bulkhead, Bessac yelled, "Up periscope."

Whirling his naked body and the periscope in a circle, he quickly found the contact. "Bearing two-six-five degrees," he said. Then, "Range?"

The captain was given the range.

"Right rudder, twenty degrees."

"Right rudder, twenty degrees. Aye, sir," the diving officer responded.

"Down periscope, and take her down to 120 feet—now!"

After steadying the boat on a heading that took it directly away from the contact, the captain slowly turned his head, scanning everyone in control. Every eye was on him, and every one about to pop out of a sailor's head.

Then Bessac turned his blazing eyes on the cringing young officer. "What do you do when you detect a contact, Mr. Dunson?"

Dunson's hands were shaking, his chin quivering. "I . . . uh, get away from it, Captain."

"Very *good*," Bessac said, sarcasm dripping from his words. "You find out his range, his heading, his speed, and you get away from him. What's so hard about *that*, mister?"

"N . . . nothing, sir."

"I agree," Bessac said loudly. "Now get up here and take the con. And if you get another contact, don't try to make friends with him."

With that, the nude skipper stepped off the platform, stomped out the door, and slammed it behind him.

The high morale that attended leaving port began to dwindle after the first two weeks at sea, and by the middle of the patrol— when we'd been submerged for a month and had another month to go—it felt endless. The continuous confinement tightened our nerves, and tempers simmered just below the surface.

Although it was seldom discussed openly, being completely out of touch with loved ones was one of the hardest things to endure. Unlike most surface ships, the boat could not transmit messages for the entire patrol, because to do so would have revealed our position to the enemy. We could, however, receive transmissions nearly anytime. Each man was allowed to receive three or four messages per patrol—approximately one every two weeks—from one person whom he had designated as his sender. These short messages, known as familygrams, came mostly from wives, girlfriends, or mothers, and they were screened by the communications officer and sometimes the captain before we actually received them.

My familygrams came from my mother. I awaited each message anxiously, because Mom was an upbeat lady with an indomitable spirit and irrepressible sense of humor. Her familygrams reflected the unconditional love that had buoyed me all my life.

My brother loved poetry, and I once received a familygram from Mom that contained a poem he had written for me. I felt very close to family as I read the poem, out there in the deep blue sea.

Submariners

You went to the ends of the earth—
not on the sea, but joined more closely
than that—
Suspended, as it were,
below the reality of its surface.
Moved by the harnessed forces of
atomic power—
and by the indomitable power of
human spirit.
—George Penley

I had conversations with my mother and my brother, although they were unaware of it at the time. How did I accomplish this? I wrote them letters while on patrol—mostly about the jokes the guys pulled on each other, the great food we had to eat, how I was feeling, and that I was thinking about them. Each one was signed, sealed, and stamped at the time I wrote it. And since I knew that the letter would be mailed as soon as we reached port—two, four, or six weeks later—I felt that I had actually talked with them. Which I had; I just hadn't yet received their response.

I've often been asked how a kid who grew up in the wide open spaces could stand the confinement of a submarine for months at a time. As Harry Truman said when asked how he withstood the stress of being a wartime president, I had a foxhole in my mind.

My bunk was my refuge, the one small space I could call my own. I could crawl onto the narrow, comfortable mattress; pull the curtain shut; lay back; close my eyes; and leave. I was no longer on a submarine, not lying next to an iron pressure hull with water above, below, and beside me, straining every square inch of metal that surrounded me. Gone from the steel cave of pipes, cables, wires, levers, and valves that threatened to enclose my mind as well as my body.

I was back on the ranch, walking the grassy plains, hunting the rocky hillsides, riding my pony like the wind, wading in the rippling creek beds of my youth. The prairie was there, beautiful in its endless expanse; the cattle and horses were there; my old dog, Sandy; my mother; my brother; and always, Dad.

I could feel the prairie wind on my face, and I could dream. Mom still owned the land, and I dreamed of going back after the navy and starting up the ranch again. Mom was aware of my dream, and I think she was holding onto the land just to give me the chance to fulfill it. The dream sustained me, as did my memories of Dad and my feelings of his presence. I could do anything when Dad was with me, and he always was.

How did a kid from the wide-open spaces cope with extended confinement inside a submarine? I went away; I wasn't always there.

There were very few officers on submarines who had come up through the ranks, but we ran into one every now and then. In my experience, officers who had once been enlisted men fit into one of two categories. Most were friendly and understanding, having once walked in the working man's shoes. Some, however, were arrogant and aloof, having risen above the masses and become legends in their own minds. We had a young officer who initially fit the latter description—an ass in his own right—but following an attitude adjustment that took him by surprise, he actually metamorphosed from one to the other in a very short time.

Mister Schultz was a lieutenant junior grade when he came aboard. Average height and thin build with a sharp, narrow face, he could have passed for one of those TV detectives who never smiles and takes his job and himself far too seriously.

Schultz had been an enlisted man who was accepted into a high-powered navy program called NESEP that paid his way through college and then awarded him a commission. Somehow the brand new officer ended up on the *Hamilton*.

I don't know what navy young Mr. Schultz had come from prior to his college tour, but he was not schooled in the ways of submarines. He could be seen sucking up to senior officers, but that wasn't altogether unusual for a junior. What was unusual was his arrogance toward enlisted men. Except for the chief petty officers, Schultz would not deign to speak to one of us. A nod perhaps, if one were having an especially lucky day. Soon, no one bothered trying to speak to him at all, not even to show him the respect commonly afforded an officer. A silent standoff ensued.

There are few secrets on a submarine, and everyone knew about Schultz's enlisted background. This knowledge only served to make the junior officer's attitude all the more repulsive, ensuring a popularity of zero among the crew. He didn't seem to care.

The other officers surely noticed Schultz's aloofness toward the enlisted men, but none of his seniors tried to clue him in to the mistake he was making. A submarine crew is an extremely close society, each man prepared to fight or die for the other at a moment's notice, but there is an underlying primal element that one must know—a feral ruthlessness that seeks out weaknesses in a man or an inability to do his job. Submariners react to such shortcomings like sharks to blood.

Schultz would have to learn on his own, or pay a higher price than he knew.

Schultz had to become qualified on the *Hamilton*. Qualifying, for officers and enlisted men alike, requires extensive study of each system on the boat, an oral exam on every system, and finally an overall exam by a committee made up of officers and senior enlisted men.

When a man was studying a system, he carried a complete diagram of it as well as a written description of every part along with its function. And as one studied the details, followed the piping, electrical connections, etc., he could ask questions of the men on watch in the compartment. Mr. Schultz didn't ask questions of enlisted men, and probably wouldn't have gotten much help if he had.

Schultz was studying the ballast tank blow system, a complex system of piping that ran along the outside margins of every compartment in the boat. The pipes, which ran inside the pressure hull but penetrated it at various points, carried high-pressure air to the ballast tanks to blow them dry and force the boat to the surface. At each point where a high-pressure pipe made a ninety-degree turn toward the hull penetration, a hydraulically operated valve was located. These valves, when opened, allowed the air to rush into the tanks.

Blow valves were normally operated remotely from the control room, the conning officer being the one to order the ballast tanks blown, all at once, when he was ready to surface. For emergency purposes, however, each valve was equipped with a small toggle switch mounted directly on the housing. If remote control were lost, as in a battle situation, a man could stand at a valve and, by moving the switch from off to on, blow an individual ballast tank. If such an instance were to occur, an operator would be stationed at each blow switch so that all tanks could be blown simultaneously on command from the con.

If a toggle switch were inadvertently thrown, God help us, a single ballast tank would be blown, causing one part of the submerged submarine to try to surface. And as the boat heaved upward on one side, it would also try to force itself to the surface at one end—either fore or aft, according to where the blown ballast tank was located—while the rest of the unbalanced boat fought to keep itself submerged, a catastrophic emergency that could sink the sub.

Mr. Schultz happened to be in AMR2 following the ballast blow system and taking notes on a clipboard. This placed him just one compartment forward of the engine room and maneuvering room, where Lieutenant Commander Green, the engineering officer and third in command on the boat, was standing watch. Three enlisted men were also on watch in maneuvering along with Mr. Green.

As luck would have it—in Mr. Schultz's case, bad luck—a first-class electronics technician named Wagner was also in AMR2, and he was keeping an eye on what Schultz was doing. Wagner was an intelligent, capable man, and as irreverent as a sailor could be.

During the course of his study, Mr. Schultz came to one of the ballast blow valves with its attached toggle switch. After reading the purpose of the switch, Schultz reached up, pinched the switch between his thumb and forefinger, and gave it a wiggle. Wagner came charging over and slapped the young officer's hand away. "Keep your hand off that switch," he said.

Schultz was mortified, his face registering surprise, confusion, and shock at such an outrageous insult. Without a word to Wagner, he turned and ran to the engine room and into maneuvering. Standing in front of Lieutenant Commander Green, with an audience of enlisted men, the young officer began to stammer out his story.

"Mr. Green, sir," Schultz said, fuming with anger. "That man Wagner just slapped my hand, right up there in AMR2."

Mr. Green, leaning back in a swivel seat, did not change expression. "Why did Wagner slap your hand, Mr. Schultz?"

"I was . . . studying the ballast blow system, sir, and when I reached up to the toggle switch on the blow valve, he slapped my hand away."

"Did Wagner say anything when he slapped your hand away?"

"Yes, he did, sir. He said, 'Keep your hand off that switch.'"

"Did you touch that switch?" Mr. Green asked.

"Yes, sir, I did."

"Keep your hand off that switch."

Following that incident, Mr. Schultz began to smile, albeit with difficulty, at every sailor on board, and a few days later, he approached me with a question about a system he'd been studying. I answered him in great detail, even walked him through the piping, and he thanked me.

Lieutenant Junior Grade Schultz had joined the crew.

Chief Kennedy did not garner high grades in Nuclear Power School, and he didn't care who knew it. He became a senior chief, and he was the first enlisted man I ever knew who qualified for the position of engineering officer of the watch (EOOW). Like most successful people, Kennedy climbed the ladder through hard work and iron determination. And a mountain of self-confidence didn't hurt, either. He ruled his world, both on the boat and at home, where a devoted wife and a houseful of kids worshipped him and obeyed his every command, just like we did. The chief was tougher than boot leather and loaded with that indefinable quality we call leadership. He reminded me of Dad, my grandfather, and not many men did.

And, like Dad, Kennedy didn't want to hear any excuses as to why a job wasn't finished. He wanted to hear that it was done, and if for some reason it wasn't, he'd better be hearing an alternative plan to see that it was.

Air compressors are an absolute necessity on a submarine; they have to work, no matter what. The damned compressors, two large multistage machines mounted side by side in the lower level, were forever breaking down—the bane of the engine room. I hated the mechanical demons, and somehow Leroy Lavender and I became the constant air compressor repairmen. Despite the maddening regularity of breakdowns, Leroy and I felt proud that Chief Kennedy trusted us to work on such important equipment—another testimony to his leadership.

When the compressors came apart time after time, I occasionally complained within earshot of the chief. He would smile, a bit of understanding in his expression, but not a trace of empathy. I'm sure he hated the things, too.

Each compressor had six pistons, or stages, all of different sizes, and the extreme pressure they all worked against often broke piston rings and sometimes even piston heads. Somehow, we kept the infernal machines running, even though toward the end of the patrol we had used up every extra piston ring in the spare parts locker and still needed more. Some stages worked on each compressor, but since neither had six operable stages, through the use of heavy copper tubing we cross-connected the workable stages on the two compressors. Thus, when both were running, we effectively had one compressor, and that's how we limped back into port.

As Leroy and I stood beside the abominable compressors, knuckles bruised, knots on our heads, and covered in grease, Chief Kennedy looked at the jury-rigged tangle of tubing running between the two machines, shook his head, and said, "Good job, guys." We felt proud. Maybe we were just dumb.

Kennedy was forever circulating memos of one sort or another among the nuclear gang, always with the heading: "All hands read and sign." After a memo made its way back to him, he would check to see that everyone had signed it, then file it in a metal box he kept on his desk in the engine room.

One day, Lavender and I snatched a sheet of Chief Kennedy's personal memo paper and had the yeoman type on it:

B.S.
All hands read and sign.

Chief Kennedy

After the memo was circulated and everyone in the engine room had signed it, we all watched as Chief Kennedy retrieved it from his inbox. Without breaking a smile, the chief looked it over carefully, checked to see that everyone had signed it, and filed it away.

If butt chewing had been an Olympic event, Kennedy would have owned the gold. The chief had it perfected to an art form, and no one was exempt. After having grown up with Dad, I thoroughly resented being chewed upon and went far out of my way to avoid situations that might ignite Chief Kennedy. I'd seen him chew out many a man, and I prided myself on never having been the object of one of his tirades—so far, that is.

Butt chewings weren't easy to avoid, either, because the chief had quirks, and it was difficult to know them all. And, as in legal matters, ignorance of the law—Kennedy's law—was no excuse. One of his quirks concerned clothing—socks, to be specific—and God help me, I didn't know about it.

At sea we wore either navy dungarees or one-piece blue, nylon jumpsuits that were issued to us all. The officers and chief petty officers could wear whichever uniform they chose, jumpsuits or khakis, but they were required to wear total regulation gear, including proper insignia denoting their rank. The rest of us, first-class petty officers and below, generally got away with wearing many items of clothing that were nonregulation.

Tooled leather belts with Western buckles, folding hunting knives that hung from our waists, and various types of nonregulation footwear were common. I always wore leather moccasins at sea, they being the everyday footwear I had grown up in on the plains. Chief Kennedy's uniform was always sharp and 100 percent regulation, but he didn't seem to mind the way his underlings dressed—except for socks.

I showed up in the engine room in dungaree shirt and pants, a knife on my belt and moccasins on my feet, as usual, but in a pair of heavy white socks. Kennedy took one look at those white socks, and I knew I'd screwed up. "What you doing in those white socks, Penley? I don't want you wearing those things any more. Sailors wear black socks, and that's all they wear."

"All right, Chief," I said warily.

I hoped the exchange was over, but I could see it in his face; he was warming up for a fine butt chewing. "I don't know what navy you think you're in, Penley . . ."

I held up my hands, palms forward. Chief Kennedy looked confused and stopped talking. I plunged on. "Chief, you told me not to wear these socks any more, and I never will."

The chief continued to look at me with narrowed eyes. Tight-lipped, thoughtful. Finally, he nodded and said, "Okay."

And that was the end of it—the closest I ever came to a classic Kennedy chewing. Few who worked for the man could claim such a record.

Bob Cantley and I would remain close friends for life. Being more aware of his inner character—unique, even for a submariner—I

Bob Cantley, on patrol in the Mediterranean, 1964.

believe I knew him better than anyone on the boat would ever know him. He was an extremely likable, popular, and capable guy, but there was a hidden side to Bob—something so deep that even the prying nature of a submarine crew could not ferret it out. Given his gregarious, seemingly laid-back nature, it was a difficult thing to know.

What was this enigma about Cantley, the paradox in his makeup that many failed to recognize? Although generous to a fault and possessing a loving, jovial nature, Bob was undoubtedly the most hardheaded individual on the boat. He detested working for other people, and he believed there was just one way to do things: Bob's way. A near impossible trait to live with on a submarine.

I knew Cantley's stubborn nature, as did a few of the guys who worked closely with him. And Chief Kennedy was maddeningly aware of it. Kennedy and Cantley butted heads often, which meant that Bob stayed in trouble with the chief nearly all the time.

Bob was smart, and he wasn't inherently lazy by any means, but he lagged behind on his qualifications most of the time. And Chief Kennedy stayed on his butt about that very thing. Cantley received many a chewing from the chief, which served only to infuriate them both time and time again.

As Bob knelt on his knees working on a piece of equipment one day, Kennedy stood over him, questioning him about his qualifications for the thousandth time. Cantley looked up, tears running down his quivering face. "Damn it, Chief, I'm doing the best I can. I know that if you decide to you can get me thrown off this boat when we get back to port, and maybe you should." Kennedy didn't answer.

As this endless clash of personalities continued, I worried that it might drive my friend insane. It did not drive Bob insane or cause him to work any harder on his qualifications; I suspect it achieved the opposite effect. Chief Kennedy never stopped chewing him out, and Bob never gave an inch.

Bob was an engineering laboratory technician (ELT), and as such, he had the responsibility of monitoring airborne radiation as well as running chemical tests on the main coolant system, i.e., the water that circulated through the reactor itself. A strict protocol attended the handling of main coolant water, and to spill a single drop was the biggest no-no in Admiral Rickover's navy.

The coolant-testing station was in the upper level of AMR2, and I happened to be in the compartment the day Cantley spilled a container of main coolant water. The spill was small, less than a pint, and looked quite insignificant. It just lay there in a clear puddle on the steel deck. Knowing Bob, I suspect he would simply have wiped it up and told no one, if Chief Kennedy hadn't come along at that very moment.

"Is that what I think it is, Cantley?" Kennedy growled.

"Yes, Chief. I'm afraid it is."

"What are you gonna do about it?"

"Well, if we just wiped it up and kept our mouths shut, we wouldn't have to do anything about it."

Kennedy exploded. "Wipe it up? That's main coolant water, Cantley. We can't just *wipe it up.* There's a protocol for cleaning it up and disposing of it. You know that."

"Yes, Chief. I know."

"And that's not all," Kennedy said. "The engineering officer will have to be informed, immediately. You stay here; I'm going forward to get Mr. Green. And don't you *dare* touch that water."

Chief Kennedy returned, steaming up to Cantley with Lieutenant Commander Green on his heels. Bob was sitting spraddle-legged on the deck like a little boy, staring at the seemingly innocuous puddle of water. He stood up as Kennedy and Green approached.

Mr. Green's voice quavered when he spoke. "How did this happen, Cantley?"

"I . . . I just spilled it, sir. Dropped it before I got the lid on it."

"Damn clumsy way to handle a main coolant sample."

"I know, sir."

"I'm going to have to file a report on this incident, you know. The report will go to the captain, to the Department of Naval Reactors in Washington when we get back to port, and probably to Admiral Rickover."

Cantley's reply floored me. "It's just going to cause a lot of trouble for everybody if you report it, sir."

Lieutenant Commander Green's eyes bulged. "Trouble! Of *course* the report will cause trouble—probably a lot of it—but if you think I'm going to jeopardize my career by not reporting a main coolant spill, you're out of your mind, sailor. If anybody's head rolls for this, it's going to be yours, not mine."

The engineering officer whirled and left.

Kennedy stood like a coiled spring, his eyes blazing. "Get the other ELTs to help you clean this up, Cantley. And it better be done properly, or I'll hang you."

Cantley sighed. "Okay, Chief. It'll get done."

I patted Bob on the back after the chief left. "I'll go wake up the other ELTs," I said.

When we returned to port, Cantley was not thrown off the boat for this transgression; in fact, he received no formal discipline whatsoever.

Submarine sailors have been described as odd, strange, weird, peculiar, unusual, different—any number of adjectives may apply. One man on the *Hamilton* crew—the only one I would never call a shipmate—I considered to be a little crazy.

Rusty Romer was intelligent, having gone through nuke school and made first-class engineman at a young age, but he was a loner, even on a submarine. Standing six foot one or –two, well over two hundred pounds, and stout as a post, he had a full head of red hair, a hard, freckled face, and dark eyes that never laughed. He walked not with a swagger, but with the solid step of a bull buffalo, untouchable. Biggest guy in the engine room, the schoolyard bully all grown up but never changed.

Chief Don Durham was the closest thing to a friend that Romer had, and even that seemed one-sided, probably occurring only because Durham was such a nice guy. Rusty befriended no one, and no one befriended him. People tended to stay out of his way, which seemed a good idea.

Bob Lee and I were both second-class petty officers, Rusty Romer was a first-class, and we were all in the same watch section. While I stood the lower-level engine room watch, Rusty was engine-room supervisor. Since Bob Lee was in training for the upper level, he stood watch with Rusty.

The open hatch that led to the lower-level engine room was in the deck near the entrance to maneuvering, and the guy in the lower level—me—had a lonely, solitary watch. The only contact I had with the upper-level guys was when I would pop up the ladder to get a cup of coffee from their community pot and maybe poke my head into maneuvering to break the monotony.

I should have noticed it before I did, but I guess I wasn't paying enough attention during the short times I was in the upper level. Then one day it dawned on me that Bob Lee was being even quieter than normal, when he was on watch and off as well. When I went up the ladder after coffee, he seldom even smiled at me, and Rusty was always sitting on his butt between the generators while Bob ran around taking care of everything. Granted, Bob was in training, but something didn't feel right.

I started going up for coffee more often and watching the interaction between Rusty and Bob Lee as much as I could. I also began sneaking up the ladder and hiding near the top where I couldn't be seen but could hear the conversations between Rusty and Bob. There wasn't much conversation; Rusty would simply holler orders at Bob in his sarcastic manner, and if Bob didn't know exactly what to do, Rusty would degrade him, make fun of him.

Bob wasn't the kind of guy to complain, so after I listened to him take this verbal abuse from Romer for a few days, I caught him in the mess hall and asked him about it. "Is Romer teaching you anything back there in the upper level?" I asked him.

"Oh, a little, I guess," Bob answered.

"Sounds to me like he's treating you like dirt."

Bob looked away. "Yeah, he gives me quite a bit of trouble," he said quietly.

"From what I've heard it sounds like he's trying to drive you nuts."

Bob looked at me in silence, gave a weak smile, and walked away.

With Romer outranking both Bob and me, I was dealing with a touchy situation. It was between meals, and there were just a few guys lounging in the mess hall. After Bob left, I sat in a booth by myself and thought it over for a while, then I went and found Leroy Lavender and asked him to come to the mess hall.

Lavender was scheduled to make chief within a few weeks. We sat down in a booth and I said, "Leroy, I need to talk to you and Chief Kennedy, in private."

"In private?" Leroy asked. "Can't you just tell me what it is?"

"No, I need to talk to both of you, together."

When Lavender returned with Chief Kennedy, the chief glanced around the mess hall one time and everybody else got up and left. The two sat down across from me. The chief leaned forward, folding his hands on the table. "What's up, Penley?"

I proceeded to tell them what I had heard and observed in the engine room, describing how Rusty Romer had been badgering Bob Lee. They listened quietly until I finished. The chief didn't look particularly surprised, but that didn't stop him from grilling me.

"Are you sure about what you're telling us, Penley?"

"Yes, Chief. I'm sure."

"You're not just trying to protect Lee because he's a friend of yours?"

"No, Chief. I'm telling you this because I think Rusty has gone over the line. He badgers Bob for six hours at a time and belittles him, and instead of teaching him anything, he may just ruin a good sailor."

Kennedy's gunmetal eyes bored into mine. "You know this is going to get Romer into a lot of trouble, don't you? And he's probably going to know that it came from you."

"I know."

Finally, Lavender spoke. "Is that why you didn't tell us until now?"

"I had to think about it," I said, "and I wanted to be dead sure before I blew the whistle on Rusty."

Chief Kennedy looked at Lavender. "What do you think, Leroy?"

Leroy looked thoughtful for a moment. "Well, knowing Rusty, I can't say I'm surprised. And I wouldn't expect Bob Lee to say anything about it himself. I'm with Penley; I'm sure he's right." Then Leroy turned to me. "And I think you should have told us earlier instead of waiting as long as you did."

I nodded. "So do I."

"I agree with Leroy," Kennedy said. With that, the chief slid out of the booth and stood up. "Thanks, Penley. Thanks for letting us know."

"You're welcome, Chief."

I don't know if Chief Kennedy and Lavender talked to Bob Lee about the situation or not. I never asked, and Bob never mentioned it.

I was working in the engine room when Lavender and the chief confronted Romer. I stayed out of the way, but I saw Rusty's face go fiery red and I could hear him hollering in protest. That didn't do him any good, because Kennedy hollered louder and shut him up. Rusty's angry eyes caught mine during the exchange, and I knew who he was going to blame.

Rusty got demoted, not in rank but in his workstation, and switched to another watch section. No longer engine-room supervisor, he now stood the lower-level engine room watch, like me. And Bob Lee got another mentor, Koslouski, an affable guy who would teach Bob instead of ridiculing him.

Rusty Romer was seething and hardly spoke to anyone for days. His one halfway friend, Chief Don Durham, passed me a warning. "Rusty's madder'n hell at you, and he's out to get you."

"I figured he was."

"Watch yourself," Durham said. "He can be a bad one."

"Thanks, Don," I said.

There was no surprise the day Rusty cornered me, down in the lower level when I was on watch, and where he knew there'd be no one else around. He came down the ladder in a rush, hit the deck plates with a bang, and strode toward me like a man with a mission. I didn't move.

He stuck his flushed face into mine. "You really screwed me up, Penley."

"No I didn't, Rusty. You screwed yourself."

"And just how did I do that?"

"By treating Bob Lee like a dog—that's how. You were supposed to be training him, helping him learn his job, but all you did was bully him and make fun of him."

"To hell with Bob Lee. I was riding boats when he was in high school. What am I supposed to do, go around kissing his young butt?"

Rusty grew louder, his eyes darker. I could feel his size as he leaned even closer into my face. "So you go and tell the chief on me, and Lavender."

"You bet I did. And I should have done it sooner."

"And now I'm standing the lower-level watch, like a peon. You're gonna pay for this, Penley. I guarantee you that."

"You gotta do what you gotta do," I said. "But right now, you can get out of my face."

Rusty shook with rage. I thought he would hit me then, but he turned and stalked away. I was not big, not stout, and not particularly skilled at fighting, but when you'd been raised by Dad, backing down was not an option. Submariners sometimes argued and got mad at one another at sea, but they never, ever, got into fistfights. This was not always the case when we got back on land, so after Romer's threat I wondered what lay in store during the next off period.

Rusty's disposition didn't improve when, a short while later, I qualified as engine-room supervisor and was transferred to his watch section. I was still a second-class engineman and he was a first-class, but he had to stand the lower-level watch under my supervision for the rest of the patrol. We didn't talk much.

Chapter Eleven

Diversions, Distractions, Disruptions

Entertainment was easy to find; in fact, it was often difficult to avoid.

Movies constituted the primary form of planned entertainment—a different one every day. After dinner had been served to both the oncoming and offgoing watch sections, the screen was pulled down at the back of the mess hall, the projector set up near the front, and one of the sixty movies brought aboard during upkeep was started. The cooks often made popcorn—tons of it—and coffee, lemonade, tea, and fruit punch, known throughout the navy as "bug juice," were always available.

The quality, age, and subject matter of the movies varied greatly. Some were relatively new, some middle-aged, and some so old they were in black and white. Nobody really cared, however, not because it was the only show in town, but because the worse the movie, the better the ad-libbing from an irreverent audience.

In the lower level of the forward battery was a small, well-stocked library and the crew's lounge where sailors could read, trade sea stories, or join in an unending poker game—a game that started when the patrol began and ended when we surfaced two months later. Players dropped out when they had to go on watch or needed sleep, only to be replaced by others who were coming off watch. There was never any money on the table, but tallies were kept, and the game was not for the faint-hearted.

Saturday nights were special. Because we had so many musicians on board—mostly Southern boys who had grown up in families that made their own entertainment—we put on live shows in the mess hall. Hootenannies, we called them, and one of the Southerners, a chief who worked in control, facilitated the weekly shows. Chief Padgett was not only a skilled guitar picker, but he could carry a fine tune in his backwoods, good-old-boy voice, and he knew the words to every country/western song that had ever been written. Standing in front of the makeshift bandstand at the back of the mess hall, strumming his guitar in a cowboy hat while talking and singing into the microphone, Padgett looked like a character right out of the Grand Ole Opry.

O. D. Walker, a first-class engine man from the hills of Kentucky, could play a guitar, a violin, a mandolin, a banjo, a harmonica, and I suspect a number of other instruments that weren't on board. And Chief Watson, an amiable fellow from the Smoky Mountains of Tennessee, could match Walker instrument for instrument and song for song. Ted Newell, a wiry guy of unknown origins, sat near the back of the band, flying fingers making his steel guitar walk and talk.

Anyone could participate in a hootenanny—singing, playing, telling jokes—whatever one had the guts to try. Officers and enlisted men alike stood shoulder to shoulder in the packed mess hall, clapping their hands, whooping out loud, and pointing at their shipmates up there making fools of themselves. For two hours each week, Chief Padgett and the boys took us away, transformed the mess hall into a live theater, a magic place under the sea.

The hootenannies were very popular, and neither the movies, the crew's lounge, nor the running poker game could compare with them. In fact, if we had had none of those many of us would have gotten along just fine.

Submariners vary in personality much like the rest of the world. Some are big, some small; some are loud, some quiet; some are aggressive, some passive; some are impatient, some patient as an ox. But one attribute is richly common: a sense of humor. With rare exception, submariners are endowed with a fine sense of humor, many stretching far beyond the norm. "Zany" is the word that comes to mind.

Practical jokes—that's where the real fun lay. Lurking in the devious mind of many a submariner is a clown, a hopeless prank-ster, a little boy who refuses to grow up. Some elaborate, some spur-of-the-moment, and some downright crazy, practical jokes were either in the planning stage or being carried out at all times.

Rat guards are not used on the hawsers that tie submarines to docks, because they aren't needed. Neither rats nor mice will come close to a submarine. I don't know what that says about the mentality of submariners, nor have I ever spent much time dwelling on it.

Despite the absence of rodents, however, a great number of uses were found for mousetraps. I could never prove who brought them on patrol, but to this day, I suspect Catron more than anyone else. As near as I could tell, there were roughly a dozen traps on board, but because of their ubiquity and constant movement throughout the boat, it was impossible to get a true count on the little machines of ambush.

Mousetraps turned up everywhere, set, of course, and placed in strategic spots to catch the intended victim unawares. Bunks were favorite spots. Many a sleepy sailor crawled into bed only to have some part of his soft young body snapped into the hungry jaws of a waiting trap. It's only pure luck that no one ever lost a portion of his genitals to the snapping wire.

The bed trick wore off, however; it was too obvious a hiding place, and soon no one dared swing into his bunk without first checking to see if a mousetrap lie in wait. Did this deter the ambushers? Not a bit. It only sparked their imaginations, forcing them to find new and ever more surprising places to hide the traps.

Big Bob Cantley, my close friend, had not only been blessed with an irresistible personality and a boyish innocence, he also possessed a naïveté that somehow begged to be victimized. An unfortunate combination in a submariner, especially when mousetraps were involved.

Cantley slept in a top bunk, as did I, and his bed was in sight of mine. When Bob was shaken awake to go on watch, he went through a little routine that never varied. Part of this invariable procedure involved reaching up and removing his shoes from his shoe locker, which hung about head high at the foot of his bunk.

One night just before the watch-waker was due to make his

rounds, I quietly removed Cantley's shoes from his shoe locker and replaced them with a mousetrap. Then I crawled into my own bed, turned out my light, and, in clear view of Big Bob, pretended to be asleep.

Right on time, the watch-waker rounded the corner, reached up and shook Bob's shoulder and whispered, "Cantley, it's time to get up for watch." As soon as he confirmed that Bob was awake, the watch-waker left.

It was a beautiful thing. It should have been set to music. Sputtering and yawning, Bob reached up, switched on his reading light, blinked in the bright glare, and ran his hands through his hair. Then, lifting himself up on one elbow, he rolled over on his side, gripped the edge of his bunk, and lowered himself to the deck. Scratching his sides and moaning like a waking water buffalo, he stumbled to the end of his bunk, reached up with his left hand, and unlatched the door to his shoe locker. When the small door dropped open, with his right hand he reached into the locker to retrieve his shoes.

SNAP! The trap got him, dead on. Roaring like a bull, Cantley shook his hand wildly and hollered, "Penley, you son-of-a . . .!"

Several guys were instantly awake, but I continued to feign sleep. After Bob worked the mousetrap off his stinging fingers, shook them several times, and stuck them in his mouth, he lunged over to my bunk. I held my eyes tightly shut.

"I know you're awake, damn you," Bob said, and slugged me solidly in the ribs.

"Wh . . . what's going on?" I exclaimed.

"You know what's going on! Putting that stinking mousetrap in my shoe locker. That hurt!" He was shaking his hand in the air.

"A mousetrap in your shoe locker?" I asked, holding my aching ribs. Then, indignantly, "Who told you *I* put it in there?"

"Nobody," Bob said. "Nobody *had* to tell me. That's just the kind of lousy thing you'd pull, Penley."

By now, everyone within earshot was awake, lying in their bunks laughing. "That really hurts me, Bob," I said. "To think that you would immediately blame me, when anyone on the boat could have done it."

"Aw, shut up," Bob said and began laughing himself.

I considered myself to be only partially civilized, and having grown up in the middle of nowhere without electricity, indoor plumbing, or a social life, I knew the reason this was so.

DeWayne Catron was not just another wild and crazy submariner, either. Oh, he was all of that and more, but something in DeWayne was less than civilized, too. I never knew the origin of my friend's aboriginal traits, but I thoroughly enjoyed them.

DeWayne and I pretty well let our imaginations run wild, but instead of pulling jokes on each other, we became a team. Not only did we team up to prey on others, we provided various forms of impromptu entertainment for the benefit of surprised shipmates who were fortunate enough—or so we felt—to find themselves involved.

Catron and I were in the same watch section—a mistake by anybody's reckoning—so we shared the same schedule. This provided us round-the-clock opportunities to exercise the products of our twisted minds. One of our favorites was taking over the boat. When certain officers had the con, we knew we could get away with it.

We'd be sitting in the crew's lounge and one of us would say, "Let's go up and take over this pig boat and show 'em how to run a submarine."

"Good idea!" and away we'd go, up to the control room.

There were about ten or twelve men on watch in control. When we swaggered into the room, in-charge looks on our silly faces, everybody knew what was coming. As Catron headed for the diving officer's chair behind the planesmen, I bounded up onto the dais where the conning officer stood his watch. Mr. Henderson, a husky lieutenant with the face of a longshoreman and the brain of a physicist, possessed a fine sense of humor.

Looking seriously at Lieutenant Henderson, I snapped a salute and said, "I'll be taking over the con, sir." At the same time, Catron informed the diving officer that he was being relieved as well.

Mr. Henderson returned my salute, stepped back to give me room, and announced, "Mr. Penley has the con . . . in a pig's rear."

The diving officer stood up, gave Catron his seat, and echoed Mr. Henderson's announcement. "Mr. Catron is the diving officer," he said loudly, "in the same pig's rear."

Then, with everyone in control listening intently but reacting to our orders with nothing but a smile or a laugh, we began our exercise.

"Flank speed," I ordered loudly. Then, "Take 'er down, Mr. Catron. Make your depth thirty feet."

The boat was already deeper than one hundred feet, but Catron repeated back my order, then gave the planesmen an impossible command. "Heave down on those planes, men. Fifty-degree down bubble, and hold 'er till you reach thirty feet."

Sitting in their chairs laughing, the planesmen gripped the controls and did nothing. After a couple of tense minutes, one of them reported, "Thirty feet it is, Mr. Catron."

"Very well," Catron answered, then turning to me, "Holding at thirty feet, sir. Suggest we keep a close watch for leaks."

"Thank you, Mr. Catron. Inform all compartments of our extreme depth, and order the leak watch set." This elicited several chuckles. There was no such thing as a leak watch.

"Aye, sir. Leak watch set. Everything normal so far. Men scared to death."

"So am I, Mr. Catron. So am I."

Standing directly behind me, Mr. Henderson was laughing out loud.

"We have a surface contact," I said. "Slow the boat down, Mr. Catron, and bring 'er up nice and easy. Periscope depth."

After repeating back my order, Catron said, almost immediately, "Periscope depth, sir."

"Up periscope," I ordered. The periscope did not move. Hanging my arms over imaginary handles, the position everyone has seen in World War II movies, I peered through the eyepieces—also not there—with great intensity. The control room stood deathly still.

"Looks like an enemy, Mr. Catron."

"How can you tell, sir?"

"I can see the captain's face, and I don't like his looks."

"Understood, sir. Good call."

"He's a big 'un, too. Ready torpedo tubes one through ten. We're gonna give him a hell of a spread."

"Readying tubes one through ten, sir." The others in control, especially Mr. Henderson, were having trouble maintaining battle silence. The boat only had four torpedo tubes.

"Tubes one through ten ready to fire, sir," Catron reported sternly.

"Thank you, Mr. Catron. Fire one, fire two . . . Aw, hell; fire 'em all."

"Aw, hell; fire 'em all. Aye, sir," Catron responded with a straight face.

It was then that I noticed everyone in control had a straight face, including Mr. Henderson.

Captain Bessac was standing about five feet from the conning platform, his hands on his hips, his forehead creased, his eyes glaring, at me.

"Down periscope," I said. No one responded to my command. Catron kept his seat in the diving officer's chair, trying to maintain a serious air but mostly managing to look silly.

Bessac looked ten feet tall. Someone had to speak, and since the captain was staring hard into my eyes, it had to be me. "Uh . . . training to take the con, Captain, in case of emergency. Catron is doing the same as diving officer."

"I see," growled the captain. "I guess if that were to happen we would have quite an emergency on our hands."

"Yes, sir. I . . . suppose we would, . . . sir."

Then, with just the hint of a smile—the only smile I ever remembered seeing cross his face—the captain dropped his hands from his hips and said, "Don't break my boat, Penley."

"I'll do my best not to, Captain," I answered smartly. Shaking his head, the skipper turned and left control.

"Mr. Henderson has the con," I said loudly, "for real."

Catron jumped up from the diving officer's seat. "I'm outta here," he said.

The control room lost control. Guys were bent over double laughing, including, thank God, Mr. Henderson. I imagined Captain Bessac having a laugh of his own; I certainly hoped he was.

The ship's medical officer, Dr. Boston, was a full lieutenant. The doctor had more than enough responsibility—seeing to the health of the crew and handling any and all medical emergencies—but since he was not assigned a regular watch, the man had too much time on his hands. His active brain brimmed with ideas.

One of his ideas to fill this extra time didn't work out well—not for the doctor, anyway.

I once had the opportunity to read a technical paper written by the chief psychiatrist at the Submarine School in New London, Connecticut. In his paper, the psychiatrist addressed problems associated with psychoanalyzing submarine sailors— or attempting to do so, that is. The shrink candidly admitted that neither he nor any other psychiatrist could psychoanalyze sub sailors in the traditional manner, because submariners just naturally tried to mess with his own mind as he questioned them. For example, the chief psychiatrist said that when he asked submariners if the confinement ever bothered them, he would commonly receive answers such as, "Oh, yeah, it drives me crazy. Sometimes I grab a hammer and chisel and try to beat holes in the pressure hull."

No matter how hard the psychiatrist tried, he could not get these men to give him straight answers. These nutty responses to verbal testing are one of the reasons that written tests were devised to weed out people who could not stand the environment in submarines. Fortunately, the written tests proved to be viable screening tools.

Evidently, Dr. Boston hadn't read the chief psychiatrist's paper. He should have.

Although the entire crew had been through psychiatric testing in sub school, and most had several years of submarining under their belts, our good doctor decided to do some screening of his own. He set out to explore how we felt about being involved in carrying missiles with atomic warheads, each aimed at a target somewhere in the Soviet Union. And the poor man actually believed he would get honest answers.

If the doctor had set out to raise morale among the crew, his psychological experiment could have been deemed a smashing success. From the first day Dr. Boston began his interviews, the word was out. The guys he had talked with joked openly about it in the mess hall, telling what the doctor had asked them and the zany replies they had given him. Not only did the news of his interviews afford a great amount of humor, it spawned even crazier answers among those who were yet to meet with him.

The doctor's interviews went on for several days. It was great fun for the crew, but the wear and tear on the doc became obvious. The man stalked through the boat without a hint of a smile, glumly making his way between the wardroom and the missile compartment where his office was located. Slump-shouldered and staring at the deck as he walked, he spoke to no one.

The doc was determined, though, and it took some time for him to figure out that the crew was messing with his mind. Until that mental illumination occurred, the man must have thought he'd been sent to sea with a crew of psychotics.

The light broke through the day Dr. Boston decided to interview Danny Dawson, a sailor who had dedicated his life to putting people on. In his slow-as-molasses Texas drawl, Danny described the interview.

"Come in, Dawson," said the doctor. "Have a seat." The office was small; besides cupboards and drawers for medicine and equipment, the simple furnishings consisted of a narrow counter and two tall stools. While the doctor did his best to look relaxed on one stool, Danny climbed onto the second and leaned an elbow on the counter.

"How've you been, Dawson?"

"Oh, I guess I've been doin' good, sir. Just fine, near as I can tell."

"Good, good. I'm glad to hear it." Dr. Boston was actually smiling.

"I'd like to ask you a few questions, Dawson, if you don't mind."

"I don't mind, sir," Dawson drawled. "Don't mind a'tall."

"Very good. Then let's get started. Okay?"

"I'm ready whenever you are."

"Let me start by asking how you feel about our mission out here, Dawson."

"Our mission? I guess I feel all right about it, sir. Not sure what you mean by the question."

"Let me clarify the subject. As you know, this ship carries missiles with nuclear warheads that are capable of being fired very long distances and wreaking a great amount of destruction in an instant."

"Yes, sir, I'm aware of that," Dawson replied.

"How do you feel about that?"

"How do I feel about that?"

"Yes, how do you feel about that?"

"I don't see that it matters how I feel about that, sir."

The doctor lost his smile, tinges of frustration creeping into his face.

"Let me put it this way: How would you feel if you were actually involved in firing a missile?"

"Well, since I'm just a second-class quartermaster, a navigator, I can't imagine that I'd ever have anything to do with firing a missile."

The doctor nervously fidgeted on his stool. "Okay. Then let me ask you this: What if you were the one who had to push the button that actually fired a missile?"

"Oh, that's ridiculous. No one would ever tell me to push the button."

The doctor exploded, his face twisted in rage. "Out!" he screamed. "Get out of this office, and don't let me see you in here again!"

Danny slid off the stool and ambled out of the doctor's office.

Dr. Boston gave up; Danny's was the last interview he ever attempted. Thus ended the saga of undersea psychoanalysis. Damn, it was fun.

The doctor wasn't the only one with time on his hands. While some watch stations kept a man on the move for six hours, others required little action. The radiomen stood such watches, and always occupied the radio room in pairs, waiting for incoming transmissions, which were normally few and far between. Though they were highly trained sailors, their duties extremely important, and their responsibilities great, the radiomen spent much of their time looking for ways to fight boredom. Alas, this bunch included Whitey and Skelton.

Whitey and Skelton were always assigned the same watch. To keep the demonic pair together seemed rather insane, but in some strange way it made perfect sense; separating them would have defied some incontrovertible law of nature.

If one of the radiomen needed to leave his watch momentarily to go to the bathroom, he had to get permission from the conning officer. When he called down to the con to ask permission to leave his station, his voice would ring out of a loudspeaker and fill control.

"Con, this is Jones in radio. Permission to go to the head, sir?"

"Permission granted, Jones."

And when the radioman returned: "Con, this is Jones. Back in the radio room, sir."

"Thank you, Jones."

I was lucky enough to be in control, chatting with the guys on watch, the day it happened. Mr. Henderson had the con, and Whitey and Skelton were on duty in the radio room.

Unbeknown to anyone but the dynamic duo, Whitey and Skelton had become engaged in an impromptu competition—a gas-passing contest. Both being fierce competitors, the contest had escalated from a friendly game to a serious endeavor.

Whitey was ahead, and despite Skelton's most stringent efforts, he had not managed to match the magnitude of Whitey's finest blast. But Skelton was no quitter. Although he was bringing up the rear, so to speak, the thought of giving up never occurred to him.

Far beyond the point of good judgment, Skelton continued to force the issue. According to Whitey, the sole eyewitness, when Skelton felt the shot forming he began to smile. And as it neared the breech, a look of triumph seized his Leprechaun-like face. Hoisting his short, pot-bellied body a few inches off the chair, he pulled the trigger.

Skelton's look of triumph was quickly replaced by one of surprise, shock, and horror. In his zeal to excel, he had mistaken the onset of what he thought to be a tremendous shot of gas for something quite different. The result was not without a gaseous element, but consisted primarily of matter less airborne.

Skelton had pooped his pants.

When Whitey finally gained control of himself, he wiped the tears from his cheeks and addressed an issue that Skelton was loath to approach: the fact that he would need a relief in order to deal with the situation. His problem required not just a short head call, but a period of time that would accommodate a shower and a badly needed change of clothing.

Skelton tried to get Whitey to call the conning officer and request a relief for him. No way, Whitey told him. Skelton had done the deed, and he'd have to call the con himself.

I still thank the powers that be that I happened to be in control to hear that historic call. We heard the mic being keyed in the radio room, then a low, tentative voice came over the intercom.

"Con?" squeaked Skelton.

"Yes, what is it?" asked Lieutenant Henderson.

"Request permission for a . . . relief, sir."

Henderson recognized the voice. "A relief? Do you need to go to the head, Skelton?"

"No, sir. I, uh, need to be relieved for a while." We could hear Whitey giggling in the background.

"Why do you need a relief?" Henderson asked gruffly.

"I'd, uh, rather not say, sir."

"Listen, Skelton, in order to get you relieved I have to wake up an off-duty radioman, make him get dressed, and come up and take your place. Before I do that, you're going to tell me why you need a relief. Now what's your problem?"

Long silence. Then, "Sir, I thought I was going to pass some gas, and, uh, something else happened."

Lieutenant Henderson looked incredulous; then, along with everyone else in control, he began to smile. "Skelton, are you telling me that you don't need to go to the head because you've already gone in your pants?"

"I'm, afraid so . . . sir."

Henderson threw back his head and howled. The laughter from control could have alerted enemy sonar fifty miles away.

The mothers, girlfriends, and wives who sent familygrams had been cautioned by the navy not to send bad news such as deaths in the family, serious illnesses, and the like. And if such messages did arrive on the boat, the communications officer would notify the captain and the intended recipient would not be given the bad news.

The inability to contact loved ones while remaining submerged for months at a time, or even to acknowledge receipt of a familygram, often placed extreme pressure on relationships.

Since we did not transmit messages, if we had sunk the day after we left port that fact would not have been known, even by the United States Navy, until two months later when we failed to return.

Submariners were said to have the highest divorce rate of any branch of the military, and I believe it was so. Although the captain could remove bad news from a familygram to save a man's sanity, even he could do nothing for a sailor who was on patrol and, for unknown reasons, received no messages at all. Sadly, this happened, and usually heralded the breakup of a love affair or the end of a marriage.

One unmarried fellow—or "single john," as we were called—was a career sailor named Shoemaker who normally spent his time ashore bouncing from girl to girl with no thought of romantic ties or, God forbid, commitment. Alas, Shoemaker fell prey to the very emotions he denied possessing. Good-looking, loud, and gregarious, Shoemaker filled up a room when he walked through the door—a man born to be a sailor. Unfortunately, as sailors were wont to do, he found his love in a dive on the infamous "Strip," a string of lowlife bars and pawnshops that stretched for three untamed blocks outside the main gate of the Charleston naval base.

Shoemaker's girl, Suzie Anne, was nicer looking than the average Strip girl—blond, slender, with a fetching figure, and a face that had weathered the storms of bar life better than most. One glaring omission stood out, however—the conspicuous absence of one front tooth, an upper incisor that left a black hole in her otherwise pretty face, a gap that became the focus of her weak countenance and tended to overwhelm any beauty the girl may have possessed. But Shoemaker could see no defects, inside or out. He was in love.

Shoemaker had rented an apartment during the previous off period and began living with Suzie Anne—a highly unusual move for a rounder such as he. And before we left on patrol, he gave her full power of attorney so that she could receive his paychecks and cash them in his absence. Leaving his shiny new car and all of his money with Suzie Anne, he had kissed her goodbye in their little love-nest apartment and gone off to sea.

Shoemaker never received a single familygram from Suzie

Anne. During the patrol, he grew quiet and withdrawn. He couldn't sleep and he didn't eat regularly. His sense of humor fell to zero, and he lost so much weight his pants would fall off when he unbuckled his belt. We all worried about Shoemaker, but nothing anyone could say would bring him out of his gloom. Not until the end of the patrol would we learn the outcome of Shoemaker's love affair.

Not all relationships went bad. The solid ones withstood the long separations, the worry of not knowing, and ultimately, the test of time. DeWayne Catron had such a marriage. While on patrol, DeWayne received a familygram announcing the birth of his first child, a healthy baby boy. I've never seen a happier man.

That same day, Catron was called to Captain Bessac's private quarters. The skipper ushered DeWayne in, shook his hand, and congratulated him on the new addition to his family. And to Catron's surprise, Bessac invited him to sit down. The captain reached in a locker, pulled out a bottle of fine whiskey, and poured DeWayne and himself a drink. They toasted the new baby, and Captain Bessac thanked him for his service to his country.

A fine moment in a fine sailor's life.

Heavy machinery within a confined space under the sea—the inherent dangers dwelt inside us as well as all around us. Like living in a cave with a wolf outside the door, occasionally scratching to remind us of his presence. Our beloved boat shielded us from the threatening sea, but she was an unforgiving mistress.

A friend of mine who sailed on the USS *Nathan Hale*, the same class of FBM as the *Hamilton*, was on patrol when their oxygen generator exploded and killed a man. They stored the man's body in the walk-in freezer, but the boat was forced to temporarily abort the patrol and steam to an area where they could safely transmit a message. They were soon met by a surface vessel that took the body back to shore. As long as their shipmate's body remained on board, my friend explained, morale was absolute zero. Most of the crew couldn't sleep, couldn't eat, and would hardly talk to one another.

As soon as the sailor's body was removed from the *Nathan Hale,* morale returned to normal and the boat resumed its patrol. No one was ever killed aboard the *Hamilton,* but we had our share of injuries, and each time a man got hurt the effect on morale was devastating.

As the patrol neared its end, at long last, morale began to soar. It was a Friday, and an especially big hootenanny had been planned for the following Saturday night. O. D. Walker, a first-class engineman, was working on some piping near the forward end of the lower-level engine room. Since the lower-level watchman was involved in a job at the far aft end of the space, O. D. was working alone.

Using a heavy, four-foot pipe wrench, O. D. was attempting to loosen a frozen pipe union located directly above his head. With both hands clamped around the handle of the wrench, O. D. pulled down with all his strength, practically lifting himself off the deck with his effort. The wrench slipped off the pipe. The heavy handle whipped downward, whacking O. D. on the top of his head—a blow that could have been fatal.

O. D. went down, his head spraying sheets of blood over the deck plates. With an unbelievable effort, he managed to pull himself to his feet and climb a nearby ladder. I saw him as he emerged into the upper level, swaying like a drunken man, holding onto a guardrail with one hand and his bleeding head with the other. His clothes, his hair, and his face were drenched in blood. He looked at me and tried to mutter something. His eyes rolled up, and he fell like a stone.

I ran to maneuvering, shouting that O. D. had been hurt, maybe killed. The EOOW quickly notified the conning officer, then asked me what had happened.

"I don't know, sir. Whatever it was happened down below, and somehow O. D. managed to climb the ladder before he passed out." The EOOW shook his head.

Dr. Boston charged through the engine room hatch, closely followed by the hospital corpsman and the emergency medical team. The doctor checked O. D.'s head, then held a large bandage over the wound while the team unfolded a stretcher and lifted him onto it. They were gone, running forward to get O. D. to the mess hall, where an emergency operating table folded up out of the deck.

I eased down the blood-soaked ladder that O. D. had somehow managed to climb. It was a gory mess down there. Looking at the position of the pipe, the wrench, and the blood, I could easily see what had befallen our shipmate. Rusty Romer, the lower-level watch, brought a handful of rags and began to clean up the blood. I got down on my knees and helped him.

Along with a great tear in his scalp, O. D. had a concussion. Even so, the man was lucky; his skull had not been broken. The doctor checked him out, sewed him up, and confined O. D. to his bunk. The cooks watched over him like mother hens, checking him often and bringing him anything he asked for. And the cooks weren't alone; everyone was constantly checking on him or asking about him. Our hospital corpsman, "Doc" Jungblut, had to tell everyone to leave O. D. alone so he could get some rest. After that, the guys started asking Doc so often he could hardly get any rest himself.

Morale plummeted. The big hootenanny was canceled and few even felt like watching movies. Men either slept too much or wandered through the boat with insomnia. A dreary bunch and, though I didn't consider O. D. a close friend, I was one of them.

After three days of gloom, O. D. showed up in the mess hall, a huge bandage on his head, wobbly but walking. A great cheer went up, and every man jumped to his feet. O. D. managed a weak smile, waved a hand, and sat down to eat.

When O. D. came up from his sickbed, morale came with him. We were one again—a crew complete.

Although morale underwent a constant upswing during the last two weeks of patrol, patience ran thin, tempers easily flared.

A young cook, Hardy, had recently made third class, which placed him in charge of preparing complete meals instead of just helping the other cooks. Everybody liked Hardy—short, thin, fast-moving, and friendly—but nobody cared for his meals. We had all been putting up with them, hoping that experience would favor his cooking, and our palates. That didn't happen. If anything, his culinary skills seemed to lag more and more as the patrol progressed. Everyone knew when it was Hardy's turn to cook, and we'd all begin to groan before it was even served.

When a meal was especially good, which many were, except for Hardy's, we would all compliment the cook as we passed by the galley on our way out of the mess hall. "Good chow, Cookie," or "Great meal, Buddy." Hardy strove to reach that status, but he never received any compliments.

The final straw: Hardy cooked a meal that consisted of the entrée, a putrid sort of chili-mac concoction, plus a side of mixed vegetables that tasted like leftovers gone bad. I was in the ongoing watch section, the first to bite into this culinary abomination. As soon as we started trying to eat it, everyone shook their heads and wrinkled their faces, some poking their fingers at their mouths as if they might vomit.

Whispering among ourselves, we quietly devised a plan and warned the mess cooks who were serving us not to tell Hardy what was going on. After piling all the chili-mac and the mixed vegetables on our plates, we started hollering for more. The mess cooks hurried the empty serving bowls into the galley and brought them back full. We continued to call for more, heaping the stuff onto our plates and even pouring it into coffee cups until we had every ounce that Hardy had made. We hadn't eaten a bit of it, and there was none left in the galley for the off-going watch section.

On a silent cue, we all stood up and began walking past the galley, dumping the entire uneaten meal into the garbage can. Hardy stood dumbfounded, watching his work slide into the garbage and listening to caustic comments, such as "That's it, Hardy. Everything you cook tastes like crap, and we're not eating any more of it."

What does an entire watch section, one-third of the boat's crew, do after it has thrown away a meal? We stood around outside the mess hall, hungry, crowding the passageway, refusing to leave.

Everyone from chief petty officers down to seamen and firemen were involved—a minor mutiny. For the moment, anarchy ruled on a U.S. warship.

Hardy, cursing loudly, charged down the steps to the berthing area and woke up Roy Scott, the first-class cook. Scott came rushing to the galley, running his fingers through his hair and buttoning his shirt on the run. After glancing over the situation, he told Hardy to go wake up the rest of the cooks.

A mob of cooks started scrambling to throw a meal together. The commissary officer showed up, a young LTJG, red-eyed and glowering at the bunch of us who had thrown away the food.

I think the executive officer got involved, too, though I never actually saw him. From the back of the crowd, a voice of authority boomed out: "You guys get out of here, now, and go relieve the watch. And I don't care if you ever get anything to eat!"

I don't know who shouted the order, but our little mutiny quickly turned into a stampede. We relieved the watch, hungry, and though the off-going guys were glad to hear we had finally rallied against Hardy's terrible food, they were unhappy about not having a meal waiting. It didn't take the cooks long to whip them up something reasonable, however, but they let us sinners suffer a while. A couple of hours later, the commissary officer had sandwiches delivered to all of us rebels who had thrown out the food—not out of the kindness of his heart, but by order of the captain.

Hardy never cooked another meal, and surprisingly, after we reached port, he reenlisted for another hitch in the navy. He signed up for a program that took him to electrician's school, thereby changing his rank and his job, from third-class cook to third-class electrician. And Hardy remained a good sport through it all, even when we expressed our hope that he ended up being a better electrician than he had been a cook; otherwise he would surely electrocute himself. He called us various uncomplimentary names and said he might come back and electrocute the lot of us—a threat not to be taken lightly from a man of Hardy's inabilities.

Practical jokes—the nonstop insanity escalated as we neared the end of our long submergence.

Shortly after we turned our nose toward the Straits of Gibraltar, still on patrol but headed for that gate to freedom, a group of us—actually more than a third of the crew—decided to pull one of the oldest pranks in submarining: a trim party.

Trim parties were not a favored form of recreation among the officers—especially the conning officer and the diving officer on watch at the time the prank went down. And, for good reason, the chief in charge of the ballast control panel harbored the same ill feelings about these "parties."

The crew loved them.

The diving officer, seated to the left and slightly forward of the conning platform, was charged with keeping the boat trim, i.e., stable in the water, as well as maintaining the ordered depth. The two planesmen sat directly in front of the diving officer while the chief at the ballast control panel sat behind him.

The boat's trim was maintained by the interaction of several different factors: the position of the diving planes; the boat's weight, which could be changed by pumping seawater in or out of internal ballast tanks; and the weight distribution throughout the boat, which could also be affected by pumping water from one tank to another.

Changing the position of the diving planes was easy, simply a matter of pushing or pulling one of the operating levers in the hands of the planesmen. But in order to pump ballast between tanks, the chief at the control panel had to open and shut valves and start and stop pumps—all accomplished remotely with switches, buttons, and rheostats on the panel. Adjustments to the trim had to be made when watch sections were changed or when the crew rushed to battle stations during drills—i.e., anytime a good portion of the crew was moving around, changing the weight distribution inside the boat.

The trim on submerged subs had always been maintained in this manner, and sometime back near the dawn of the submarine navy, some clever sailor had come up with a way to simultaneously drive the conning officer, the diving officer, and the control-panel operator mad: the trim party.

This is how it worked. The party had to start during a quiet time, when the boat was in trim and everything was running smoothly. Guys would start wandering toward the rear of the boat, one or two at a time so as not to attract attention, and after a few minutes, twenty-five or thirty of them would be in the engine room and AMR2. This extra weight aft would necessitate holding down on the diving planes to keep the boat level while pumping from aft tanks to forward ones to balance the ballast and equalize the trim. The diving officer and the chief running the control panel were kept busy for several minutes until a proper trim was reestablished.

Then, when the pumps stopped and everyone knew the trim had been adjusted, the guys would start easing forward, again just a few at a time, and after several minutes they'd all be gathered in the torpedo room. Now the nose of the boat would be heavy, causing the diving officer and the chief to reverse the procedure they had just done, adjusting the trim once more. After a couple of these cycles, the perpetrators usually dispersed, quickly, before the conning officer got suspicious enough to track them down.

Trim parties were usually impromptu—begun on the spur of the moment, pulled off quietly with mouth-covered giggles, and quickly ended, with nothing but the chagrined suspicions of the officers in control left in its wake.

The trim party conceived on the way out of the Mediterranean was to be the mother of all trim parties. It was a planned event, and therein lay the problem; somewhere in the planning we got carried away.

Nobody seemed to remember who first thought up the idea, nor could anyone understand how the word spread so quickly, but the effect was galvanic. The scheme was uncomplicated; we simply planned to hold the trim party when Lieutenant Henderson had the con, because we all liked him—lucky him— and we planned to include a large number of guys so we could affect the trim more than had ever been done before. To go where no trim party had ever gone.

We enlisted plenty of guys to join in the party—too many. A number of them even stayed awake during their off-watch time just to be a part of it. One fellow summed it up succinctly shortly before we gave the "Go" signal: "No way we're gonna get away with this, Penley; Mr. Henderson isn't dumb, you know."

"I know," I said, nodding gravely. Then we laughed ourselves silly.

The preset time came, and guys stood up and started wandering out of the mess hall, the crew's lounge, and the berthing area— all spaces located amidships—and moseyed toward the engine room and AMR2. When we had all gathered back there, trying to look like we were not a crowd, I couldn't believe the number of bodies involved.

Chief Kennedy, standing at his work desk in the engine room, glanced around and instantly figured it out. I tried to act nonchalant when the chief looked at me. He just rolled his eyes and shook his head.

We had great chuckles as we felt the aft end of the boat trying to sink, heard the ballast pumps starting, and water pumping furiously through the pipes from the after tanks to their forward counterparts. When things had settled down and the pumps had stopped, we slowly began making our way forward, all the way to the torpedo room. This took a while, but after several minutes, we were all packed into that most forward compartment, a space much smaller than the engine room and AMR2.

Right on cue, the nose of the boat tried to drop. Again the pumps whined, desperately pumping the same water back to the aft end. We were all having great fun, when the phone rang in the compartment. The torpedoman on watch lazily answered the phone: "Samuels." Then he jerked upright. "Yes, sir," he said. He looked at all of us and mouthed, "Henderson."

Uh-oh.

"Yes, sir. He's here," the torpedoman said. Then he held the phone out to me. "Mr. Henderson wants to talk to you."

"To *me?*" I asked.

"Yep. He asked for you, Penley."

Busted.

I took the phone, automatically standing at attention as I prepared to address the lieutenant in control. "Penley speaking . . . sir."

"Penley, this is Mr. Henderson, up in the con."

"How are you, sir?"

He ignored my greeting. "How many of you characters are there in the torpedo room?"

"There are . . . quite a few, sir."

"The boat feels like there must be fifty or sixty of you up there."

"I'd say that's a good estimate, sir."

"Is Catron in there?"

"Yes, sir. He is."

"And Whitey and Skelton?"

"Yes, sir. Them too."

"And probably Danny Dawson and Paul Ashford, and Bob Cantley and Bob Lee and Koslouski?"

"Yes, sir."

"Sounds like a rogue's gallery. Are you the leader of this thing, Penley?"

"I, uh, wouldn't really call myself the leader . . . sir."

"Just an innocent participant, huh? I'll bet they about had to twist your arm off to get you to go along with it."

"You've got it, sir," I said. "That's exactly how it happened."

"That's awful, Penley. Whoever forced you into such a thing should be court-martialed."

"I agree, sir."

Pause. "Well, for the moment, let's have you act as the leader, Penley, and I want you to pass along a message to those little boys gathered up there with you."

"All right, sir."

"I'm not interested in wearing out the pumps while you kiddies charge back and forth through the boat. Got that?"

"Yes, sir."

"Now, sixty guys must make it pretty packed in the torpedo room. Correct?"

"Yes, sir. It's pretty crowded up here . . . sir."

"I've got a fairly good idea who the rest of the bunch is in there besides the ones I named. I want you to tell them, Penley—as their temporary, innocent leader—that if this trim party should continue, you'll all be spending the next forty-eight hours in the torpedo room. Every minute that you're not on watch elsewhere, all of you will be in that compartment.

"It'll probably be pretty tight quarters in there for two days, especially when you're trying to sleep. Wouldn't you agree, Penley?"

"Yes, sir. Sixty guys living in here for two days would be a little tight." I spoke loudly, so that everyone in the small compartment would understand Mr. Henderson's threat.

"Okay," he said, "you pass that word along, Penley, and try not to let those nasty guys twist your arm any more."

"I will, sir. I mean . . . I won't. I mean, I will pass your message on, and I won't let them twist my arm any more."

"Good man. Thanks for your help, Penley." He hung up the phone. I'd love to have seen his face at that moment.

I didn't have to pass on the message; they already knew. We all laughed ourselves hoarse, then slowly dispersed. And so ended the mother of all trim parties.

We slipped out of the Mediterranean the same way we had come in: shutting down reactor power and hitching a ride on a thermal current. The crew had been ordered to keep the noise down during our exit, lest shore-based sonar pick us up. A difficult task for a boatload of caged animals about to be set free, but we managed to pull it off.

A number of guys got so excited they suffered from insomnia the last several days at sea, a common condition known as "channel fever."

Everybody wondered about the possible hole in a forward ballast tank, or tanks, but few talked about it. The young trainee—the one who had been in the engine room the day we collided with an unknown submerged object—caught me alone in the power plant shortly after we cleared the Straits. "What do you think about that hole that may be in a ballast tank, Penley, or maybe even in a couple of ballast tanks?"

"I don't know any more about the hole, or holes, than I did the day it happened," I told him.

That didn't seem to appease the young fellow, so I went on. "Okay, this is what I think. I don't think we're going to have much trouble surfacing, and I feel sure we're not going to sink."

With that, a big smile crossed his face. "Thanks!" he said, and walked away. I had no idea why my words, which were based mostly on nothing but optimism, should have affected him so, but I was glad to have brightened his day.

The diving alarm sounded throughout the boat—A-ooo-ga!, A-ooo-ga!, A-ooo-ga!—followed by the finest phrase we knew: "Surface! Surface! Surface!"

High-pressure air rushed into the ballast tanks with a loud whoosh, blowing them dry—all of them, thank God. Our nose planed upward and water rushed off the sides, cascading down into the swirling sea as the big boat surfaced. A great shout went up, big smiles, high-fives all around. We had done it, again.

Air. Air from the outside began to circulate through the boat— sweet, cool, clean. The smell of the earth.

Something had begun to happen within me as we neared the end of the patrol—something that I could neither understand nor acknowledge. A fear began to abate, a fear whose existence I could not admit, even to myself. The fear that one day I would not return from a patrol, that my life would end on the bottom of the sea, inside a steel tube.

The fear was a ghost that lived inside me, a shadowy entity that would not reveal itself clearly for years to come.

Chapter Twelve

Show Me the Way to Go Home

After threading our way through the ever-present Soviet trawlers, merrily outrunning them and leaving them bobbing forlornly at the three-mile limit, we were greeted by the welcoming strains of a navy band and the vigorous waves of the Gold Crew as we tied up alongside the *Holland*.

Within a day of our return to Rota, we maneuvered the *Hamilton* into dry dock to check for hull damage. The boat looked immense perched high on blocks, and sure enough, there was a long, wide gash low in a forward ballast tank—the tank's thick skin torn completely through.

Speculation was that we may have collided with a submerged log, just waterlogged enough to keep it floating at a certain depth. I never heard any other theories voiced, except those in my own mind—the ones that questioned how a wet log could tear a large hole through a heavy metal tank.

We all got paid the minute we hit port. Then, after the reactor was shut down and the engine room secured—liberty time. Wild animals, uncaged. Guys dove into their dress uniforms, cocked their white hats like the salts they were, charged up the ladder, and sprinted for the gangway. One man hollered his favorite Latin term as he exited the open hatch: *"E scrotum danglus!"* Loosely translated "Let it all hang out."

The manager of the Acey-Deucey Club had been warned of our arrival. Gently but firmly, he herded us to the Stag Bar, away from the civilized folk in the main club. That was fine with us; at that point, we considered everyone else on Earth to be wimps anyway.

After months of nothing but water, tea, and bug juice, the first beer tasted marvelous—liquid ecstasy. Of course, after a dozen or more, interspersed with straight shots of 100-proof whiskey and other fierce libations, one could hardly taste anything.

The fastest way to get from the submarine docks to the Acey-Deucey Club was via a dirt footpath—half a mile long, four feet wide, and lined with drainage ditches on each side. We usually hot-footed it up there rather than wait on irregularly scheduled busses. And we practically ran all the way the first night in.

Bob Lee and I left the club sometime around midnight, heading down the footpath back to the boat. Since neither of us could walk on our own, we locked arms, leaned on one another, and managed to weave our way down the path. It worked well, for a while.

It was a warm, starlit night, so beautiful it induced Bob and me to start singing, something. Thinking we sounded pretty good, we began a little dance step—kicking out our feet in semi-unison as we zigzagged down the narrow path, arm in arm and crooning like Bing Crosby and Bob Hope in one of the old *Road* movies. Somehow we zigged when we should have zagged and fell off the side of the path into the drainage ditch.

The ditch was dry, thankfully, but the sides were steep, and the bottom grown over with tall weeds. Our singing briefly interrupted, we tumbled down the bank and into the weeds. The ditch was only about three feet deep, but we were submariners, not mountain climbers. And to compound the problem, we discovered that neither of us could get up. After threshing around in the weeds for a while, we gave up, sitting at the bottom of the ditch looking at each other.

"I've got an idea," I said. Inebriated as he was, the even-minded Bob gave me the "Look," a stare that invariably said one of two things: Have you completely lost your mind, Penley? or Oh, boy, here we go again.

Ignoring the Look, I said, "Some of our guys are still back in the club, and they'll be coming along pretty soon. Let's just wait for them, and they can pull us out."

Bob thought it over, emitting a loud burp that bounced his head as he contemplated my proposed solution. "That is a good idea," he said. We began to sing again, this time minus the dance steps, of course.

We sat on our butts, arms around one another's shoulders, our dress whites covered in dirt, and sang until we saw the shadowy figures of our shipmates coming down the path. Reacting to our melodious voices, they stopped and peered down into the darkened weeds. Somehow, one of them appeared to be reasonably sober. "Who's down there?" he asked.

"It's Penley," I said, "and Bob Lee."

"What're you doing down there?"

"Singing."

"Yeah, we heard."

"We can't get up."

"Can't get up?"

"Nope. That's why we been waiting for you guys, to help us out of this ditch."

They all roared. "Well, I'll be damned. This is a new one even for you two."

"Shut up," I said, "and get us out of this hole."

Sub sailors scrupulously avoided getting into fights at sea—the very idea of it being a mortal sin—but they tended to make up for it on shore. After months of elbow-to-elbow isolation, pent-up animosities were strained to the limit—ready to blow. And blow they did, every time we hit port.

We delighted in fighting the surface craft sailors from the tender, as the scarred and patched Stag Bar at the Acey-Deucey Club could attest, but surface sailors were not an imperative ingredient. If need be, sub sailors could find reasons to fight among themselves. These battles usually took place in the clubs, but a couple of nights after Bob Lee and I tumbled into the ditch, two of our boys decided to bring their differences back to the boat.

Jack Wright, a first-class cook, had been a good friend of mine since sub school. Average height, stout, low-key, and likeable, Wright was a fine cook and popular among the crew.

Rick Bellar, a second-class torpedoman, was Wright's opposite. Small, shrewish, and an inveterate troublemaker, Bellar's wiry body seemed to be in constant motion, like a two-year-old, which seemed to fit his emotional maturity. He was self-centered, loud, and so vulgar that the executive officer once issued him a stern warning about his language—a first among submariners. Bellar knew his job and did it well, but that didn't keep him from being considered a world-class ass by much of the crew.

When I got back off liberty that night, I found Jack Wright and Rick Bellar squared off in the galley. A sizable crowd had gathered to watch. Seeing my friend Wright involved startled me; he was the last person I expected to find in a fight, especially aboard the ship. I didn't know who had started it, but I naturally assumed it was Bellar. Like the rest of the onlookers, I found a good place to watch through the door of the galley, hoping to see Wright knock Bellar's teeth out of his head.

Neither of the pugilists were sober, but Wright remained quiet, focused, moving determinedly as they sparred. Bellar jumped around, spouting a nonstop string of profanity as he moved. Most of his punches missed the mark, his swings wild and worthless.

Wright landed two good jabs to Bellar's jaw. Bellar screamed in rage and grabbed a butcher knife. The heavy, foot-long blade protruded wickedly from his right hand. Holding the knife over his head in a stabbing position, Bellar charged into Wright. And I charged into the galley.

I approached Bellar from the left, reached high, and clamped his knife wrist in my right hand. Reaching around his middle with my left, I pinned his other arm to his side.

Wright let fly. Seeing Bellar momentarily subdued, my friend slugged him in the face, hard, half a dozen times. Bellar sagged in my grip, barely able to stand, and I took the knife out of his hand. I stepped back, and Wright hit him again. Bellar flew like a limp rag.

I screamed at Wright. "Stop hitting him, Jack! I didn't come in here to help you whip him; I just wanted to take this knife away from him."

Jack stopped swinging, but Bellar was finished anyway. Slammed against a steel bulkhead by Wright's last punch, he slid to the floor—his lips split, his nose bleeding, his mouth silenced at last. And although I hadn't planned to become an active participant, it was a pleasing sight.

The spectators stepped aside as I walked out of the galley, holding the big butcher knife in my hand. Bob Lee, who had just arrived on the scene, said, "What the hell were you doing in the middle of that, Penley?"

I shook my head. "Trying to get myself killed, I guess."

Note: I would meet Rick Bellar years later, after our navy experience was history, and to my utter surprise, find him to be a well-adjusted man—friendly, considerate, likable. Maybe all that aggression was just his way of dealing with the confinement and danger of submarining. I suspect so.

When the crew change was complete and the Gold Crew once more in command of the *Hamilton,* again we split the crew in halves and boarded two planes—U.S. Air Force jetliners. The captain's plane took off first, then the one I was on, with Lieutenant Commander Rawlins, the executive officer, in charge. Jim Nelson sat beside me, as usual, thinking somehow I could keep him safe while we were airborne. Danny Dawson sat directly across the aisle from me. Poor Danny had started worrying about the flight back to the states even before we surfaced. Since both confided their fears to me prior to every flight we made, I didn't have the heart to tell them I didn't care for flying myself.

We took off late in the afternoon, happy to be on our way home, or so we thought. Sometime that night, my sleep was disturbed by a cabin announcement that I didn't catch. Jim Nelson took hold of my shoulder. "Gary, we've got engine trouble."

"Engine trouble?"

"That's what the pilot said," Jim said nervously. "Engine trouble."

I was very tired and had been sleeping hard. "Let me know what happens," I said, and fell back asleep.

A few minutes later, Jim shook me again. "Gary, they're turning the plane around; we're going back to Spain."

"That's strange," I said, sitting up and rubbing my eyes. Now

I *was* concerned, but I didn't want Jim to know it. I noticed that Danny Dawson was sitting up straight as well, worriedly listening to Jim and me.

Jim had fallen in love with a wonderful girl named Betty during our previous off period, a girl whom he would soon marry and remain with forever. "Think about Betty," I said. "That's a better place for your mind to be."

My words didn't seem to placate Jim very much, and the usually raucous Dawson still looked like he was preparing to meet the grim reaper.

"Aw, don't worry," I said. "These things will fly on one engine. It's stupid to be turning back."

Jet-powered airliners were relatively new at the time, and I knew we were somewhere far out over the Atlantic in a plane that would drop like a rock if we lost power. That's what was really on my mind as I spoke all that bravado to my shipmates. I looked out the window, at the black night, and hoped they believed what I had said. I sure didn't.

I feigned sleep for what remained of the night and listened to the engines. I heard nothing unusual; however, not knowing a thing about jets, I didn't know what I was listening for anyway.

We didn't return to Rota; instead we landed at an SAC (Strategic Air Command) Air Force base in Madrid. It was early morning, a bright, cheery day, but Lieutenant Commander Rawlins was anything but cheery. Seated in the front row of the aircraft, our fiery exec was mad at the entire air force—mad being an understatement. Rawlins had looked furious ever since we turned back toward Spain. By the time we landed at the SAC base, the man was seething.

One of our stewards, a young air force enlisted man, stepped toward Rawlins as if he might be approaching an angry lion. We all watched as the fellow leaned over and spoke lowly into the exec's ear. The exec turned on him, fire shooting from his eyes. The young man reeled back, nearly losing his balance. Rawlins stood up, his voice echoing from one end of the cabin to the other. "Well, they tell me we've got to get off of this damn thing!"

The young steward backed away, obviously unaccustomed to hearing such language from an officer whose rank matched that of an air force major. "I'm . . . sorry, sir," he mewled.

Rawlins roared. "You're not as sorry as I am!" He turned and stomped toward the open door. We all stood up and followed.

The SAC air base's terminal was nicely done—large, roomy, a décor of comfortable colors. The building contrasted greatly with naval facilities, whose stark structures readily revealed where the navy spent its money: on ships.

Commander Rawlins stormed into the terminal like General Patton leading a blitzkrieg on Berlin, the junior officers trying to keep up with him, the rest of us gawking around like country hicks come to town.

In the terminal, an apologetic air force officer rushed forward to greet the exec. Unfortunately, Rawlins outranked him. "Sir, I . . .," the officer began, but stopped when Rawlins glared at him as if he might be a bug.

"I want to speak to the top man," Rawlins said.

"You mean the commanding officer of the base, sir?" the wide-eyed officer asked.

"That's right," Rawlins said, and then he waved an arm, encompassing us all. "And see all these sailors here; they've been at sea, underwater, for several months."

The officer's jaw dropped. Rawlins continued. "I want two busses to take them to the NCO Club, now."

"The NCO Club? It's still morning, sir."

"I don't care what time it is," Rawlins said. "I want my crew bussed to the NCO Club, and if the club isn't open yet, *open it.*"

"Yes, sir!"

Two busses arrived within minutes. Air force blue, their waxed finishes gleaming in the sun, they looked brand new. We stormed out of the terminal and piled on board. Our driver, an air force sergeant, looked at us as if we might be aliens from outer space.

The entire SAC base gleamed in the sun—clean, trim, neatly landscaped—the facility itself standing at attention. Jet fighters and bombers crouched in formation: flying warriors, poised for battle at a moment's notice. The pride of America's air defense.

The only things on the base that lacked a proper military bearing were two busloads of submarine sailors. The NCO Club was open, but didn't look like it had been for long. We weren't sure what rank constituted an NCO (non-commissioned officer), but we guessed it was probably E-4, the same as third-class petty officer in the navy. There were several E-3s with us, and since we couldn't disregard our shipmates, we decided to disregard rank instead. The bartender took notice of the younger guys and their minimal stripes but wisely chose not to challenge us on the issue. We settled in, from seamen to chiefs, and ordered about sixty drinks.

Compared to any navy club we'd ever seen, the NCO Club was plush. And the glistening wooden bar showed no scars or repairs. Evidently air force NCOs didn't fight in their clubs—a strange concept, difficult for us to comprehend.

As news of our invasion spread through the base, we drank, made ourselves at home, and refrained from fighting. I don't know what our exec was doing during this time—stirring the pot, to be sure—but news of Rawlins's vocal arrival had also spread quickly.

Air force NCOs began dropping in the club, supposedly on work breaks or off duty, but mostly curious—wanting to get a look at the submarine animals they had heard about. The NCOs stood back and watched, reluctant to say much as we raised our glasses and hollered underwater adages such as "A-ooo-ga!, A-ooo-ga! Take 'er down steep and deep. Make your depth thirty feet."

And another favorite, most often voiced by Joe Birkle, a wildly tattooed torpedoman with the eyes of an aborigine and arms like a Louisville slugger: "Submarines once; submarines twice. Holy jumpin' Jesus Christ!"

The big torpedoman's hollering routine usually began with his standing up on a chair and throwing three or four beer bottles across the room—a rather informal introduction to the verbal portion that followed. Some of the NCOs frowned on this practice, not being accustomed to having missiles hurled across the width of their club, but who was going to try and curtail the wildman Birkle? No one in that place.

Catron and I managed to strike up a conversation with a tall sergeant who was leaning against the bar. Nice fellow, sharp, just grinning and watching the show. "I understand you boys have been underwater for several months," the sergeant said.

"Yep," said Catron, "right about now it seems like we were down there forever."

The sergeant smiled and nodded. "I can imagine." Then he shook his head. "No, I take that back. I can't imagine that at all."

After a few more questions about submarining, the sergeant said, "I heard that your commanding officer actually cursed out loud on the plane. Is that true?"

I laughed. "Yeah, Commander Rawlins has been known to *curse* quite a bit."

After we'd been there a few hours, an air force man stepped in and said something to one of our guys who was seated near the front door. The sailor stood up and hollered, "The busses are here; we're supposed to go to the terminal for muster."

One guy groaned. "Why don't we just muster here? They know where we are."

Doug Dunn, the chief of the boat, had downed at least as much as anyone else, and more than many. Reeling to his feet, Dunn gave his age-old spiel, one that we could all have repeated verbatim. "All right, nobody here's drank any more than I have, and I doubt any of you could. But we're submarine sailors, and we do what has to be done. Now get yourselves out there on that bus."

"Aw, stick it, Chief," somebody said.

Dunn just grinned.

While the bartender and a number of air force NCOs looked on aghast, we all laughed and headed for the busses, taking our drinks with us. The bus driver, a sergeant, watched in astonishment as we climbed aboard with drinks in our hands. When the bus was about half full, the driver spoke, loudly. "You are *not* allowed to bring drinks on this bus. You'll have to take them back into the club and leave them."

For a moment, the world stood still. Then a sailor raised his arm, denoting a signal, and dropped it swiftly. "Screw you!" we all chimed in unison, and sat down with our drinks. The driver looked up and down the rows, anger, disbelief, and finally resignation on his face. He turned around and stared out the windshield, shaking his head.

Off we went, down through the base, hoisting our drinks and singing our theme song: a take-off on the old Beatles hit "Yellow Submarine." "We all live in a stinking submarine, a stinking submarine, a stinking submarine!"

At the terminal, we tossed down the last of our drinks and left the glasses under our seats. Piling off the busses in a stumbling disarray that looked anything but military, we weaved our way into the building. There we were supposed to fall into formation. All eyes in the terminal were glued on us, including those of Mr. Rawlins, our proud exec, and his clutch of junior officers. They stood off to the side as the chief of the boat attempted to bring us to some sort of order—an endeavor tantamount to trying to herd cats.

Reeling on his feet while trying to appear sober—a comedy in itself—Chief Dunn hollered, "All right, get yourselves squared away and stand on that line." Pointing at a line on the terminal floor, he said, "Put your toes on it."

We all struggled to toe the line, a blurry, wavy thing that mostly eluded our focus. Several guys could not stand on their own, let alone find the elusive line. Their standing problem was easily solved; other sailors stood shoulder to shoulder against them and held them upright, somewhere in the proximity of the line.

Lieutenant Commander Rawlins, our commanding officer at the moment, was to be commended. Impeccably dressed and standing straight as a mainmast, he gazed calmly over our ragged ranks and nodded a stern approval, as if we might have been the most stalwart group of men to ever don our country's uniform.

The swaying chief of the boat, trying without success to match Rawlins's steady stance, decided to bring us to attention—a courageous idea, though seriously lacking in logic.

"Atten-hut!" Chief Dunn growled, and sixty pairs of eyes stared at him as if he had spoken in an alien tongue or perhaps given some sort of wild bird call.

Dunn repeated the order. "I said, ATTEN-HUT!"

Amidst looks of bewilderment, smirks, grins, and muffled giggles, we tried to come to attention—an awkward, shuffling thing that would have made many a military man shudder. Then one of the guys in the front row took it upon himself to speak for the group—a question: succinct, concise, directly to the point.

"What the hell's goin' on, Chief?"

The junior officers turned away. Rawlins could barely suppress a grin. Chief Dunn could not.

"We're gonna be staying here tonight," Dunn said. "You're going to get back on the busses and go check in at the base hotel."

Base hotel? We'd never heard of such a thing.

Despite frowns, groans, and mutterings of "Base hotel?" the chief continued. "After you check into the base hotel, you can stay there or go back to the NCO Club. There'll be busses back and forth between the hotel and the club until late tonight. And *nobody* is allowed to leave the base and go into town. Nobody. Got that?"

Some of us nodded and some of us groaned, "Yeah, we got it, Chief." Not many cared about going to town, anyway. The NCO Club was closer.

Instead of simply telling us to get back on the busses, Chief Dunn decided to continue our impossible display of military maneuvers.

"Left face!" Dunn barked, so forcefully he lost his balance and nearly fell down in the process. Some guys turned left, and others actually turned to the right, ending up face to face with the next sailor in line. The guys who couldn't stand without assistance fell in various directions when they tried to turn left *or* right. Amazingly, none of them made it all the way to the floor, each being caught and pulled back upright by one or more of his buddies.

"Forward, march!" said Dunn, and everyone started forward. It might have worked if we'd all been facing the same direction when the chief gave the order. As it was, individually we were all in motion, but as a group we weren't going anywhere.

The chief shook his head and waved a hand. "Aw, hell. Just get back to the busses, if you can."

Lieutenant Commander Rawlins and the other officers left for their own quarters, undoubtedly thankful that they were separate from ours.

The base hotel had been alerted of our coming, but no staff could have been adequately prepared for such an onslaught. The manager did place us all in one section of the hotel—on the second floor, away from civilized folks. A prudent move.

A large lady behind the desk must have been hand-picked. Square-jawed and steely-eyed, she looked us over coolly as we crashed through the front door and crowded into the lobby. Holding up a beefy hand, she extended two fingers. "Two to a room," she barked. "Pick your own poison, and put your names beside a room number, or make an "X" if you can't write." Somewhere, she had dealt with sailors before.

Catron and I, both able to stand on our feet and sign our names, albeit illegibly, took a room together. Whitey had not been aboard our plane, so Donny Skelton teamed up with Bob Cantley—an equally volatile combination as it turned out.

Some of us had our seabags, with extra clothing, toiletries, etc., which had been delivered to the hotel. Others had nothing but the clothes they were wearing, their seabags having ended up on the other plane when we left Rota.

Most of the guys quickly found their rooms and deposited their gear, if they had any, then headed back out to the busses to return to the NCO Club. Some of the married men, and a few responsible single souls among us, elected to stay at the hotel— reading books, watching TV, and other boring activities. Leroy Lavender remained reasonably sober during our entire stay in Madrid, and I don't think Jim Nelson ever did go back to the NCO Club. He just sat around his room gazing at Betty's picture like a fawn who had lost its mama in the woods.

Another young chief, a good family man with a wife and three kids, had received no familygrams during the patrol. He laid around the hotel staring at the ceiling, talking to no one.

Neither Cantley nor Skelton had their seabags, but together the two hatched an idea for getting their dress white uniforms washed and pressed. They asked a Spanish maid if she could take their clothes home with her, wash and iron them, and return them to their room, promising to pay the woman for her labor, of course. A good idea, except for the fact that the maid could not speak a word of English, nor did Cantley or Skelton have any knowledge of Spanish.

Somehow they got the message across to the Spanish maid, whose nods and smiles assured them that they had a deal. And they did have a deal, except that neither of them understood the meaning of the Spanish word *mañana*. Cantley and Skelton stepped into the bathroom, took off their uniforms, and handed them to the smiling maid who quickly took them away. They then sat down in their white hats, shorts, T-shirts, and shoes—the only clothing they had left—and awaited the maid's return, blissfully unaware that she had promised to bring them back *mañana,* tomorrow.

After another extended session at the NCO Club, we heard the familiar call, "The busses are here!" Again we picked up our drinks and climbed, clambered, and crawled aboard our chariots. At the same time, other busses were picking up the rest of the crew at the base hotel, so we could all muster once more at the terminal.

Chief Dunn was still standing and still barking, but he had given up on trying any fancy military moves. Same drill—some guys sober, many reeling on their feet, and a few being held up by others. Cantley and Skelton highlighted this particular muster. Having no uniforms, they had each managed to borrow a pair of blue denim dungaree pants from someone else. So there they stood, in line and at some form of attention, in white hats, T-shirts, dungaree pants, and black shoes.

"What happened to your uniforms?" I asked them.

Cantley grumbled something about, "How were we supposed to know what *mañana* means?"

Again, all eyes in the terminal were on us as our less-than-sober chief of the boat stood in front, slurring his words. Mr. Rawlins and the other officers looked on, doing their best to keep straight faces. We were told that the plane would be ready to fly us out the following morning, and that we could return either to the NCO Club (the destination of choice) or to the base hotel.

As we fell out and left the terminal, I saw Cantley and Skelton climb onto a bus headed for the NCO Club. "Hey, Bob," I said, "I don't think you and Donny can get in the club dressed like that."

Bob barked back at me, "The hell we can't! What are we supposed to do, sit around the hotel all day while you guys are over at the club having fun?" I knew better than to argue with him.

It was getting toward evening now, and the NCO Club becoming more crowded. Cantley and Skelton turned every head when they walked in half-dressed, and in dungarees at that. The bartender looked at them and muttered, "If they don't get your plane fixed pretty soon, you guys are gonna be coming in here naked."

And, Bob being Bob, the bartender was soon laughing and handing him free drinks. Cantley was a friendly drunk, to say the least. A mental picture one could never forget: Big Bob standing at the bar in a T-shirt and dungarees, entertaining a room filled with folks in full dress uniform or dress casual civvies.

"Man, you guys got a nice club here," Bob would holler, too loudly and too often. Throwing an arm around the shoulders of a perfect stranger, "How you doing tonight, Bubba? Havin' a good time? Good for you." Slapping him on the back and moving on to another new friend who could not escape, and didn't want to.

Passing by me, Bob would strain my eardrums. "Gary, have you talked to that sergeant over there?" pointing at a smiling, half-embarrassed fellow whom I hadn't met. "He's really a good guy; go say hi to him." Bob elicited laughter from the crowd as if we had brought him along solely for entertainment, and the NCOs competed with the bartender to pay for his drinks.

I went back to the base hotel long after dark, on the next-to-the-last bus of the evening. Catron stayed at the club longer and took the last one that ran. When DeWayne's bus unloaded, I was standing on a second-floor balcony that overlooked the main entrance, the lights from the entryway lighting up the sidewalk nearly all the way out to the street. It was a pleasant evening, and several other sailors were out on the balcony with me, along with a number of air force men and their families.

One sergeant and his wife, standing right beside me, couldn't withhold their laughter as Catron came staggering down the walk toward the hotel's front door. He looked up at us with an idiotic grin and waved, losing his balance and reeling off onto the lawn, still waving as he disappeared into the darkness. We heard him run smack into the trunk of a tree, stop short, and giggle. Emerging once more into the light, he wended his way back to the sidewalk.

It took DeWayne a fuzzy moment to get himself oriented and pointed once more toward the hotel. Then he leaned forward and determinedly headed for the doorway, directly under the balcony where we all stood watching.

On either side of the entryway below us sat a large pot, each the size of a wooden barrel. In these pots were planted decorative trees, tall, thin, and neatly groomed. With two- to three-inch diameter trunks reaching up to the second story where we stood, the slender trees had been trimmed of branches nearly all the way to their tops, where a domed shock of leaves formed their only adornment.

As Catron neared the entrance below, I hollered down to him. "Hey, DeWayne, come up here with us."

"Okay," he said, and walked over to one of the potted trees. Reaching up above his head, he grabbed the thin trunk and hoisted himself up until he was standing on the edge of the pot.

"Here I come," he said. Reaching up higher yet, DeWayne took hold with both hands and began to shinny up the little tree. He only made it three or four feet when the trunk began to bend. Undaunted, DeWayne continued to climb until the trunk was bent far over in a precarious arc, suspending him in a horizontal position about ten feet off the ground. The trunk snapped, dropping him facedown on the lawn.

The tree broke off near the bottom, leaving only a couple of pathetic feet protruding from the pot, the rest lying flat on the lawn along with DeWayne. As my friend raised his head and struggled to get up, the sergeant's wife beside me muttered something about "animals" and turned to leave. She grabbed her husband's arm to lead him away, but he was bent over laughing and refused to go.

As our hero made it to his feet once more, I hollered down to him, "Are you all right, DeWayne?"

"Yeah, I'm all right," he said, looking up at us with that silly grin. "Wussy tree wasn't strong enough to hold me."

"Try the other one," I said.

DeWayne turned his head and eyed the second tree, standing innocently in its pot. "Good idea," he said.

More people had gathered on the balcony by now, and the sergeant whose wife had left gazed wide-eyed as DeWayne lurched toward the second tree. "Oh, no!" the man said, turning to me in disbelief.

"Yep," I said, "he's gonna do it."

And DeWayne did it, exactly as he had done the first, and with the same predictable result. When the second tree snapped the sergeant laughed himself hoarse, along with myself and several other sailors on the balcony.

It looked like a crime scene: DeWayne and the two murdered trees all lying flat in the grass. One of the chiefs on the balcony finally spoke up. "Some of you guys better go down there and get him. If he tries the stairs he might take the whole building down."

The Spanish maid brought back Cantley's and Skelton's dress whites early the next morning. Clean and freshly pressed, their uniforms looked considerably better than their red eyes and puffy faces. One last time, the busses took us to the terminal and the chief of the boat lined us up for muster.

A sad bunch. Yesterday we had had on a head of steam—or so we had felt. This morning we were simply hung-over sailors. Chief Dunn, who looked as though he might be suffering some sort of terminal illness, gave us his boring and age-old speech about being able to drink more than any of us and still do his job. We paid no attention, until the chief directed us to the plane.

I'm sure everyone on the SAC base was watching as our plane lifted off the runway, watching and wondering if submariners were all insane or just acted that way. We didn't know the answer to that ourselves.

A while after we were airborne, Lieutenant Commander Rawlins walked back to where DeWayne Catron sat, directly across from me. Stopping in the aisle between us, he looked down at DeWayne. "Catron, I heard you tried to climb some trees on the air force base. Is that true?"

"No, sir," Catron replied. "I did not climb a single tree on that base."

A narrow smile creased the exec's face. "Glad to hear it," he said. "It didn't sound like something you would do."

Chapter Thirteen

Between Patrols:
The World According
to Submariners

At long last, we landed in Charleston. Good old South Carolina, U.S.A. As soon as we deplaned we found ourselves caught up in a horde of screaming, teary wives and girlfriends running with open arms to clutch their returning heroes. Children tripping over their own feet. Tiny voices yelling, "Daddy! Daddy!" Babies staring at their fathers for the first time. Tough submariners fighting to hold back tears.

Others were not met by anyone: some single sailors who had no steady girlfriend, and one memorable married fellow whose wife didn't show. The young chief who had received no familygrams walked in distraught circles through the terminal, searching in vain for his wife and children. Overcome with grief, he looked around every corner, down every corridor, and in every waiting area, unable to accept what he already knew: his family was gone. His wife, a good woman whom I'd had the pleasure to meet, had become unable to deal with the long absences and the not knowing if her husband was dead or alive from the time the boat submerged until it surfaced months later.

Shoemaker's girlfriend from the Strip was nowhere to be found, and the former girl-in-every-port guy who had made the mistake of falling in love was a basket case.

No one was there to meet me, either, and that's the way I wanted it. Not that I didn't enjoy female companionship on occasion; I certainly did, but in my mind long-term attachments did not jibe with a submariner's life.

The married men left for home with their families, while we "single johns" boarded a bus that took us to our quarters on the base. Serving in the nuclear submarine force had its perks; during the nearly three months of our off period we lived in some of the finest barracks the navy owned.

Unlike most navy barracks, our two-story structure was divided into separate rooms. Four guys to a room, with extra privacy provided by lockers, head-high and very wide, that separated the room into halves. It was like having just one roommate in a space that submariners considered huge, with lockers that held ten times as much as our tiny personal boxes aboard the boat.

Our new homes may have been wonderful, but we didn't hang around the barracks for long. The Strip awaited. We quickly stowed our gear, exchanged our dress white uniforms for civvies, and called cabs to take us to that playground of the devil.

Most of us owned cars, which we put in storage while on patrol. And we left them in storage for three or four days after we returned to Charleston. It was time to raise hell, and cars didn't fit in, not into the *right* places, anyway. Oh, our cars would fit into, and around, a lot of things: telephone poles, fire plugs, parking meters, and the like. And parking was no problem; they could easily be parked up on curbs, sidewalks, and in illegal spaces that blocked private driveways. That's why we left them in storage and rode in taxis.

The Strip: an unholy place where one could find sailors and civilians of every breed—con men, pickpockets, bullies, slashers, shooters—and get sliced up or killed over a game of pool or the honor of a woman who had long since forgotten the concept. When a fight occurred, any onlooker with a bit of sense stayed out of it, for to try and interfere or break it up was not worth the risk.

The Strip consisted of a great number of bars, all lowbrow and very rough, cracked and weathered and all looking like they needed a good cleaning and painting, both inside and out—or even better, a working over with a wrecking ball. The roughest on that mean street were submarine bars, establishments that catered almost exclusively to submariners. There were three or four sub bars on the Strip, the most famous being the "525 Club," or, as it was commonly known, the Five-and-a-Quarter.

No one knew where the Five-and-a-Quarter got its name nor what it signified, and nobody cared. Hundreds of photos of submarines were tacked up behind the bar, along with pictures of chiefs, petty officers, and hard women who had made themselves famous there. A diving alarm could be sounded by the bartender with a quick pull of a short rope. Two strong boards, two-by-fours, spanned the large front window—body catchers. The boards, darkly stained by ancient varnish and cigarette smoke, were reasonably unobtrusive in front of the smoke-fogged window that had not been washed in years. And they served their purpose well; I witnessed many a sailor's body bounce off the two-by-fours during one of the frequent fights that took place in the Five-and-a-Quarter—a regular occurrence, and the dusky window was never broken.

The place was not large but just roomy enough. A badly scarred bar with a line of worn vinyl stools, two pool tables, a number of chairs, and enough free floor space to accommodate two fights at the same time. Most of the bars closed at midnight or 2:00 a.m., but not the Five-and-a-Quarter. The dim neon sign that stuck out over the door—525 CLUB—burned round the clock, seven days a week. It never closed.

A skinny, old boozer named Toby ran the place with Terri and Jeanne, a couple of big old gals who looked like forty miles of bad road. I don't think they ever got any sleep, except when one of them dozed off in a rusty metal chair that sat behind the bar.

The Five-and-a-Quarter, our exclusive club. We loved it.

Whitey had flown on the captain's plane, and so he had not accompanied us on our adventure to Madrid. He arrived in Charleston a day and a half ahead of us, and by the time our plane rolled to a stop in South Carolina, Whitey had been in the Five-and-a-Quarter for thirty-six hours straight—a good start.

It was late evening when we walked into the Five-and-a-Quarter. Bob Lee, Bob Cantley, Ted Newell, Donny Skelton, myself, and Rich Dominy, a new fellow who quickly fit in to our group—a dubious honor at best.

Whitey was in uniform, and going strong. "Hey guys! Where ya been? Tearing up Spain, I hear."

Whitey pointed at us and turned to Toby. "Give them guys a drink," he said. "Aw, hell, set 'em up for everybody." He pulled a huge roll of bills out of his pocket, peeled off several, and tossed them on the bar. "Take what you need," he said.

Toby picked up the money, took out the exact amount, and handed the rest back to Whitey. The old drunk had many faults, but he would never cheat a sailor. And he seldom threw a submariner out of his bar, regardless of what the infraction may have been.

Most of us stayed all that night and the next day as well. We were more than tired by that evening, having been there twenty-four hours, so we called a cab and headed back to the base, our comfortable barracks, and our soft beds. Whitey did not; he stayed on at the 525 Club. The wild little guy had now been there sixty hours, 2½ days—drinking, eating sandwiches that were heated up in a toaster oven behind the bar, buying rounds for the house, occasionally napping in a chair with his head resting on a table, or standing like a little boy while the barmaid wiped some spill off the front of his white jumper.

Back at the barracks, the rest of us got a full night's sleep, woke the next morning with terrific headaches, downed a handful of aspirins, and cleaned ourselves up. That day we visited some other bars that, though not as famous as the Five-and-a-Quarter, boasted noteworthy reputations of their own: the Amvets, the Candlelight Club, the Fountain Inn, the Loading Zone, and others whose names are lost in antiquity—a shame.

We ate huge meals at Mom Rhino's, one of the few restaurants on the Strip, a delightful bistro with poor lighting, cobwebs in every corner, torn linoleum floors, broken and patched booths, plastic-topped tables and vinyl-covered chairs reminiscent of the 1940s and 1950s, and water-spotted plates and silverware that one prayed had been washed with soap sometime in recent history.

Mom Rhino's, named after the giant of a woman who ran the place, boasted a surprisingly large menu, serving about everything one could imagine, and some things one could not imagine. Somehow, most of it tasted pretty much the same regardless of whatever name Mom Rhino might have attached to the particular dish. It was the only place in Charleston where one could order a beef taco and, being from the West, that alone was enough to ensure my frequent return to her establishment. They actually tasted somewhat like tacos, although they were messy to consume, and the juices that dripped from them defied description.

A memorable fight occurred at Mom Rhino's that afternoon, a mammoth conflict between two women, both of whom were mighty hefty and mighty strong. The battle would live in infamy, due not in small part to an unforgettable line mouthed by one of the female combatants.

The two portly ladies—one in pants so tight they looked as if they might rip wide open at any moment, the other in a broad flowered dress, which should have been much, much longer—were regular inhabitants of the Strip, and therefore acquainted with one another. Friends they were not, however. I had seen them argue before, but never dreamed I'd be fortunate enough to witness a clash of the titans, right there in Mom Rhino's.

Most of the guys had already gone to the Five-and-a-Quarter, leaving just Rich Dominy and myself to finish our meals. Rich was a small, blond-headed fellow with a nonstop sense of humor, an adventurous soul, and a wild streak yet to be fully developed. Being new to submarines and new to the ways of the Strip, Rich was about to get a valuable initiation into a side of life he'd never known existed.

The women were seated in separate booths, by themselves, when the verbal part began. The exchange quickly grew in volume, the crux of it turning out to be the fact that one of them had a boyfriend and the other one didn't. The one who had the boyfriend bragged loudly about this fact, and the other yelled back that her boyfriend was a no-good SOB. That did it.

The one in pants, who supposedly had this absent boyfriend, jumped up from her booth, ran to the other one, who was still seated, and started beating her about the head and shoulders with both fists. The one in the dress fought back, but fighting from a seated position badly hampered her ability to retaliate. The one standing landed several telling blows, then grabbed the seated one by the hair, two handfuls, and dragged her out of the booth onto the floor, flat on her back. The one on the floor began to wail, presumably because the hair pulling hurt. I couldn't blame her; it kind of hurt to watch it.

Caring not a whit about her downed opponent's screams and

cries, the enraged Amazon kept hold of her hair with both hands and began to drag her across the floor. The woman on the floor being so heavy, the other had to pull her along with a series of jerks, each jerk looking as if it would rip the hair out of her head. Being yanked along in this manner caused the woman's dress to begin to tear down the back, ripping it apart and pulling the entire garment down below her waist.

At this point the obvious victor, the one in the tight pants, let go of the other's hair and began to strut around her in a circle, yelling, "I'll stomp a mud hole in your butt, and walk it dry!"

As the floored woman's wails tapered off to blubbery sobs and the other continued to stomp a track around her, repeating the infamous line over and over, Mom Rhino walked out of the kitchen and stopped with her hands on her hips. The world stood still. The one on the floor stopped crying, and the other stopped walking around her. Like lumpish bronzes frozen in place, they stared at Mom Rhino, fear having replaced all their anger at sight of the largest woman on the Strip.

Mom Rhino pointed at the standing woman. "Stop that," she said, "or I'll stomp a mud hole in *your butt* and walk it dry." She didn't even raise her voice.

The woman scurried back to her booth and hurriedly slid into it. Mom Rhino looked at the one on the floor and said, "And you get up from there, and get back in your seat. I ain't havin' no more of this."

With great effort, the whipped woman heaved herself to her feet, doing her best to hold her tattered dress up, her nose and lips bleeding, her hair a hopeless tangle. I marveled that she hadn't been scalped during the battle.

Mom Rhino walked into the back and returned with a handful of safety pins. Dropping them on the table in front of the battered loser, she said, "Here, fix your dress." Then the giant woman turned to look at Rich and me. "How you boys doin'?" she asked.

Rich was speechless. I smiled and said, "We're doing fine, Mom."

"Good. How's the tacos?"

"Delicious, Mom. Just delicious."

Still wondering at the unexpected show we had happened onto at

Mom Rhino's, Rich and I drifted over to the Five-and-a-Quarter. It was evening by now, things were lively, and Whitey was still on his feet. His white navy jumper had gotten so soiled that he'd taken it off and was wearing only a T-shirt and white dress pants. His white hat, somewhat spotted itself, remained perched on the back of his head. He had now inhabited the club around the clock for eighty-four hours: four days and three nights and was going on night number four.

Somewhere along the way, we had lost Donny Skelton and Ted Newell. Bob Lee and Cantley and I had decided to get our cars out of storage the following day, and so we didn't plan to stay too late at the Five-and-a-Quarter. Sometime that evening Whitey took me aside and said, "Gary, I've got a lot of money on me. Would you take some of it back to the barracks with you when you go?"

"Sure," I answered, and then I gasped when Whitey pulled a roll out of his pocket and handed me twelve hundred dollars: twelve one-hundred-dollar bills. I shook my head in amazement, stuck the money in my pocket, and ordered another beer.

An hour or so later, Whitey got concerned that he hadn't kept enough money for himself. He took me aside again and asked me to give some of it back to him. Since it was his money, I couldn't exactly say no, so I gave him two hundred dollars. Shortly after that I left, fearing that Whitey might decide to try and get even more of it back from me.

The following day, mid-morning, I looked out of my room in the barracks and saw Whitey, trudging down the hall like a refugee from a concentration camp. After four days and four nights in the Five-and-a-Quarter, he was pale, his face drawn, his eyes so red it hurt to look at them. He appeared to have died and forgotten to fall down.

I ran out into the hall and caught Whitey. "Welcome home," I said. "Did you have a lot of fun?"

He managed a wan smile, then shook his head. "Oh, man," he said. "I feel like crap warmed over, and you can't imagine how much money I spent down there. I took every bit I had when I went to the Five-and-a-Quarter, and now I'm flat broke."

I stood and looked at him for a long moment, frowning, pretending to commiserate with him over his plight. Then I smiled, took him by the arm, and said, "Whitey, you're going to love me."

"Love you?" he said. "That'll be the day."

"Well, today's the day," I said, leading him to my locker.

I opened my locker door, reached inside, and handed Whitey a thousand dollars. His bloodshot eyes popped wide open. "What's this?" he asked.

"It's your money," I said. "You gave it to me down at the Five-and-a-Quarter. Asked me to keep it for you." Fingering the stack of hundred-dollar bills, Whitey broke into a grin.

"You love me now, don't you?" I asked.

"Damn near it," he answered. "But if you think I'm gonna kiss you, forget it."

The first thirty days of the off-period were mostly free time. One could go home on leave or anywhere else he might choose to travel, and those who elected to stay in Charleston were only required to muster a couple of times a week. That just took a few minutes.

After raising hell for about four days and then retrieving my car from storage, I drove to the airport and headed for Colorado.

Military personnel could fly for half-price in those days—on any airline—the only catches being that we had to travel in uniform and every flight we tried was on a standby basis. Sometimes the plane had a seat for us, and sometimes not, and we stood the chance of being bumped off at every stop we made. A little harrowing at times, but still a great deal, making air travel affordable for virtually all men and women in the armed forces.

My flights from Charleston to Denver routed me through Augusta, Georgia; Atlanta; Chicago; and then to Denver. I took off from Charleston at night, landed in Augusta, and immediately lost my seat—bumped off the plane. This meant I wouldn't make my connecting flight in Atlanta, unless I did something unorthodox. I bought a flashlight, went out on a dark highway, and started hitchhiking. Got picked up by a couple of Georgia good ol' boys who had a case of beer, which they gladly shared with me, and drove one hundred miles an hour through the black night.

The two young guys were nowhere close to sober, and they kept asking me about submarines and telling me what a hero I was. I didn't disagree with them. They went out of their way to get me to Atlanta so I could make my flight to Chicago, and they insisted I take another bottle of beer with me, into the Atlanta airport. I thanked them profusely and managed to ditch the beer before airport security got me.

On to O'Hare International in Chicago, where again I was bumped off my flight. In fact, I got bumped off of five or six flights, spending all day charging from one gate to another in O'Hare and waiting at each one to see if I would get a seat on that plane, only to be bumped off again. Miles of running inside that giant airport with a heavy seabag over my shoulder. Exciting.

I finally caught a plane to Denver sometime that evening. All the airline had left was a first-class seat, which they let me have at no extra charge. Full meal, pretty stewardesses, and free drinks. The excitement continued.

Denver, at last, far after midnight. A skuzzy bus station filled with homeless schizophrenics and bums, and several hours wait for the bus to Lamar. I wrapped my arm through the strap on my seabag, fell into a rock-hard chair, and slept like the dead. I woke just long enough to board the bus, which took another five hours to reach Lamar—five more glorious hours of sleep.

Home. As always, Mom met me at the bus station, along with a number of her lady friends. That way she knew I couldn't escape being shown off in uniform and treated like a returning hero. Since I had known the ladies since birth, and they showered me with homemade candy and cookies, I went along with the returning hero thing until I could get to Mom's house and change into civvies.

Lamar. The little town in the southeast corner of the state hadn't changed much, but I had. No more high school buddies to run with; they had either left town, gotten married and settled down, or both. That was okay; I was a sub sailor, and at that point, none of them would have understood what made me tick.

The old ranch and the wide, wide prairie. That's what I wanted to see. The antithesis of life on a submarine. I drove Mom's old pickup truck out there and bounced across rough sod composed of buffalo grass, cactus, yucca, and sand. Rocky hillsides rose up to break the broad horizon, rounded buttes stood like fortresses. It looked like a setting for a Western movie, and right there, on those harsh plains, I had been raised by a man bigger than life: a real cowboy.

Dad's spirit still dwelt in that hard land. I could see him—a grizzled old man in an aged Stetson, walking board-straight in high-heeled boots or eating up the miles sitting astride a galloping horse, a favorite sport that he had fearlessly followed until near the age of eighty.

I drove down the old dirt road, now sodded over, where Dad and I and a heroic horse had nearly perished in a blizzard when Dad was seventy-eight and I was twelve. The old rock house in which I had spent my childhood—a rustic homestead that dated to the 1880s—still stood there alone, fighting the elements as it had for nearly one hundred years. The open porch where I had slept outside in the summer, wondering at the ocean of stars overhead and listening to the howls of coyotes—a thrilling sound, wild and free, as the animals sang me to sleep.

I walked through the decaying home where Mom and her father had taught me how to live, and I gazed long into Dad's old room, where he had showed me how to die. The kitchen that had never seen plumbing, where buckets of water had stood on a bench, buckets that froze over during winter nights, right there in the house. My childhood had been a study in survival, bolstered by the love of some mighty tough folks. A treasured experience that I would not trade with anyone.

Late in the afternoon, on a rise overlooking the old rock house and remnants of the outbuildings, I sat on the hard prairie and watched the western horizon, knowing that a spectacular sunset would bid farewell to a perfect day. Western sunsets are one of the natural wonders of the world. Even if one watches closely, these wondrous events seem to occur in a moment. One minute it looked almost clear, only a streak of light clouds clinging to the edge of the earth. Then suddenly God reached down and ignited the sky. The broad horizon came ablaze. A fiery red that burned like molten metal stretched across the west, a bright, shimmering gold edging the red. And for the few minutes that it blazed, until it faded into a somber twilight, it possessed me. A moment of perfect beauty that I could carry with me under the sea.

Back in Charleston, another week of free time remained. After that, we'd all start attending specialized classes five days a week. We nukes took short courses designed to update us on the latest reactor technology, to train us to operate essential tools and machinery in case of emergencies at sea, and always—safety measures. Most of the enginemen and machinist mates, myself included, were taught how to weld, operate a machine lathe, and take apart and repair the most complex pieces of equipment and advanced fire-fighting techniques and first-aid for virtually every type of wound imaginable.

We did have liberty every night during these courses, and since they were all hands-on training, most of them required little homework. This lack of homework provided a financial boon to the community. If we'd had assignments that occupied our evenings and weekends, it would probably have bankrupted the Strip.

Having just returned from Colorado, I reported in to officially end my leave time, ran to the barracks to change into civvies, and headed for the only place that seemed logical: the Strip.

I cruised the Strip for a while, saying "Hi" to proprietors and barmaids with whom I was acquainted, but found none of my *Hamilton* buddies. I happened to run into Suzie Anne, Shoemaker's ex-girlfriend with whom he had entrusted everything he owned and then received no familygrams while we'd been at sea. It turned out that Suzie had wrecked his car during the patrol and sold its remains to a junkyard. She also sold his clothes, abandoned the apartment they had shared, and spent all of his paychecks. Upon arrival back in Charleston, Shoemaker rescinded the power of attorney that he had so foolishly given her but found himself penniless and without a car.

I saw Suzie Anne walking toward me and stopped her on the sidewalk. "Hi, Gary," she said cheerfully, the dark gap from her missing front tooth dominating her otherwise decent face. "How was the patrol?"

"The patrol was fine," I said bluntly, then anger rose in my voice. "There's something I want to ask you about, Suzie. Why did you do that to Shoemaker? Ruin his car, sell everything he owned, and spend all his money. What possessed you to do such a thing to him?"

Suzie Anne let out a big sigh, then began to explain. "Well, I told him not to do it. I told Shoemaker I wasn't worth a damn, and that he'd regret leaving me all that stuff and having his paychecks sent to me. I told him more than once he shouldn't do it, but the guy was in love with me, and he insisted. And, just like I said I would, I screwed him over. And that's all there is to it."

My anger faded. I shook my head, and then I had to laugh. "Well, I guess if you told him all that, then he hasn't got anybody to blame but himself."

Suzie agreed. "Nope, he doesn't," she said.

I turned to leave. "Take care of yourself, Suzie Anne."

She flipped a curvy hip at me and said, "Oh, I'll be okay." I figured she would be.

After downing a plateful of Mom Rhino's famous tacos, which practically slid down my throat via their own lubrication, I wandered over to the Five-and-a-Quarter. The old haunt was busy, but none of my buddies were there. In fact, just one of the *Hamilton* crew was there, sitting alone. Rusty Romer, the engine room bully who had vowed to get revenge for my having turned him in to Chief Kennedy and Lavender for badgering Bob Lee. His threat still stood.

Rusty was seated on a barstool near the door, looking sullen, when I walked in. He turned his head and our eyes locked. His brow knitted and his gaze narrowed—looking mean, as he always did. He had on a short-sleeved shirt that accentuated his powerful biceps and stout torso, a physical significance not lost on me. We exchanged a long stare, and then I walked past him as if he didn't exist.

Although my running mates were absent, there were sailors

in the Five-and-a-Quarter whom I knew, and old Toby and the barmaids were there, of course. I ordered a beer, spoke to everyone I recognized, struck up conversations with several, and shot a few games of pool.

I drank a few beers, slowly, so as not to impair myself. I felt sure I would have to fight Rusty that night, and I wasn't looking forward to it. I moved around the room talking with folks, laughing, and telling jokes to everyone but Rusty. He never moved from his seat at the bar. This went on for two or three hours, Rusty occasionally looking at me, and me occasionally looking at him. At times our eyes met in a mutual glare, malice traveling both ways.

I was standing at the far end of the bar looking directly at Rusty when he stood up. To my surprise, he headed toward the door. After a few steps, he stopped and looked back at me. Again we stared, for an eternity, until at length he turned and left.

Unbeknown to me, Rusty Romer was leaving Charleston the following day, being transferred to another sub with a different home port. I never saw him again.

As the off period continued and we began attending regular classes, our partying slowed a bit, although weekends remained open season for nearly anything imaginable.

We learned that we would not be going back to Spain, but instead to Scotland. There the Gold Crew would dock the boat following their current patrol. We knew that Scotland was a beautiful country, so it sounded like a nice change of pace. We didn't really think much about it at the time; we were returning to a submarine, not to a place.

Our submarine family changed somewhat during our two and a half months in Charleston: while some men left for other duty stations, new ones arrived.

Senior Chief Kennedy, one of the finest natural leaders I would ever know, retired from the navy after more than twenty years—retired on a Friday and went to work for the Electric Boat Company in Groton, Connecticut, the following Monday, building submarines. I would miss that tough man more than I realized at the time.

Another senior chief, Chief Spence, a competent leader but less intense, reported aboard to replace Kennedy as king of the engine room.

Chief T. K. Russell, a good man whose contribution had been dimmed by the long shadow that Kennedy cast, left to become an instructor at one of the nuclear prototypes in Idaho.

Danny Dawson, my slow-talking friend from Texas who could make me laugh any time he chose, left for another boat. I would sorely miss him, and would find him later in life, back in Texas, the same funny guy he had always been.

Bob Lee and I both made first-class, but remained on the *Hamilton* Blue Crew. The odd couple lived on.

Whitey and Skelton also stayed on, as did big Bob Cantley and DeWayne Catron. I couldn't have imagined a patrol without them.

Chief Don Durham was supposed to remain on the *Hamilton* as well, but the Vietnam War was heating up, and Don wanted to join in the fray. Because of his nuclear training, however, the navy department wouldn't let him go. Don figured out a way to outfox them; he joined the army. Being a career military man with about fifteen years in and five to go for retirement, Don talked to the army and made a deal to spend his last five years as an army warrant officer, with orders to command a river gunboat in Vietnam. He must have been good at it; he was later reported to have retired as one of the most decorated warrant officers in the army.

Jim Nelson, whom I had always figured to be a career submariner, married his beloved Betty in a small chapel on the base shortly before his discharge was due. I had the honor of being best man in their military wedding. Jim left the navy, went to work in a civilian nuclear plant, and never looked back.

Chief Padgett, the guitar-picking, country/western-singing leader of the Saturday night hootenannies, also got transferred. It was a major concern to most of the crew, myself included. What would we do on patrol without our weekly live entertainment?

Mr. Green, the chief engineering officer, left to become exec of another sub, allowing Lieutenant MacKinnon to move up to the position of engineering officer.

The serious Dr. Boston was replaced by the zaniest officer I would ever know. Tall and young, his thin face filled with laugh lines, Lieutenant Nance had graduated near the top of his class in medical school, but I was never sure if he had been sent to watch over our health or to keep us laughing around the clock. I couldn't wait to make a patrol with him.

Lt. Cdr. Robert Rawlins, our fire-breathing but popular executive officer, was promoted and transferred to a command of his own, replaced by Robert Chewning, a low-key lieutenant commander who only breathed air.

And Captain Bessac, the walking tower who could make brave men shudder with a flicker of his eyes, was replaced by C. D. Summitt, a commander who appeared to be Norman Bessac's opposite.

We all knew that Summitt had never commanded a missile submarine, and a number of things about our new captain puzzled us. He was a short, straight man with a round friendly face, a warm countenance, a soft Tennessee accent, and a voice that was never raised. He set about getting to know the name of every man in his crew as quickly as possible and spoke with a smile every time he passed one of us, seemingly unconcerned as to whether or not he projected a commanding image. We didn't know what to make of him.

During the last couple of weeks before we were scheduled to fly back across the Atlantic and retrieve our boat from the Gold Crew, the school assignments began to slow down and we were again given more free time. Three-day weekends: we mustered on Friday mornings and were turned loose until the following Monday.

Why all this free time? Was it a reward for the stressful job we did at sea, or was it something the navy department deemed necessary for our psychological well being? The latter, beyond a doubt.

Not only did Bob Lee understand applied engineering as well as any of us, he also had the mind of a businessman, an attribute that would lead him to wealth in later years. Even now, instead of staying in the barracks, he had invested in a mobile home and lived in an upscale trailer park in the suburbs. He rented his extra bedroom out to Ted Newell when we were in Charleston, and when we went to sea, Bob rented the trailer to some members of the Gold Crew, thus paying for his investment with rent money.

One night, late, I decided to surprise Bob and Ted with an impromptu visit. Actually, it was about 2:00 a.m. Bob and Ted were both sober and asleep, and I was neither. I had simply planned to knock on their door and give them a big "Howdy," but a chicken changed my plan.

Several chickens regularly wandered the trailer park in which Bob lived—decorative, multicolored birds, the kind people keep for their beauty instead of their taste. One of these colorful birds, a rooster, walked in front of my car as I neared Bob's trailer. The chicken stopped, blinded by the glare of my headlights.

For reasons I'll never understand, I decided to catch the rooster. Stopping my car and quietly opening the door, I approached the mesmerized bird, stealthily, at least as stealthy as a drunken sailor can be, that is.

The chicken stood still in the headlights until I got very close, then it sensed me, saw me, or something. It darted under Bob's trailer, and I darted after it. The bird was used to walking under mobile homes, but apparently it wasn't accustomed to being pursued under them. As I dove under Bob's trailer, rolled onto my back, and began pumping my legs to push myself farther under it, the confused chicken stopped, and I caught it.

Being a country boy, I knew to grab the chicken by both legs, and that's what I attempted to do. Being a chicken, it knew the proper defense for this maneuver: squirming in my grasp, flapping its wings, raking me with its spurs, pecking me profusely, and squawking loudly enough to wake the dead.

Along with the dead, the bird's squawking woke Bob and Ted. I heard the door slam as they charged out to see what was going on under the trailer. Two flashlights lit up the scene—me flat on my back holding the chicken in the tight space above me. By now, I had both its feet in one bleeding hand and its neck in the other. This put a stop to its spurring, pecking, and squawking, but I found myself bleeding from scratches and pecks on both hands and well up my forearms.

Bob and Ted took a long moment to assess the situation. Then Bob, in his unflappable manner, asked, "What the hell are you doing under there, Penley?"

"Catching this chicken," I said.

"What for?"

"I don't know."

Ted Newell broke into uncontrollable laughter. Bob Lee grinned narrowly and gave me the Look, the one that said, "Are you totally insane?" At that point, I'd have had a difficult time defending the accusation.

"Is the chicken hurt?" Bob asked.

"I don't think so," I said, "but I am."

"You'd better turn it loose," he said, "it belongs to one of my neighbors." That's when I noticed that more lights had come on in the trailer park, and I could hear voices inquiring as to the nature of the disturbance.

I released the chicken. Loosing another loud squawk, it charged out from under the trailer and into the night. I crawled out, climbed to my feet, and followed Bob and Ted inside.

While I stood over the kitchen sink, bleeding, Bob got out a bottle of mercurochrome and about a dozen Band-aids and began patching me up. "What are you doing out here at this time of the morning?" Bob asked.

"Came out to see you guys. How you doin'?"

Bob shook his head, and Ted went back to bed.

Donny Skelton was an interesting fellow to watch. Since he and I slept in the same room in the barracks, I had a ringside seat for many of his antics.

One night about 10:00, I was lying in my bunk reading when Donny staggered in, barely able to stand on his feet and move in any clear direction. I had to help him open his personal locker, the combination lock proving too complicated to operate in his condition. As I lay back down and resumed reading, the little pot-bellied leprechaun undressed down to his boxer shorts, got his toiletry bag and a towel in hand, and headed unsteadily for the showers. Shortly after he wobbled out the door, I turned off my light and went to sleep.

Next morning, a little after 6:00, I woke up and glanced over at Skelton's bunk. No Skelton. His bed was still made, and obviously hadn't been touched since he'd left for the showers the night before. I decided I'd better go on a scouting mission.

Donny was easy to find. Seated on a toilet, his shorts down around his ankles, he was leaning against the side of the narrow stall, snoring. He'd been sleeping there, on that toilet seat, for eight hours.

When I shook him awake, he slowly opened his eyes, which looked like they might start bleeding at any moment. He blinked several times and looked around to see where he was, then attempted to stand up from the toilet seat. That didn't work. His stiff legs and joints could not raise his body from his eight-hour perch.

I reached out and gave Donny a hand, slowly pulling him to his feet. He stood, but not up. When he made it to his feet, totally dependent on my support, he remained in the same position at which he had occupied the toilet—bent over at a ninety-degree angle and unable to straighten himself up. Only two things about him changed upon standing: his face and his butt. His face twisted in pain, while his bare rear revealed an embedded ring, rosy red, that perfectly matched the outline of the toilet seat.

"Oh! Ooh!" Donny said, holding onto me lest he fall backward onto his tender behind or forward onto his face. After I got his shorts pulled up, I began walking him back to our room. Slowly we went, Donny taking bent-over baby steps, one hand on my arm and the other in the middle of his back, gathering a laughing crowd as we proceeded down the hall. I stopped and, against his wishes, pulled down his shorts to show the rest of the guys his neon backside. In his stiffened state, Skelton was unable to do anything about it, except to groan and direct uncomplimentary names in my direction. I wiped the tears from my eyes and walked him the rest of the way back to his bunk.

A few days after Skelton spent the night on the toilet seat, Whitey showed up in the barracks, unable to take a single step under his own power. Being held up by two tall shore patrol, one on each side, the little guy was taking slow, uncertain steps down the hall, each movement at the urging of his captors. Whitey's eyes were blank, his face expressionless, his body hanging in the arms of the shore patrolmen. A large bandage covered the top of his round head, sprigs of blonde hair sticking out all around it, thin rivulets of blood seeping from under the tape and gauze.

Several of us appeared in the hall, stopping short at sight of our wounded mate. "What happened to him this time?" I asked. The two shore patrolmen, one a first-class petty officer and the other a second-class, looked a little sheepish, embarrassed. As they struggled to hold Whitey's limp body upright, the first-class began to speak.

"We're sorry," the man said. "We didn't mean to hurt him." Then, under the angry glares of the group of us, he went on to explain what had happened.

It seems that Whitey had stumbled out the front door of the Five-and-a-Quarter, crossed the sidewalk, fell down in the parking strip, and passed out. Sometime later, the two shore patrolmen had come along, reached down, and shook him awake.

Whitey looked up at them, struggled partway to his feet, poised his hands in front of his body, karate style, and hollered, "I'm a trained killer!" The shore patrol quickly subdued him by rapping him on the skull with their clubs, knocking him unconscious once more.

"A trained killer!" I said. "Hell, he's just a crazy submariner." At that, Whitey looked at me dumbly and grinned a little.

"We know that now," said the shore patrolman, "but when he jumped up we thought we might be dealing with a martial arts expert or something. After we knocked him out, the people who run the 525 Club told us who he was and that he was on the crew of the *Alexander Hamilton.* The two girls who work at the club patched up his head and then we brought him back here."

Whitey was still hanging in the two men's grasp and grinning stupidly. I shook my head. "Is he charged with anything?" I asked.

"No, he's not," the patrolman said. "We just wanted to get him back here safely. Can you guys take care of him?"

"Sure," I said. "If you can just walk him to his room, we'll lay him down." I led the way as they shuffled Whitey down the hall. He immediately fell asleep when they dropped him on his bunk.

"Thanks, guys," I told the shore patrol. As they turned to leave they again apologized for clubbing our shipmate, but we waved them off.

Looking down at my wild little buddy, sleeping like a babe in his bunk, his battered noggin still bleeding, I figured we were about ready to go back to sea.

Chapter Fourteen

Upkeep:
The Calm Before the Storm

Holy Loch, Scotland, a large, circular inlet off the Firth of Clyde on the western edge of the country. A perfect bay framed by rounded hills that looked to have been smoothed and shaped by the hand of a great sculptor. Small two- and three-story houses of stone with steep roofs for shedding snow, thin spirals of smoke curling from tall chimneys that rose out of the wooded hillsides—a quaint, inviting place whose people greeted American sailors with more warmth and sincerity than we might have expected.

There was no naval base per se, but on one side of the bay nestled the little town of Dunoon. There our officer's and enlisted clubs were located as well as navy stores, shore patrol headquarters, and the like. Directly across the water from Dunoon was another friendly village named Gourak. In the middle of the bay, halfway between the towns, sat a submarine tender at anchor, the USS *Hunley* (AS31), with its flock of subs tied outboard on either side, their low-lying hulls dwarfed by the tall mother ship that nourished them and readied them for their next patrols.

The same as we had done in Spain, we took bunks on the tender the evening we landed, and anxiously awaited the arrival of our sub the following day. Fog was no stranger to Scotland, and again we stood on the high decks and cheered as our great warship appeared out of the mist.

Once more I was filled with strong, opposing emotions: pride and honor to serve my country on this deep-diving machine of deterrence and an underlying dread of the upcoming patrol. And again I buried this dread—this unspoken fear that I would die at the bottom of the sea—during a solitary inspection of the boat from the farthest point forward to the farthest aft. By the time I reached the engine room, I was acclimated, transformed, ready to laugh my way through another long patrol.

The twenty-eight-day upkeep—a time we referred to as "Rickover's Period"—proceeded well, with the tender *Hunley* providing the same fine support as the *Holland* had done in Spain. Our revised command had a less intense feel about it but appeared no less effective than before.

Senior Chief Spence, our new head of the engine room gang, was quiet, hard working, and comfortable with himself. A career submariner, lanky and thin-faced with a fine sense of humor, Spence was easier on the nerves than our old boss, Chief Kennedy, had been. The fiery Kennedy, being convinced that no mere mortal could replace him, had left a long letter explaining in detail how everything should be conducted during upkeep. Chief Spence looked the letter over, chuckled, and passed it around for all of us to read. We referred to it as Kennedy's "What Happens After I Leave" letter.

Lieutenant MacKinnon, the newly appointed engineering officer, maintained the popularity he had enjoyed prior to his promotion. Unlike the strange, socially inept Mr. Green whom he had replaced, MacKinnon joked with us, laughed a lot, and was fun to work for. He loved his job and his engine room crew, and he dished out no punishment that was not deserved. He also took no crap from anyone, and no one gave him any.

Lieutenant Commander Chewning, our new exec, a man of average height and build who seldom smiled, epitomized the term "low key." Handling the job of executive officer was a demanding task—in some ways tougher than that of the captain—but Mr. Chewning accomplished it with an ease that made it look simple.

And then there was the captain, C. D. Summitt, the small, friendly commander that one could not help but like. But nice guys are a dime a dozen, and commanding officers are not. At sea, it is imperative that a submarine crew have complete faith in the skipper's abilities and judgment. We watched and waited.

Same work, same schedule: eight hours one day, twelve the next, and liberty every other night. Chief Spence doled out the tasks with the same type of posted list that Kennedy had. Most jobs, except the specialized ones or the particularly dangerous, could be checked off the list and done on a volunteer basis.

The upkeep proceeded smoothly, with not a single man injured during the entire month. Perhaps we should have viewed this as some sort of omen—a portent of danger in our future—but we were young and invulnerable and immune to such thoughts.

I had the rare opportunity to perform maintenance work on the emergency diesel, a large engine located in the lower level of AMR2. The diesel was seldom even started, and I had not had the chance to work on such an engine since leaving the old LST in Japan several years before. The engine was much like the ones that powered the older diesel submarines, many of which were still in service, and little did I know that this experience was a harbinger of things to come. It's just as well I didn't know.

The diesel could power the boat if need be, either on the surface or at periscope depth. A snorkel system, also akin to those on the old boats, provided air to the engine when submerged through a large mast that could be raised from the top of the sail like a periscope. When raised and opened, this snorkel mast, a pipe about three feet in diameter, dumped outside air into the main ventilation system—the same piping that pumped the air we breathed—and carried it aft to the diesel.

The snorkel mast, a piece of equipment that was virtually never raised on patrol, could also be used without the diesel running. In that configuration, it would simply bring surface air into the boat at periscope depth in case the interior atmosphere became fouled by some contaminant and needed to be purged. Since our location remained top secret at all times, this system would allow us to take on "new air" if necessary without having to surface, the new air being dumped out of spot coolers throughout the boat.

When running shallow and snorkeling, a large valve atop the snorkel mast stood open to allow air to enter the boat. For safety purposes—life and death, actually—the valve was designed to close automatically in case the boat slipped below periscope depth.

Captain Summitt would often wander back to our spaces with his coffee cup in hand, pour himself a cup from the large engine room pot, speak to each of us by name, and ask how the work was going. Sometimes the captain would have one of us explain in detail the task on which he was working—a unique style of leadership for a commanding officer.

In my experience, when the skipper set foot in the engineering spaces—or anywhere else on the boat—everyone would stand at attention until he left. Not Captain Summitt. When he stepped through the engine room hatch, someone would holler, "Attention on deck!" and everything would stop. Summitt would look around, smile, and say, "Carry on, men." Then he'd fill his coffee cup and we'd all go back to work, feeling strangely at ease in his presence.

I brought up the subject once to Lieutenant MacKinnon, the engineering officer. "I've never seen a captain act like that," I said. Mr. MacKinnon just smiled and didn't reply. I should have known better than to even mention it; whatever his thoughts concerning the captain, the engineering officer wasn't about to share them with me.

And then there was Dr. Nance—Lieutenant Nance, to be precise. We'd never seen anything close to his like. Dr. Nance was an officer, but like all navy physicians, he was not a line officer. That is, he could move up through the ranks as an MD, but not in the line of a ship's command. He didn't care; he was a reserve fulfilling his active duty time and had no aspirations for a military career. Too bad—the man was a born submariner.

When a sailor stuck his head into Dr. Nance's office, the doc's eyes would widen and bulge like a madman. He would then reach out to his patient, both hands extended like twisted claws, and utter, "Heal, heal!" No respecter of rank, he did this to everyone who visited him, from the lowest seaman to the captain. After this ghoulish greeting, the doctor would then settle down and ask what the man's medical problem might be. On one visit when we reached this point, I asked him, "Dr. Jekyll, where did Mr. Hyde go?" He reached out, grabbed my throat, and immediately brought the fiend back for my enjoyment.

As did his predecessor, Captain Summitt required his officers to be in proper uniform at all times—be it khakis or blue jump suits—complete with insignia. The officers obeyed the skipper's directive, of course, except for Dr. Nance. Nance wore a pressed khaki uniform, with insignia, right down to a pair of high-heeled cowboy boots—his khaki trousers neatly stuffed into the tops of them. The captain just shook his head and laughed.

Our good doctor could be a questionable influence on his fellow officers, especially on liberty. He and Lieutenant Commander Bonham, our weapons officer, accomplished an unheard of and quite illegal act one evening. They entered an enlisted men's club in Dunoon, something I had never known an officer to even want to do.

Hamilton officers were allowed to wear civilian clothes on liberty, while we enlisted were not. However, enlisted men from the tender *Hunley*, who were permanently stationed in Scotland, could wear civvies into the Acey-Deucey Club. When one of the *Hunley* sailors did so, he was required to sign in, spelling out his name and rank in a guestbook that rested near the front door.

The Acey-Deucey Club in Dunoon was a popular place, boasting a live band, a large dance floor, and numbers of comely Scottish girls who loved to go there and meet sailors. Dr. Nance and Lieutenant Commander Bonham, having heard how much fun we had at our club, decided to pay it a visit. This idea, which occurred to them after consuming a goodly amount of Scotch whisky, was the brainchild of Dr. Nance, I'm sure. Dressed in civvies, the two submarine officers made their way to the Acey-Deucey Club and signed themselves in, as Gary Penley and Bob Lee, first-class petty officers.

They got away with it for a while, drinking, dancing, and generally whooping it up, probably drawing more attention to themselves than they should have. Evidently, someone recognized one or both of them and tipped off the shore patrol, enlisted peacekeepers who were always on duty at the club. Discovering that two senior officers were more than a little inebriated and posing as enlisted men was a shore patrolman's worst nightmare.

The head shore patrolman, a first-class petty officer from the *Hunley,* had the career-threatening task of questioning the errant officers. Two other shore patrol stood nervously beside him during the confrontation. Lieutenant Commander Bonham immediately fessed up and, wanting to get out of there as quickly as possible, promised they would leave that minute and never return.

Dr. Nance had different thoughts.

"What the hell's going on?" the doctor protested, his slurred words loud enough to be heard all over the club. "We aren't doing anything wrong."

"I'm . . . sorry, sir," the shore patrolman said, "but officers aren't allowed in enlisted clubs."

Nance wouldn't give up. Mr. Bonham grew increasingly uneasy as the doctor continued his tirade. "Why don't you guys just get outta here and leave us alone?" he said, waving his hands in the air. "Can't you see we're having fun?"

Before the jittery shore patrol could reply, Mr. Bonham grabbed the doctor by the shirt collar and propelled him out the door, Nance cursing and dragging his feet all the way.

Such news traveled fast. By the following morning, the entire crew was aware that Dr. Nance and Lieutenant Commander Bonham had sneaked into the Acey-Deucey Club—an act for which the two free-wheeling cowboys could have been court-martialed. And everyone also knew that they had signed themselves in as Gary Penley and Bob Lee.

Sometime around mid-morning, I stepped into Dr. Nance's office. For once he did not greet me with his ghoulish impersonation. Instead, a sheepish, little-boy smile creased his guilty face.

"Boy, I thought I'd heard it all," I said.

"Aw, shucks," he said. "It weren't nuthin'. You're just trying to make me feel good, Penley."

"Nuthin'! If it was nuthin', then why did you sign my name in the guestbook?"

"Yours was the first name that came to mind. You should feel honored."

"*Honored,*" I said, shaking my head. "Thank you, sir. I can't remember ever feeling so honored."

"You're very welcome," Dr. Nance replied and laughed out loud.

There were no Guardia Seville hats for DeWayne Catron to steal, and as far as I know, he never climbed any Scottish trees. But being ever the resourceful sailor, DeWayne didn't need props to provide more than his share of entertainment during upkeep.

Catron slept in a top bunk, directly across the narrow aisle from me. This gave me a ringside seat to a show that, had I missed it, would have left my entire life incomplete.

This was the setup on that night of nights. It was around 10:00 p.m., and I lay reading in my bunk, directly across from Catron's. Catron had gone on liberty. Another fellow, a big man named Dick Reed, was also reading in his bunk, down at the bottom of the tier in which Catron slept. This placed Reed at floor level, and he happened to have his shoes sitting on the floor, right beside his head.

Enter Catron, so sloshed he could not stand without holding onto a bunk or a handrail. God only knows how he made it back to the boat, but here he was, staggering like a disjointed dummy in the aisle between Dick Reed and me. Reed and I couldn't help but laugh, and Catron began laughing with us, his eyes unfocused and a goofy smile on his face.

"How you doing, DeWayne?" I asked him.

"Good," he said, leaning directly into my face. "Reeeally good." His breath would have taken down a horse, and he managed to spit on me a bit as he spoke. I didn't ask him anything else.

DeWayne began to undress—a reeling, swaying, falling endeavor that woke up several other guys and practically had Reed and me in tears. Catron actually fell to the floor two or three times before he managed to get his clothes off, finally stuffing his dress uniform into his locker in a wad.

Now wearing only his skivvies, he tried to climb into his bunk. The bunk being head high, in DeWayne's condition this was tantamount to attempting to scale a vertical rock face barefooted. He fell a couple more times but continued a valiant struggle, finally managing to gain a purchase on the middle bunk, which was empty at the time, and heave himself up onto his own.

Reed and I, along with a half dozen other guys, were still laughing and thinking the show was finally over. Not so. Catron lay down flat on his back, turned his head sideways toward the aisle, and puked. The vomit went cascading downward but didn't make it to the floor. Instead, the stream landed in Reed's shoes—a bull's eye—and splashed widely, splattering Dick Reed, his bed, and the book he was reading.

"Son of a bitch!" Reed roared, jumping up from his bunk. At the same time, Catron rolled out of his, his body crashing to the floor one more time. DeWayne struggled to his feet and stood facing Reed, who was now in a blood rage, both of them spotted with vomit, and Catron reeling like a wino in the wind.

I, still lying in my bunk and feeling sure that a fight was about to ensue, backed as far away from the two of them as I could. DeWayne, balancing himself by holding onto his bunk and mine, looked pitifully at Reed. Reed, red-faced and boiling, stood with his jaw clenched and his fists doubled at his sides. After glaring at DeWayne for a long minute, Reed turned and stomped away, cursing loudly.

I looked at DeWayne and asked him if he thought he was through vomiting. "I . . . think so," he said. I got out of bed and, being careful where I placed my hands, helped him to the showers. While Catron and Reed washed themselves off, I went and got a mop and cleaned up the mess that my crazy friend had made. Then I helped Catron into his bunk once more, where he mercifully fell asleep.

The following morning Reed looked at DeWayne and said, "I was gonna hit you, but you just looked too nasty."

Upkeep was nearly finished, morale was soaring, and the crew more than ready to take our big boat into the deep. A week or so before departure, a first-class nuke named Wagner was told that, for medical reasons, he could not go on patrol. Although whatever he had contracted was not contagious, Dr. Nance feared that it could escalate after we went to sea and endanger Wagner's life.

Instead of going on patrol, Wagner would fly back to Charleston to his waiting wife and children. He asked to stay aboard until the day we departed, and he was granted permission. Defying the doctor's orders to take it easy, Wagner worked alongside the rest of us during that last week. I'd never seen a shipmate more depressed.

I had line-handling duty the day we backed away from the *Hunley* and headed out to sea, and so I was able to remain topside until we left the Holy Loch. I waved at Wagner, who was leaning against a rail on the tender. He looked like a little boy who had been told, at the last minute, that he couldn't go to the circus with the rest of the class.

Chapter Fifteen

The Unforgiving Sea

Out of the Holy Loch, into the Firth of Clyde, and toward the open sea. And the ever-awaiting trawlers. What a boring job those Soviet sailors must have had—like counting sheep leaving the corral for pasture and then counting them again when they returned.

Miles away, with land far behind, the double A-ooo-ga!, A-ooo-ga! of the diving alarm set up a cheer throughout the boat. The vent valves opened in the tops of the ballast tanks, air rushed out with an audible hiss, and our big iron fish nosed down, slipping into its natural habitat beneath the waves.

We headed north and east, above the Soviet Union, and into ice-cold water. We were toasty warm in our undersea world, though; a steam plant generates plenty of heat inside an airtight tube. Air conditioning remained as necessary in Arctic waters as it had been in the Mediterranean.

We quickly fell into the routine of patrol—except for those infernal drills—and happily caught up on our sleep after the long work hours during upkeep. There were few differences between patrolling in cold water versus warm, and those weren't enough to worry about.

We were told not to concern ourselves with heavy clothing in the unlikely event that we should have to abandon ship. Why? Because no matter what one was wearing, a human could survive for only about eight minutes in that water. That was not a worry, anyway—if the boat went down, we would all go with it. Submariners don't dwell on such things; we just continued to have dreams of unorthodox and unrealistic ways to escape from a sinking sub.

Lt. George Dewhirst, a tall, handsome officer whom I had known and respected for some time, had the con one night when I wandered up to control to chat with the guys on watch. I noticed Mr. Dewhirst staring intently through the periscope, and when he looked around and saw me, he invited me up onto the conning platform.

"Hey, Penley," the lieutenant said, "come and look at this."

I bounded up onto the platform, hung my arms over the steel handles of the periscope, and peered out into the Arctic night. A wondrous sight—huge, colorful, spectacular—a mental image that will remain with me as long as I live.

Great streamers of light rose from the horizon to the top of the sky—immense, some bright, some shadowy, all moving—a slow serpentine dance of ever-changing ghostly light. Both bright and dim at the same time—awesome, surreal—the Arctic sky filled with this undulating thing of ghostly colors that changed as I watched. It seemed alive, and I could not look away.

At length I turned from the periscope and looked at Mr. Dewhirst in amazement. "My God," I said, "it's the *aurora borealis.*" The northern lights, up close, through a periscope.

Dewhirst smiled. "You may never again see such a thing in your life."

"I know," I said. "Thank you, sir."

Drills. Captain Summitt had never commanded a Polaris missile submarine, and he appeared to be schooling himself as quickly as possible. He held a great number of drills—battle stations— so many that we began to grow tired of it. And the captain was growing tired of the crew, because we started to rebel: deliberately slowing down so that each time the boat manned battle stations it took longer than the previous drill had. This head butting continued: more drills from the captain, and slower reaction time from the crew.

Chief Dunn, the chief of the boat, saw what was going on.

After discussing the problem with a number of the crew, Dunn reluctantly requested a meeting with the skipper. At this meeting, Chief Dunn attempted to explain to Captain Summitt that we, the crew, thought we had done well at manning battle stations on previous patrols, that we considered ourselves quite skilled at this maneuver, and that we felt his drills were excessive and disruptive.

Chief Dunn came back with the captain's reply, which went something like this: "There is one captain on this ship, and that is me. And there is one man who will say how many drills will be held and one man who will judge when battle stations are being properly manned—the captain."

The news spread quickly through the boat, and Chief Dunn told us we'd better get ourselves in gear, because he wasn't about to face the captain with any more complaints from the crew.

The drills continued, even more often than before, and our little rebellion came to an abrupt halt. Living with our nerves on a razor's edge, when the first gong of battle stations sounded, whether awake or asleep, we could jump up, throw on our clothes in seconds, and run through the boat like banshees, diving through hatches without missing a beat. Within two days, we were manning battle stations faster than we had ever imagined possible. Captain Summitt continued the drills long enough to make sure the message stuck, then finally he slacked off. He maintained his habit of strolling through the boat and chatting with the crew, and he came back to the engine room to drink coffee with us just as before. The captain was still a nice guy, and we were probably the fastest crew that ever manned battle stations.

The Saturday-night hootenannies. What to do without Chief Padgett to organize, perform, and act as master of ceremonies? I had become so concerned about this during the off period that I decided to take over the job myself. Shouldn't be any problem, I figured. Other than the insignificant facts that I could not play a single instrument, had no singing voice, and possessed no musical talent whatsoever, I considered myself a shoe-in for the job.

Back in Charleston, I had bought a guitar, some music books that I could not read, and began to teach myself. I mastered three chords, which, much to the chagrin of my barracks mates, I practiced endlessly. I also began to memorize the lyrics to scores of country/western songs, and soon learned enough to play along, kind of, with any tune in existence. Most of the guys within earshot of my room would likely have disagreed with this conviction, but what did those barbarians know of music? I told the biggest complainers to get earplugs for themselves, and they did.

Now, on patrol—as many had feared—I proclaimed myself a musician and began to schedule hootenannies. I put up signs throughout the boat advertising the event, and coerced everyone I could into participating. A surprising number agreed to appear in the show. Even the officers put together a singing group and joined in a couple of practice sessions.

The first scheduled Saturday soon rolled around. The show was to be that evening after dinner, and I, with no public-speaking experience and no musical ability, would act as MC. I was so scared I couldn't eat.

The electricians set up microphones, speakers, and even footlights, and the mess hall was packed. Everyone except those on watch had come to see the new version of the Hamilton Hootenanny.

I walked on stage, cowboy hat on my head, guitar slung jauntily around my neck, and grabbed hold of the mic. With my heart stuck somewhere up around my throat, I leaned forward and spoke in my best Johnny Cash imitation. "Hello, I'm Gary Penley."

The crowd roared. I bowed and said, "Thank you. Thank you. Thank you." Then, as the laughter began to subside, I said, "Well, since I know you've all been waiting for this, I'm going to start out with a solo—an old Hank Williams number that I know you're going to love." I think someone might have groaned at that point, but I chose to regard it as a gesture of encouragement.

I strummed my three chords and sang like a pig with its tail caught in a fence, but it worked. By God, it worked. I received a standing ovation and laughter that would not stop, for two reasons, I believe. One, because I sounded so funny; and two, because everyone knew the Saturday night hootenannies were back.

Whitey and Skelton sang a duet that was not quite ready for prime time, the officers belted out several numbers that proved their good sportsmanship beyond a doubt, and Leroy Lavender and I put on a parody that made fun of the officers. Chief

Watson and O. D. Walker, our natural musicians from the hills of Tennessee and Kentucky, respectively, each played some real music on guitars, violins, and a mandolin. Ted Newell played a very professional solo on his steel guitar.

Dr. Nance, our wild MD, surprised us all. Walking into the mess hall carrying a classical guitar worth thousands of dollars, he sat down in front of the microphone, smiled, ran his hands over the instrument as if it were gold, and gave a performance that stunned the crew.

Wednesday afternoons were reserved for cleanup throughout the boat—the only day that everyone was awake at the same time. All hands changed the sheets and pillowcases on their bunks as soon as lunch was finished, then went to their workspaces to clean equipment, scrub dirt and grime, and polish the decks for the next several hours. This was usually a good time in the engine room, with everyone clowning and joking to make a dirty job as much fun as possible.

Hootenanny, submerged in North Atlantic, circa 1965. Left to right: two unknown officers, Gary, "Whitey" Kutzleb, Leroy Lavender, Donny Skelton, (first name unknown) Gill, unknown officer.

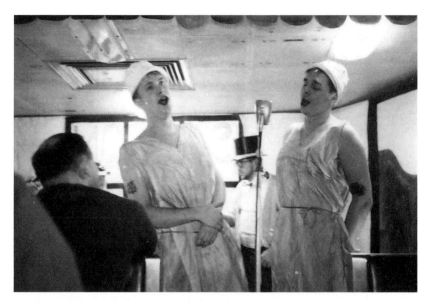

Performing in Hootenanny with Leroy Lavender while submerged on patrol in North Atlantic. USS Hamilton, circa 1965.

Whitey Kutzleb performing in Hootenanny. He is the wildest man I ever knew.

Performing with Whitey Kutzleb.

When I headed back to the engine room that day, I had no idea that a near disaster awaited me.

The dirtiest job, done only once each patrol, had been scheduled for that afternoon. Cleaning the bilges. Although nuclear-powered machinery generally ran cleaner than conventional power plants, over time the bilges still collected grease and grime. In order to clean them, a few guys—the lucky ones—worked up on the walkway, handing buckets of water, cleaning equipment, and detergents back and forth to the ones who had to crawl into the bilges and scrub them down.

We drew straws to see who got lucky and who didn't, and that day I lost. Donning dirty coveralls, rubber gloves, rubber boots, and rags tied around our heads, I and the rest of the "scrubbing slobs" dove into the bilges and began the filthy job. We had buckets of water, piles of rags, scrub brushes, hoses equipped with spray nozzles, and plastic containers of a powerful detergent designed to cut heavy grease. We mixed the strong detergent into the buckets of water, scrubbed the bilges with the toxic mixture, and then rinsed it off with a pressurized hose.

We scrubbing slobs were really getting with it—singing, splashing each other with cleaning water, and spraying one another with the hose, all the while crawling around on our bellies in the muck.

Suddenly, one of the guys up on the walkway looked down at me and said, "Penley, come up out of there. Get out of there now!"

"What's wrong?" I asked.

"Your eye—it's flaming red."

The others looked at me then, all with concern in their eyes. Rich Dominy reached down to help me out of the bilges, and Leroy Lavender hollered, "Somebody call the doctor and get him back here."

Somehow I had gotten the powerful detergent splashed into my left eye. Dr. Nance dove through the engine room hatch at a dead run, never missing a step. When he tilted back my head and looked at my eye, his expression told me it was bad.

Nance quickly read the label on one of the bottles of detergent, then said, "We've got to get you to my office, as fast as we can."

The other guys helped me strip off my coveralls, gloves, boots, and headband, and the doctor rushed me forward to his office. By now I was terrified, and even more so when I looked at my eye in his mirror. It was blood red, all of it.

Nance quickly sat me down and began to rinse my eye with several solutions. The doctor was working quickly and efficiently, and for once, he was not joking at all.

"Does your eye hurt?" he asked.

"A little," I said, "but not too much."

"Good," he said, and continued to wash it out.

He kept inquiring as to how much pain I could feel in my eye, and it never did hurt badly. At length he treated it with some sort of medication and then covered it with a thick bandage. He sat back, staring directly into my good eye, and said nothing.

I looked down at his cowboy boots, then back up into his eyes. "Okay, Doc," I said, trying to sound braver than I felt. "What's the verdict?"

He hesitated before he spoke. "I believe the detergent took the outermost protective layer off your eye. At least I hope that's what it did, and no more. If that's the case, it should heal without any damage."

"What if that's not the case?" I asked. "What if it's worse?"

"I don't think it will happen," he said, "but if you want to hear the worst case, I'll tell you."

I nodded.

"Worst case: it's possible you could lose your eye. And as you know, we still have another month and a half of patrol ahead of us. Even if you were to lose it, the captain couldn't abort the mission. We would still complete it."

He leaned forward, concern and compassion in his normally laughing eyes. "I'm not an eye specialist, Penley, but I assure you I'll do everything in my power to save that eye."

"I know you will," I said. I left his office and trudged toward my bunk, aware that everyone in sight was watching me. I was terrified.

The doctor wouldn't let me stand watches, and he told me to get all the rest I could. He checked on me often, even coming to my bunk and shaking me awake to ask if my eye was hurting. When I jokingly complained about his telling me to get plenty of rest and then waking me up to check on me, he said, "Go back to sleep, Penley. Doctor's orders. And I'll wake you up when I damn well please." We both laughed.

During meals in the mess hall, Catron, Cantley, Dominy, Lavender, Bob Lee, and other close friends would sit with me and inquire about my eye, and nearly everyone would walk by my booth and tap me on the shoulder. "How you doing, buddy? Hang in there, pal."

Even the captain and the exec asked me about my eye, and the morale on the boat took a dive. I was still scared to death, and bored. And although Dr. Nance kept my eye bandaged for more than a week, after three days I practically demanded that he let me stand watches again. He reluctantly agreed, although if he'd known how often I ran into steam pipes trying to navigate the engine room with one eye, he probably wouldn't have.

There was no hootenanny that Saturday; it was canceled without mention.

Nance changed my bandage every day or two, but he wouldn't let much light hit my eye. I could sense the light when he took the old bandage off, but he covered it up too quickly for me to really tell how well I could see. Finally, after about a week and a half, he removed the bandage, cleaned out my eye, and told me to open it wide.

I could see! No permanent damage had occurred. I thought the doctor was going to cry. Everyone on the boat was elated at the news, and morale soared as a result. Captain Summitt stopped me in a passageway and smiled. "I'm sure glad your eye is all right, Penley."

"Thank you, Captain," I said. "I'm pretty glad about it myself." We laughed.

"You ready for the next hootenanny?" Captain Summitt asked.

"You bet," I replied. "I'm more than ready."

"Good," he replied. The captain did not attend hootenannies so as not to inhibit the entertainment with his presence, but he made sure that everyone knew he supported them.

At the next hootenanny, I opened with, "Sure glad to *see* you all again," a line that brought the house down, much more than did my opening song.

This would be my last patrol on the *Hamilton*, by my own choice. I would have one year left in the navy at the end of this run, and Lieutenant Dewhirst, who was my division officer at the time, had offered me an opportunity for a new adventure in my final year. Near the end of the last off period, Mr. Dewhirst had approached me and told me that following the next patrol he was to be transferred to a fast-attack nuclear sub where he would serve as engineering officer. The lieutenant said that if I wanted to accompany him onto the fast attack, he would put in a request for my transfer as soon as he arrived on the boat.

Fast-attack submarines were just what the name implied. Smaller and faster than boomers, these boats carried no missiles, being designed specifically for torpedo attacks and covert spy missions on enemy shipping, military installations, and communications. What an adventure for my last year in the navy! After only a day or so of pondering the decision, I told Mr. Dewhirst, yes, I would love to accompany him on the attack sub.

All this wasn't as simple as it sounded. There was a strange catch to my making the decision to be transferred. If a sailor had enough boomer patrols under his belt, which I did, he could ask to be put on the drop letter, an action that would ensure his transfer off the *Hamilton* after one more patrol. The catch: once one's name went on the drop letter, it could not be removed for any reason. When I opted to have my name put on that list, I *would* be transferred, even if subsequent circumstances might make me want to change my mind.

So prior to leaving on this patrol, I had told Lieutenant Dewhirst that I would put my name on the drop letter, which I did. Exciting—another adventure in the making. And an adventure it would be, with twists and turns I could not foresee at the time.

I still dreamed of returning to the old ranch in Colorado—land which my mother still owned—but as I became more proficient at my job on the boat and continued to pass rating exams and advance in rank, thoughts of higher education began to creep into my mind. Scary thoughts, because no one in my family had ever attended college. Neither of my parents nor the grandfather who raised me had even finished high school.

For a time, I tried to bury the thoughts of college, to tuck them away in a place where they wouldn't bother me. It didn't work; they kept sneaking back and tapping me on the shoulder. I guess I must have let them slip out, because several officers, all of whom had engineering degrees, began to encourage me in that direction. During one of these discussions with Lieutenant MacKinnon, our popular engineering officer, he asked me something I would never forget.

I was lamenting my age to Mr. MacKinnon. "Why, if I were to go to college after I get out of the navy, I'd be over thirty years old when I graduate."

MacKinnon smiled. "How old will you be if you don't go to college?" The question floored me, and would return to me often in years to come.

The amiable Captain Summitt demonstrated a different style of leadership to be sure, and one that few ship's commanders could have pulled off. And there in the icy waters of that wild north sea, we learned how stubborn the man could be.

North of Russia, where the eastern reaches of the Atlantic, the Barents Sea, and the Arctic Ocean all run together into one frigid expanse, Mother Nature can unleash storms that make the gods tremble. And sailors too.

We encountered a savage storm that forced us to take the boat considerably deeper than normal to escape the effects of surface turbulence. Down below, somewhere around five hundred feet, we found the water reasonably calm. Surface detection sonar told us what was going on up above, so we knew the magnitude of the storm raging on the surface, and we felt quite smug lurking down there in the quiet depths. The perfect place to ride out the storm, if we had stayed there.

Captain Summitt, however, had his own ideas about where we should be.

At regular intervals the skipper took precise navigational fixes in order to calibrate various equipment—a procedure that required bringing the boat to periscope depth and stabilizing it for a short time. Heedless of the storm, the captain decided to go up and get his navigational fix. He took over the con himself.

The mess cooks were setting the tables in preparation for the upcoming meal when we started angling toward the surface. I was on watch in the engine room, and surprised when the boat nosed upward. The turbulence began to rock us a bit, and then all hell broke loose.

The boat rolled heavily to port, bucked and jumped like a bobbing ball, then heaved over to starboard. The mess hall became an instant wreck—dishes, cups, saucers, and silverware all dumped off the tables onto the deck, sliding from one side of the compartment to the other in a shattered mess.

Back in the engine room, I hollered, "What's going on?" and ran to maneuvering. Lieutenant Reed, the EOOW, was on his feet, clinging to pipes with both hands to maintain his balance. Reed looked at me and sighed. "I think the captain is trying to get a navigational fix."

"Oh, wonderful," I said, and headed for the middle of the engine room where I could get my hands on a safety rail. In covering the few feet and climbing a couple of steps to get to the handrail, I was thrown from side to side and up and down, bouncing off the deck and collecting a few bruises along the way.

I hollered down a voice tube to Rich Dominy, the lower-level watch, "Hang on. The old man's trying to get a navigational fix."

"Oh, no," was all the reply I heard.

I could hear the roar of the Arctic storm through our thick hull and feel the powerful waves slamming the sides like a sledgehammer. The big sub heaved and bucked like a wild bull, the crashing sea tossing it about like a raft in a hurricane. One moment we were thrust to the surface, and the next moment the storm threw us down, a hundred feet deep. Then back to the surface, then back down.

I clung so tightly to the handrail that my hands ached. Swinging in a wobbly arc like a broken pendulum, I slammed against the steel rail with first one side and then the other, gaining bruises on my legs, hips, arms, and a couple of knots on my head.

Up front, guys sleeping were rudely woken, some thrown out of their bunks. After insightful exclamations such as, "What the hell!" all agreed that the turbulence seemed excessive.

The crazy ride went on for about ten minutes, though it felt like ten hours. Finally, the captain took the boat back down to five hundred feet. He had not gotten his navigational fix. I let go of the handrail and walked to maneuvering, rubbing my sore arms and sides. Mr. Reed was still standing, and laughing at the whole affair.

"That was a lot of fun," I said.

"Sure was," Reed replied, then he looked at my arms. "Did you get hurt?"

"No," I lied.

He didn't believe me, so I came clean. "Actually, I've lost fights and come out in better shape."

We laughed.

Since every man in the boat was awake, and the mess hall not yet in shape to serve a meal, everyone who worked back aft started gathering in the engine room, laughing and discussing what had happened to them during the wild ride.

Unbeknown to most of the crew, the captain had ordered the cooks not to set up the mess hall again. About fifteen minutes after he took the boat back to the deep, his voice came over the speaker in maneuvering, a determined edge in every word he spoke.

"This is the captain. We did not get our navigational fix on the first attempt. We've spent some time studying the prevailing direction of the storm and adjusted the boat's heading accordingly. We are going back up, to obtain a navigational fix."

Mr. Reed rolled his eyes, then reached up and grabbed hold of the overhead pipes. The three guys at the control panels in maneuvering jumped up and stood behind their chairs, which were fastened tightly to the deck, and hugged the backs of them for support. I stepped out into the engine room and hollered, "Y'all better grab hold and hang onto this buckin' bronco. The old man's gonna take 'er back up."

Somebody groaned, "We're going up there again?"

"Yep, that's what the man said, and he's the driver."

Once more, the boat turned its nose up toward the storm, and every man in the engine room found a handrail and gripped it like a pipe wrench. One did not dare sit down, lest the thrashing boat crack your tailbone or break your back.

With all due respect to Captain Summitt's calculations, our new heading felt no better than the first one. The storm grabbed the boat and slung it like a cork in a raging river. Plunging, bucking, rolling, we heaved far over from one side to the other, nosed down, nosed up, dove uncontrollably to one hundred feet, then whipped back to the surface like a porpoise at play—again and again and again.

There were a lot of guys in the engine room for this ride, hanging tightly to every handhold available. There are many words to describe our situation; ridiculous is the one that comes to mind. Ridiculous is the way we all tended to see it, and the way we played it out.

We began to holler.

"Yahoo!"

"Ride 'em, cowboy!"

"Stay with him, boys!"

Even stoic Bob Lee was laughing. Some guys let go with one hand, whipped off their caps, and began to swing them wildly as they yelled like rodeo riders. Having grown up on a ranch, I'd been bucked off horses many times, but these guys seemed to be doing well, riding this big iron bronc.

Lieutenant MacKinnon, the engineering officer, had come

back to maneuvering before the second ride started. Now he too was holding on and being tossed around like a ragdoll. I could hear him laughing loudly and hollering "Yahoo!" along with the rest of us.

This time the skipper fought to stabilize the boat at periscope depth for fifteen long minutes, a valiant stand, but the raging storm would not be conquered. At long last, we felt her heading for the deep, and the quiet that awaited us there.

Again the captain's voice sounded over speakers throughout the boat—disappointed, and more than a little ticked. "Once more we did not get our navigational fix; the storm wouldn't allow it. All hands stand down. We won't be trying it again today."

A cheer went up throughout the boat. "Yaaay!" I don't think the captain joined in.

I stuck my head into maneuvering and found Mr. Reed and Mr. MacKinnon still laughing. "Did you get hurt that time, Penley?" Reed asked.

"I don't think so, sir. You can't bruise a bruise."

The big storm passed, or we passed it, and the cold sea calmed around us. Rising to periscope depth was no problem, and Captain Summitt got his regular navigational fixes. He seemed content when he joined us in the engine room to help drink our coffee.

After filling his cup, the captain grinned and asked, "How'd you guys like that ride I gave you the other day during the storm?"

"Oh, we loved it, Captain. Just loved it."

Summitt laughed, not believing us for a second. The skipper had gained our respect and our friendship as well. He had that wild something in him that all submariners must possess, and now we knew it.

One would think that, after having tossed us about like a giant's play toy, the sea would have had enough fun with us for one patrol. Not so.

Leroy Lavender was a chief now, and I was a first-class.

Nothing had changed between us, though; we still worked jobs together, bitched at one another, and laughed it off as soon as we said it.

During a routine test of the emergency air conditioning system, a main bearing inside one of the units failed. As a result, the main shaft was scored, rendering the unit inoperable. Air conditioning being an absolute must inside a nuclear sub, the machine had to be repaired. Lavender and I volunteered for the task, or maybe Leroy volunteered both of us.

It was an unusual job, made even more interesting because we didn't have all the parts we needed. The ruined bearing was easily replaced from our spare parts locker, but we carried no replacement for the main shaft, which had been deeply gouged in several places. Leroy and I disassembled the unit, studied the damaged shaft, and then studied each other, each knowing that the phrase "It can't be done" was never uttered on a submarine. We would have to improvise.

The scored shaft, being somewhere between two and three feet in length and approximately two inches in diameter, would fit in our machine lathe. Both Leroy and I had taken short courses in welding and in operating the lathe, but neither of us had ever taken on a job that required such precision fitting. When we pointed this out to Chief Spence, he acknowledged our concerns, then replied, "Nobody on board has experience at anything like this, so it's up to you guys to do it." End of discussion.

I was a better welder than Leroy and he was better at running the lathe, so we divided up the work accordingly. My job consisted of filling the gouges with welding material. This resulted in a shaft with irregular bulges where the gouges had been—bulges made of different material than the shaft itself. Leroy then had to fasten the piece into the lathe and machine the bulges down to the exact diameter as the rest of the shaft—a more difficult and nerve-racking job than the welding had been.

Each of us stood over the other as we worked—operating on the theory that two heads were better than one—until the job was done. Then, saying a silent prayer with every move we made, we reassembled the unit. We started it up, and to our great relief the machine worked perfectly. With its jury-rigged, rebuilt shaft, we couldn't have described it as "good as new," but it would do in an emergency, which had been our goal.

Chief Spence was pleased, and maybe a little surprised, when he saw how well the repaired air-conditioning unit ran. After demonstrating it for the chief, we shut the machine down and left it in standby mode, its normal status. Leroy and I went forward to get some sleep before our next watch.

I got only a couple hours of sleep before my watch section was called. Lavender, being in the section that followed mine, blissfully slept on.

While eating dinner in the mess hall, just before going on watch, I learned that we were running at periscope depth and snorkeling, though the diesel was not running. While Leroy and I were repairing the air-conditioning unit, it had been necessary to release a small amount of refrigerant, Freon, into the boat's atmosphere—a rather insignificant event in our minds, but something that had to be reported to the captain.

Captain Summitt had decided to raise the snorkel mast and, using the main circulation system, purge the Freon from the boat's atmosphere. Guys in the mess hall were making jokes about the skipper taking on a supply of "new air."

Back in the engine room, I took over the watch as engine room supervisor. Lieutenant Reed, a smart young officer whom I considered a friend as well as my boss, took over as engineering officer of the watch (EOOW).

Nothing much was happening: just steaming slowly at periscope depth and snorkeling. I stuck my head into maneuvering and joked with Mr. Reed, "Still taking on new air, huh?" He nodded and smiled.

An hour or so later the entire boat was relaxed. Dinner was finished up forward and a movie showing in the mess hall. So many guys had opted to watch the movie that several were sitting in the aisle between the booths, their butts resting flat on the deck.

The engine room watch was boring, so I spent much of the time standing in the doorway to maneuvering chatting with Mr. Reed and the three other guys seated at the control panels.

A garbled voice came over the intercom—something that I didn't catch. Mr. Reed jumped to his feet, his eyes bulging. "Oh, no!"

"What's wrong?" I asked.

"Stand by for collision!" Reed said.

"*Collision?*" I hollered.

"That's right," Reed said, and then I heard the high-pitched Whoop! Whoop! Whoop! of the collision alarm wailing throughout the boat.

I ran out into the engine room and yelled, "Stand by for collision!" wondering how in hell we had gotten close enough to another vessel to be in danger of collision.

The boat took a sharp down angle, which made sense. We were trying to dive under the other ship, I surmised. I ran through the engine room, shifting pumps to high speed, knowing that we might need full power for whatever maneuver the captain had in mind. And flashing through my mind was the knowledge that colliding with another vessel was one of the worst things that could befall a submarine.

Then the boat turned it nose upward—sharply upward. *What are we trying to do, ram the other ship?* I asked myself as I raced for maneuvering. Then I realized that, although we had assumed a steep up angle, the boat continued to slide downward. Then the boat abruptly tilted and we nosed down again, hard, sinking fast. The captain gave maneuvering an all back emergency order—an attempt to slow our descent. The propulsion panel operator whirled the steam controls like a madman, reversing the screaming turbines and the big screw that drove us, praying that it would pull us out of the uncontrolled dive.

"What's going on?" I yelled at Mr. Reed.

He yelled back, "We're not colliding, we're flooding!"

Flooding. For a quick moment, a strange sensation—relief. Flooding was not as bad as collision. My feeling of relief didn't last a second. Seawater poured into the engine room—tons of it. Water from above—a deluge—drowning the men and every piece of equipment in sight.

"Water pouring out of the spot coolers!" I yelled. "Ventilation piping running full!"

"Close and dog the engine room door," Reed ordered.

The entire ventilation system was flooded, water pouring from every duct into every compartment on the boat.

Up forward, the men sitting on the deck watching the movie were suddenly waist deep, the flood covering them before they could even jump to their feet. Rich Dominy swung out of his rack, his feet landing in six inches of icy water. The stairwell leading from the mess hall down into the berthing area looked like Niagara Falls.

One man in the mess hall went berserk. Overcome by panic, he screamed, "This is it! We're going to die! We're all going to die!" He had to be subdued, held down, and sedated.

Men grabbed wool blankets off bunks, more than fifty of them, to plug the floor-level hatch leading down into the battery compartment. If seawater encounters the battery, chlorine gas forms, quickly killing everyone in the boat.

Unknown to us back aft, the leak was somewhere amidships, and it was huge. The guys up forward were fighting to close an emergency valve that would stop the flood, but the drenched men couldn't overcome the pressure of the sea, pressure that increased with every foot we sank. The water poured in, and the valve would not move.

I slogged through the engine room, both levels, running in water ankle deep on the walkways, and reported to Mr. Reed: "No leaks in the hull, sir. Spot coolers still running full." He nodded gravely.

We continued to sink and to wonder what in hell was going on up forward.

Deep now—close to seven hundred feet. Then faintly, we heard something—above the screaming turbines and the roar of the incoming water, air, entering the ballast tanks. The high-pressure air fought to push its way into the tops of the tanks, working hard to force the compressed seawater out the open ports in the bottom.

The boat slowed its dive, then stopped, struggling against the weight of the flooding water that had pulled us down—water that still poured in, making us heavier by the second.

Then the big sub shuddered, and the high-pressure air won the battle. The ballast tanks began to blow, and with that wonderful whoosh, the *Hamilton* headed for the surface. Slowly at first, then picking up speed as the tanks emptied and the pressure subsided around us.

We hit the surface, and my knees nearly buckled.

An all-stop order. The turbines whined to a halt, and the flooding water stopped.

The *Hamilton* lay low in the sea, heavy with the water inside.

The gong sounded for general quarters. Everyone rushed to their stations, sealed the compartments, and waited. Our flooded sub rolled gently on the surface.

Within minutes, a voice came over the intercom. That wonderful Tennessee drawl, as calm as could be. "This is the captain. The leak is stopped and sealed. The snorkel valve stuck open and would not shut, and that's where all the water came in. The valve is now closed and the snorkel mast has been lowered, so we have no more problem with flooding.

"Our problems are not over yet, though. It appears that we took on about thirty-five tons of water, and since our location is top secret, we have to dive again, immediately. With the flood water inside the boat, we'll be thirty-five tons heavy when we dive. I have a plan that I feel confident will allow us to accomplish this safely, and I have confidence in all of you to carry it out. Prepare to dive."

"Jesus Christ!" I heard somebody mutter.

I looked into maneuvering and caught Mr. Reed's eyes. "The fun never stops," I said. He gave a nervous chuckle, then shook his head and laughed.

The captain initiated his plan before we dove. Maneuvering received an order to proceed forward at one-third speed. When we had stabilized at one-third, a second order told us to accelerate to flank. Soon we were churning at top speed, on the surface.

The diving alarm sounded. A-ooo-ga! A-ooo-ga! "Dive, Dive." And hurtling as fast as the boat would go, we dove. Being thirty-five tons heavy, the boat tried to drop like a rock. But flank speed made the diving planes more reactive than normal. The captain ordered the diving officer to turn the planes upward, as if attempting to surface. Flying through the sea at greater than twenty knots, the upward tilt of the diving planes counterbalanced the weight of the water inside the boat—the planes alone preventing our sinking.

Bob Lee was at the drain pump, doing his usual masterful job of operating the complex manifold that enabled him to empty out every compartment on the boat. It took about thirty minutes to pump all that seawater back out where it belonged. Then the captain slowed the boat and once again spoke to us all.

"We did it, or rather, you did it. The water is out, the boat is sealed, and we have resumed patrol. Congratulations; I commend you all."

A great cheer resounded through the boat. Laughing, joking, and backslapping that I thought would never stop. We had done it. We had flooded and fought back the sea and lived to tell the tale.

Most of the blankets on board had gotten soaked with salt water after being packed around the battery hatch. They had to be rinsed out with fresh water and then hung up to dry, all over the engine room. We started calling the engine room the ship's laundry, and the humidity that hung in the compartment for days while the blankets dried made it feel more like a laundry than an engineering space.

Everyone on board had his own story of where he had been when the water came in, and what had happened to him in the minutes following. Most of the stories were told with the teller laughing at the situation and at his own desperate reactions.

Wild Joe Birkle, the tattooed torpedoman, had qualified as diving officer just before the flood. He was standing his first watch when the water began pouring on his head and on the planesmen seated in front of him. Joe didn't flinch. He and Captain Summitt saved the boat, and our lives. It was hilarious just to listen to Wild Joe tell the story.

Rich Dominy, a master of understatement, shared some vital knowledge with me. "I think I've figured out the key to submarining," Rich said.

"Oh, what's that?" I asked.

"The water should always be on the outside of the boat, never on the inside."

One man's story was not funny—the one who had panicked in the mess hall and had to be subdued. Such behavior is abhorrent on a submarine and not to be tolerated. The man had lost control under pressure and could not be trusted to give his all to save the boat and the lives of his shipmates.

Submerged on USS Alexander Hamilton, *my final patrol on the boat.*

We had a month left to go on the patrol, and the man was ostracized for the entire time. He was relieved of all duties and, except for a few guys who had worked directly with him, no one would speak to him or sit in the same booth with him in the mess hall. He never watched movies nor showed himself in the crew's lounge, and when the patrol ended, he was escorted off the boat and thrown out of the submarine service. I'm sure he didn't mind that.

As for me, after surviving the flooding, I felt certain I had endured the most frightening event I would ever experience. How could I have been wrong about that?

The end was in sight—two weeks to go before we would surface, inhale the smell of sweet land, and set foot on terra firma. Once more morale began to soar with thoughts of docking in Scotland and returning to Charleston. I felt the same familiar anticipation, but this time a degree of melancholy tempered my mood. It was my last patrol on the *Hamilton*. She had been my home for years—my home and my weapon—my reason for living. But she was more than a home, she was a close friend and a mighty warrior with whom I had shared many battles, and I would never set foot on her again.

I wandered through the boat, taking in every valve, every pipe, every switch, every familiar thing in sight—which amounted to every square inch of her, of course. I sat in places I normally hadn't inhabited often—the radio room, the torpedo room, the missile fire control station—and traded sea stories with the guys on watch. I slept little, preferring to savor my last days and hours with my shipmates and my boat.

I had requested and received permission to ride into port on the bridge, the command station high at the top of the sail. There I accompanied Captain Summitt, Lieutenant MacKinnon, and the two enlisted men who were assigned as lookouts—sharp-eyed seamen who visually scouted the seas for signs of enemies on the surface or submerged—a critical watch station that had existed since the first submarines went to war.

I climbed the ladder inside the sail as soon as we surfaced, far out at sea, and stood on the bridge behind the skipper and Mr. MacKinnon all the way into the Holy Loch.

My high ride on the surface turned out to be a lot of fun. It was a chilly day but not foggy, and Mr. MacKinnon was wearing, of all things, a Russian-type fur hat. On the front flap, which turned straight up over his forehead, MacKinnon had attached a bright red star, making it look exactly like a Russian hat, Soviet insignia and all.

In the distance, we spotted the waiting Russian trawlers, a large group of them, sitting still in the water and spread out so as to force us to steam through the middle. Captain Summitt headed for the center of the pack where a narrow corridor could be seen that would allow our passage. As our approach brought us within approximately a quarter mile of the long line of trawlers, one of them pulled directly in front of us and stopped.

The captain smiled wryly, then ordered the boat to flank speed. Our big propeller kicked up a wake as we accelerated, churning directly toward the trawler at twenty knots. We closed fast with the smaller craft, now sitting dead in the water with the *Hamilton* speeding toward it like a giant torpedo aimed for its center. This ride atop the sail was getting exciting.

As we neared the trawler, we could see Russian sailors leaning over the rail, their faces filled with more than a little concern as we bore down on them like a Melvillian nightmare—a giant sperm whale churning toward a rowboat filled with terrified men. The skipper gave a command for left rudder, turned to miss the trawler, then straightened out the boat and sped past them.

The Russians were running up and down the decks of the trawler, looking through binoculars and snapping pictures as fast as they could point their cameras. Captain Summitt posed for them, flashing a toothy grin in their direction and holding it for the Soviet cameramen. Lieutenant MacKinnon stood board straight beside the skipper, his silly Russian hat with the red star perched atop his head, his eyes grim.

I had to laugh. "They're going to think they've got a spy among us, Mr. MacKinnon."

MacKinnon grinned. "That's what I'm hoping for." Then we all laughed, the captain too.

As we raced past the Russians, maybe fifty yards away, I held my right hand up high and gave them the finger. What a moment: the Cold War raging and I got to give the Soviet Union the bird, up close and personal.

A few short days while we turned the *Hamilton* over to the Gold Crew, a couple more nights of liberty in scenic Scotland, and then it was time to leave. I ran my hand over her hard iron sail as I walked across the deck and headed for the gangway, and from the plane, I gave the big boat a fond salute as she faded from view

Part Three

Snafu

Diesel boat, much like the Thornback *and* Amberjack.

Chapter Sixteen

The Best Laid Plans

Back to Charleston, three or four days of raising hell, and home to Colorado. As always, I visited most of Mom's lady friends—the ones I couldn't escape—and then drove out to spend time alone at the old ranch. I wasn't so sure now that I would return and start it up again after my discharge, but Mom was holding onto the land anyway—just for me, I believe.

I had planned to stay in Colorado for two weeks, but after only a few days, I began to feel strangely distracted, preoccupied. The anticipation of being transferred to a new submarine dominated my thoughts. *What would it be like living on a fast-attack nuclear sub? How much smaller than the* Hamilton *would it be? Would the attitude of the crew be different, and that of the officers, and the captain? How fast would the boat go? How deep would she dive? What kinds of clandestine operations would I find myself involved in?*

I left Colorado and flew back to South Carolina several days before I had planned to. In Charleston, I made the requisite visits to the Strip—watching fights at the Five-and-a-Quarter and downing gourmet meals at Mom Rhino's—but all the while anticipating transfer orders to the fast attack on which Lieutenant Dewhirst was now serving as engineering officer.

The transfer orders never came. Instead, I received a phone call from Mr. Dewhirst. The moment I heard his voice, I knew something was wrong.

The lieutenant began with a sincere apology, then went on to explain a problem that had arisen concerning my transfer.

Because I had only one year left in the navy, the executive officer of Mr. Dewhirst's sub refused to accept me into his crew, unless I would agree to extend my enlistment another two years.

The lieutenant explained the reason for his exec's position: I would have to renew my qualifications on the boat, which would take a few months, and by that time I'd be too near my discharge to warrant the time taken to requalify.

"You've got to be kidding," I said, choking on the unexpected news.

Lieutenant Dewhirst assured me it was no joke. "Are you interested in extending your enlistment for two more years, Penley?"

"I'm . . . not sure," I said. "Can you give me some time to think it over before I decide?"

"Yes," Dewhirst said, "but not very long, I'm afraid. I need your decision within two days. I'm sorry to rush you, Penley, but if you decide not to extend I'll have to hurry and get another engineman, because we'll be going to sea shortly."

Two days, in which to make a life decision. It wasn't just a matter of two more years, it was a major career choice. I'd been in the navy six years, had one more to go for a total of seven, and I was twenty-five. Two more years would make a total enlistment of nine, almost halfway through to the twenty it took to retire with a lifelong pension. And, if I extended I'd be eligible to take the chief's test in one more year. I felt I could pass the test and make chief petty officer, which would only provide one more temptation to stay in for twenty.

I liked the navy—in many ways I loved it—but I had never planned to make the military a career. I wanted more education, or to become a rancher, or something. I wasn't sure what.

Was there any way I could get my name off that damnable drop letter and remain aboard the *Hamilton* for another year? I talked with Mr. Reed, Mr. MacKinnon, and even Captain Summitt. They were all sympathetic to my situation, but there was nothing they could do. The drop letter was cast in stone, irreversible, and unless I agreed to extend my enlistment, I could not be assigned to any nuclear sub in the navy.

I did the only logical thing: I went to the Strip and stayed most of one day and all that night in the Five-and-a-Quarter. Whitey kept me company.

Whitey listened closely as I outlined both sides of my dilemma, then he provided a stunningly brilliant summation. "Well hell, Penley, you gotta either stay in or get out. What so complicated about that?"

Amazing. How often does one find a friend who can share such insight? I bought him another beer.

I finally ended up back where I'd started; since I had never planned to make a career of the navy, I'd have to take my chances on where I spent my final year. I called Lieutenant Dewhirst and told him my decision. He wished me luck.

More waiting, this time with an open-ended outcome. Would I end up on a destroyer, a heavy cruiser, an aircraft carrier, or another shore base in some God-forsaken place?

I didn't have to wait long for the orders. The navy made my transfer easy on itself, and seemingly easy for me. My new command was literally within walking distance of the *Hamilton* barracks.

A small squadron of diesel-powered submarines remained at the Charleston Naval Base. These older boats, tied up to a pier along with the sub tender that serviced them, were still in commission and still operative. I received orders to one of them—the USS *Thornback* (SS 418)—a sub of WWII vintage that had served its country both in peacetime and war for more than twenty years.

I emptied out my locker in the *Hamilton* barracks, loaded my belongings into my car, and drove to my new duty station—a three-minute ride. The long pier jutted far out into the bay, and out near the end I could see the big tender tied up on the left and a number of diesel subs tied directly across from it. I couldn't read the numbers on the sails from where I stood, but I knew that the *Thornback* lay among them.

Crouched low in the water, the dark boats comprised a fierce pack of warriors, their ominous hulls reminiscent of battle photos from WWII, when these savage machines had become the scourge of the Axis powers, fearlessly holding the enemy at bay during the early days of the fight while the United States readied itself for all-out war. And throughout the big war these seagoing predators had torpedoed hundreds of ships, sending untold tons of enemy shipping to the bottom of the world's oceans.

I was aware of all this impressive history as I walked down the pier in dress uniform, but as I neared the squadron of diesel subs one thought dominated my mind: *They sure look small.*

Through the submarine grapevine I had already contacted some *Thornback* crew members and learned that she was considered a good boat—a good crew and a good command— and so I had determined myself to make the best of the snafu that had brought me here.

Unbeknown to me at the time, of course, this particular snafu would build and build upon itself for the entire year I had left in the navy. And had I known where it would ultimately lead, I would undoubtedly have turned and raced back down the pier, never to set foot on a submarine again.

I located the *Thornback*, tied up among the pack of iron wolves, and looked her over closely. I had seen a number of diesel subs, of course, even been to sea on them in sub school years ago, but I had never contemplated living aboard one.

The *Hamilton* had been 425 feet long and displaced more than 8,000 tons submerged. The *Thornback* was much shorter—312 feet—with a submerged displacement of a scant 2,400 tons. At that moment, I was wishing I hadn't memorized those statistics; the comparison did not comfort me.

The primary difference in the outward appearance— besides being much smaller than a nuclear sub—was the shape of its bow. Whereas the bow of a nuclear boat resembled the tapered end of a cigar and lay underwater even on the surface, the bow of the *Thornback* knifed up out of the water like a razor's edge, the sharp blade rounding at the top and streaming aft to merge with the deck, enabling the boat to slice through the water when running on the surface. Why this difference? Unlike nuclear boats, which were designed to remain underwater indefinitely and could actually run faster when submerged than on the surface, diesel boats could stay down only for a limited amount of time—a few hours, or a couple of days at the most—and they could run much faster on the surface than down below.

The boat may have been outdated compared to the nuclear sub I had ridden for the last three and a half years, but she still looked formidable, threatening, a silent viper coiled to strike. Standing there on the pier gazing at her dark outline, I had to laugh at myself for rehashing a conclusion I had come to years before: all submarines look mean.

The exterior of the boat may have appeared sleek and deadly, but the inside just looked tight. Whereas the greatest interior diameter of the *Hamilton* had been thirty-two feet, the widest spot in the *Thornback* measured a narrow fourteen feet. And within that fourteen feet, which spanned the forward engine room, rested two giant diesels separated by a walkway some three to four feet wide.

A tight, narrow tube jammed full of piping, engines, torpedoes, and a jungle of other equipment. And within this maze—much of which appeared too tight for a small ape to clamber through—a crew of eighty men worked, ate, and slept.

I found an open hatch somewhere near amidships and climbed down the ladder, stepping onto the deck in the after part of the mess hall—a cramped space with narrow tables and narrow benches to match. From there I walked forward, passed through an oval hatch that made me glad I was thin in those days, and stepped into officers' country. There I found the tiny ship's office and handed my transfer orders to a first-class yeoman, a tall, slim, irreverent clerk who introduced himself as Rotten Roan. I started to ask him how he had gained such a nickname, but then decided maybe I didn't really want to know.

Rotten Roan introduced me to Capt. Douglas Williams and the exec, both self-assured, competent submariners. He also introduced me to the engineering officer, Mr. Leischer, a stumbling lieutenant who was known as "Crash" among the crew for continually banging his head on nearly every piece of equipment in the boat. The enginemen had awarded Lieutenant Leischer his own cranial protection, a steel hard hat labeled "Crash" that hung in the forward engine room. The engineer turned out to be a likeable fellow and a lot of fun to watch.

Then came the chief of the boat, a stout, laughing man whose only known name was Wabbit. The chief, whose protruding belly made him all the more humorous, had been a submariner for more than twenty years. He had gained the name Wabbit early on because of a speech impediment that rendered him unable to say the word "rabbit"—that and many other words he could not pronounce correctly. Wabbit was known throughout the submarine service, and he liked his name—thought it was funny. Living proof that it takes all kinds.

After getting those introductions under my belt, I went to the farthest point forward and started a self-guided tour through the boat. There were two torpedo rooms, one forward and one aft, which enabled the *Thornback* to fire its lethal fish from either end. Virtually all diesel boats were designed this way.

The forward torpedo room, where I began my solitary tour, was rounded on the sides due to the shape of the pressure hull, the small compartment narrowing toward the front like a cone, the room terminating in six torpedo tubes that protruded from outside the hull—two stacks of three tubes, each one over two feet in diameter and mounted side by side. A myriad of levers, valves, wheels, and pressure gauges filled the space around them. I grinned to myself, envisioning sweating men firing these very tubes at a ruthless enemy during the big war.

Besides the tubes all being loaded with torpedoes, an additional supply filled the room. The big fish, twenty-one feet long and nearly two feet in diameter, were strapped in place throughout the compartment—side by side, end to end, and stacked atop one another, each one resting on rails that could be slid from side to side in order to line it up with a tube for reloading in battle. And nestled among the tightly packed fish were bunks where men slept. The bunks rested anywhere from deck level to high above the torpedoes, the heads and feet of the men who slept in these hanging beds practically touching the top of the pressure hull.

Next aft came the forward battery, named for the giant battery that lay under the deck in the bottom of the compartment. Because diesel boats were propelled by batteries when submerged, they had two: one in the forward battery compartment and one in the after battery.

The forward battery housed the officer's quarters, the chief's quarters, and the wardroom where the officers ate, relaxed, and conferred. The officers slept in small stacked bunks, the only person on board with his own room being the captain. The skipper's closet-sized stateroom held a single bunk, a locker, a small fold-down sink, and a depth gauge. There was not room for more than one man to stand in the skipper's personal space, but it did offer him a bit of privacy, a nonexistent commodity for everyone else on the boat.

Then came the after battery, the largest compartment. It housed the control room in the forward one-third, the mess hall and galley in the middle, and the main crew's berthing area in the after one-third. The mess hall, although only about a fourth the size of the one on the *Hamilton*, along with the smallest galley imaginable, turned out meals that rivaled the finest restaurants.

The crew's berthing held several rows of bunks stacked three and four deep, some so tight that one could not turn over in them. This necessitated making the choice of sleeping on your back or your stomach before climbing into bed. The lowest-rated men slept in those.

The control room contained the diving officer's station, the diving plane controls, the ballast control panel, radar, sonar, the radio room, and much more. Directly above control, in the bottom of the sail, sat the conning tower, the only compartment located above all the rest. From here, the captain or the conning officer drove the boat. A soup-can-shaped compartment, convex at each end, the conning tower was about eighteen feet long by eight feet wide, a claustrophobic space that housed the periscopes and torpedo aiming and firing equipment. No less than a dozen men manned the conning tower at battle stations. Each had his own job, his own space, and no one ever got in another's way.

Continuing aft, I passed through the forward engine room and the after engine room, the spaces where I would work. The forward engine room held two diesels and a maze of piping that practically filled the compartment. The after engine room held one diesel and countless other equipment. Besides the diesels that powered the boat and all of their associated piping, the engine rooms housed electrical generators, air-conditioning units, water-distilling units, lube oil purifiers, diesel purifiers, air compressors, tool storage bins, and small workbenches. Some of this equipment was down below the main walkway, in a space where one had to bend over to creep through.

The diesels could power the boat on the surface or when snorkeling at periscope depth—a snorkel system nearly identical to that on nuclear boats. The engines also recharged the batteries after they had been depleted from running submerged.

The smell of diesel fuel overwhelmed the engine rooms, but in reality, the odor was not much stronger than in the rest of the boat. Every compartment smelled like diesel, and like the rest of the crew, I would soon grow used to the odor and learn to disregard it.

Near the aft end of the boat, directly behind the after engine room, was maneuvering, a compartment that housed the large electrical components that controlled the boat's diesel-generator plant. Here, two electricians took orders from the con and controlled the speed and direction of the twin screws that propelled us.

The after torpedo room was practically a mirror image of its forward counterpart, complete with a large supply of torpedoes and bunks nestled among them and above them. The only difference: there were four torpedo tubes instead of six.

I chose a bunk in the after torpedo room, up high on the port side. Resting between a torpedo on the bottom and the pressure hull directly above, the left side of the bunk was fastened to the hull with steel clamps, the right side being suspended from vertical chains. Climbing up there to check out the bed, I found that I had room to turn over comfortably and, because it was above head high, a modicum of privacy, or at least the illusion of it.

The overhead lights were normally left off in the after torpedo room, and there was no pass-through traffic, providing a comfortable atmosphere for sleeping. A torpedoman was always on watch in the compartment, but he generally had nothing to do except ensure that the torpedoes remained securely fastened in their moorings. The torpedoman spent most of his time sitting at the aft end by the tubes, silently reading a book by the dim glow of a flashlight. A boring watch.

On diesel boats, the engine room gang had no electronics

technicians or electricians; all were either enginemen or machinist mates. Both were mechanical rates who did the same job on submarines, and the two in charge of the engine rooms were good guys—good enough to save my butt when they didn't have to.

Gary Reynolds ran the forward engine room and Jim Barnes the aft. Both were first-class petty officers. Reynolds and Barnes answered to Dick Green, the top dog chief engine man. As was common on submarines, especially diesels, all three had acquired nicknames.

For obvious reasons, Jim Barnes was known as Barney. And since Gary Reynolds hailed from Arkansas, and looked and sounded the part, he had become Arky. Green was known simply as Chief Dick.

Arky was a career submariner—a thin, wiry guy with a raw-boned face and a sense of humor that made his entire world a fun place to live in. Barney was a young fellow—blond, round-faced, a bit fleshy, and one smart mechanic.

Barney and Arky had several underlings—most of whom were junior petty officers—working for them in each engine room. I was put to work in the after engine room, reporting to Barney, a situation in which I felt quite comfortable.

Being new to conventional subs, I had to study all the systems on the boat and requalify on the *Thornback*, and since I hadn't really worked on diesel engines since I'd been a third-class, years before on the old LST, I had some fast learning to do. As it turned out, I had to learn even faster than I had planned.

Chief Dick, an average-sized fellow who laughed a lot and was a good man to work for, had a penchant for doing things by the book—a trait that I could have done without. A couple of weeks after I'd begun working for Barney, the chief pulled me aside and gave me a shocking assignment.

"Penley," the chief said, "you're a good worker, and you seem to be a fast learner."

"Thanks, Chief," I said. "I try to do my best."

"I know, and you've been working hard for Barney."

"Barney's a good guy. I like working for him."

"Did you know that Barney is junior in rank to you?" the chief asked.

"Yes, I know. I've been a first-class longer than he has, but working for him doesn't bother me a bit. Barney knows a lot more about diesel boats than I do."

"Well, that's not the way the navy works," Chief Dick replied. "A senior man does not work for one junior to him. I want you to take over the after engine room. You're going to be in charge of it."

My mouth dropped. I couldn't believe what I was hearing. "Chief," I said. "I know I'm a first-class engineman, but I've been running nuke plants since I was third-class."

"I know," he said.

I went on, "As you know, the navy doesn't give nukes a different rate; I remained an engineman and was just given a special job code number that designated me as a nuke. And every time I came up for advancement I just studied the engineman manuals and took the tests."

The chief nodded and kept listening.

"It's a crazy system, Chief, but here I am, a first-class engineman who hasn't worked on engines in years. It's Barney's engine room, and I don't want to take it away from him. He knows a hell of a lot more about it than I do."

The chief shook his head. "I know, and I agree it's a crazy system. I guess the navy should have given you nukes different rates instead of keeping you as enginemen, but they didn't. You're senior to Barney, and I won't have a senior man working for someone junior to him.

"You're going to take over the engine room, Penley, and Barney will be working for you. I'll give you two months to get up to speed, and then the job is yours."

The problem amounted to more than my lack of diesel experience. I was a nuke—a navy brainchild—and nukes were not always the most popular among those who hadn't gone to Nuclear Power School. And now I was supposed to take over the engine room from Barney, and he and the rest of the guys under him would be working for me.

Chief Dick told Barney and Arky what was going to happen in two months, and the word quickly spread through the engine rooms. Barney was a popular boss, and the guys who worked for him showed an unquestionable loyalty. I was a stranger, and a nuke—the only nuke—and I could see the resentment in their faces as soon as they got the news.

I discussed the dilemma with Barney, and asked Arky to join in the conversation. I wished I had known them longer than just two weeks, but that's the way things stood. I explained to Barney that I had no personal desire to take over his engine room, and that I had argued against the chief's decision.

"I know," Barney said. "When Chief Dick decides something you might as well save your breath rather than argue with him."

"Listen guys," I said, "I haven't known you very long, but I need your help. You both know a lot more about the machinery than I do, and I can already tell that the younger guys don't like the idea of me taking over an engine room. I can't say I blame them, but the chief didn't give me any choice."

Both Barney and Arky nodded their understanding, and told me they'd try to help me as best they could. I appreciated that, but I knew it wouldn't provide a cure-all for my problem. An unspoken reality lay between the three of us: I also had to prove myself to them.

I had to requalify on the *Thornback*—as did every submariner after being transferred to a different boat, though they were usually given a more reasonable time period in which to complete the task. In my case, this meant learning the basics of every system on the boat from forward to aft, along with every last thing in the engine rooms—every pipe, switch, screw, nut, bolt, and every handy place to bang my head in frustration. And Chief Dick had allotted me two months to accomplish the entire program. I studied like a fiend while my comfortable rack in the after torpedo room saw little use.

The *Thornback*, along with all the other diesel boats in the squadron, had a small barracks assigned to it, a building that was located not far from the pier where we tied up. This allowed the single johns a more roomy place to sleep when they didn't have night duty, a locker in which to keep their civilian clothes, and a place to change in and out of civvies when going on liberty or returning to the boat. As usual, enlisted men were not allowed to wear civvies on the boat at any time.

I seldom stayed in the barracks. Working on the high-speed learning curve the chief had assigned me, when I got the chance to grab a few hours of sleep I just climbed into my rack on the boat.

My efforts impressed Chief Dick, I'm sure, and Barney and Arky as well, but among the younger guys, I think my hard work and fast learning only served to confirm their suspicions that I was just a brainy nuke who thought I was better than the rest of them. Occasionally I overheard mutterings about the "damn nuke," but I disregarded them.

Somehow I had to convince the engine room gang, second- and third-class petty officers as well as young firemen, that I was a regular guy—not an arrogant nuke who had come to take over their work space and make their lives miserable. The most senior man below Barney and Arky and me, a big second-class named Berewski, resented me the most. Strangely, I liked Berewski, but I knew the feeling was not mutual. I'm sure I had found myself in worse situations, but at the moment I couldn't think of many.

Most of the engine room guys were married and spent their liberty time at home, but Barney and Arky were single. One night, I suggested that the three of us go out to the Strip and play some pool. I was a good pool player—a darn good one, in fact—and after Arky discovered this, he became determined to best me at the game: a determination that would never wane for the rest of his life. He did beat me sometimes, and when that happened we both had a good laugh. Then he would try again, harder than ever. Barney mostly sat and watched these pool-playing marathons, drinking beer with an amused look on his face and marveling at Arky's dogged determination.

The three of us started running around together, inhabiting old submarine haunts such as the Five-and-a-Quarter, Mom Rhino's, and the Candlelight Club, a popular dive among diesel submariners. Sometime during this period, Barney and Arky decided I was okay. It wasn't something stated, it simply became understood between us. They were good submariners, and good shipmates.

The boat stayed in port most weekends and went out on

maneuvers—playing war games with our own navy's surface ships—during the week. It was certainly different from riding a nuclear boat, because diesels had to spend a lot of time on the surface, recharging their batteries or keeping them fully charged in the event that a battle situation should arise, and such situations arose often when playing war games.

As one might expect during war games, the surface ships were our enemies and we were theirs. If we won a round, it meant that we had lined up on an unsuspecting ship and simulated firing at it with a spread of torpedoes. We considered ourselves invincible—seagoing dragon killers. Sometimes, however, the dragon won. A surface ship, or ships, would detect our sub, position themselves above us, and drop depth charges on us. They were not real depth charges, but hand-grenade-sized explosives that were set to go off at a certain depth, the same way that depth charges work. The grenades made a loud bang and could be disconcerting when one went off near the boat. We knew if it had been the real thing, we would be dead.

At times, we had real torpedoes fired at us, torpedoes with dummy warheads that would not explode. The torpedoes were set to run at depths either shallower or deeper than we were operating. That way the heavy fish, traveling at thirty to forty knots, would pass either below us or above us.

Many things differed from life on a nuclear boat, the availability of fresh water being a major one. Because the *Thornback* carried a very small distilling unit—a machine capable of providing only enough water for cooking and drinking—the crew could not take showers at sea. I'm sure we smelled a bit rich at times, but we couldn't really tell. We all smelled that way, and the diesel fumes that permeated the boat tended to overpower all other odors.

Chief Dick okayed me to stand engine room watches even though I hadn't finished my overall qualifications on the boat, nor had I yet taken over the after engine room from Barney. I was nearing both of those goals, however, and therefore able to get a bit more sleep—a welcome luxury.

I had never imagined anything so loud as those giant diesels pounding away inside a fourteen-foot pressure hull. In order to talk to one another we had to holler as loud as we could directly into the other's ears. The vibration, which could nearly bounce one off the deck, also added to the ambience of the engine room, not to mention the 120-degree heat that forced us to stand watch in nothing but a pair of shorts, sweating like pigs on an August day.

Because of an inherent design characteristic, a submerged diesel boat could not surface during turbulent weather. Therefore, every time we ran into a storm we had to ride it out on the surface. This even applied to hurricanes, which, thank God, we never encountered.

Riding on the surface inside a narrow pipe filled with machinery in a stormy sea without incurring bodily harm requires special skills—skills normally acquired after incurring bodily harm.

And how does one stay in a bunk that's suspended eight feet above a steel deck without being catapulted out and entangled in torpedoes, pipes, valves, and other metallic objects capable of piercing human flesh? Here's how: I lay flat on my stomach and scooted my body as far outboard as possible, so that my left side and leg were almost touching the pressure hull. I then held tight to the bunk frame, a round steel pipe, with my left hand, and gripped the suspension chain with my right. I bent my right leg into a ninety-degree configuration and extended it outward onto the remainder of the bunk. Thusly positioned, my clamped hands held me in the bed while my right leg acted like an outrigger on a canoe, keeping me from being tossed around in the bunk, or out of it. In this manner, I could sleep through any storm, never changing position and never releasing my grip on the bunk frame and the suspension chain. Almost like being strapped in.

A cozy arrangement, nestled tightly within the piping and above the torpedoes while the storm heaved the boat up and down, slammed it sideways, and rolled it from side to side like an erratic metronome. The good life.

The time came for the *Hamilton* Blue Crew to fly back to Scotland to take over the boat, and for the first time in years, I wouldn't be going with them. The *Thornback* happened to be in port the day they left, and Chief Dick gave me special liberty so I could go to the airport and see them off.

I stood at the boarding gate and shook hands with every one of them as they passed by. I would remain in contact with a few of the guys for all of our lives, but for many of the others, we would be past middle-age, thirty of forty years hence, before we met again.

I fought back tears as I bade farewell to Bob Lee, DeWayne Catron, Whitey, Skelton, Bob Cantley, Rich Dominy, Ted Newell, Leroy Lavender, Chief Spence, and Wild Joe Birkle. Also Dr. Nance, Lieutenant Reed, and Lieutenant MacKinnon, officers whom I considered personal friends. There were dozens of others with whom I had lived and laughed for months beneath the sea, every one a man I could trust with my life.

I felt as though I was leaving home, or maybe home was leaving me. They flew away in two planes. I watched until both faded from sight.

There was little time to lament the parting of the *Hamilton* crew. Within days I would be taking over the after engine room on the *Thornback*, and the boat was preparing for a long run to Puerto Rico, to participate in more war games, of course.

One evening, I left the engine room as an underling working for Barney, and the next morning I walked back in to the stares of everyone under me. I was the man in charge.

When we returned from a run at sea, we always had scheduled maintenance to do on various pieces of machinery and usually a few repairs as well. Following in the footsteps of my hard-nosed mentor, Senior Chief Kennedy, I began posting a list of jobs to be done in the engine room. Some of these tasks could be accomplished at sea, while others had to wait until we returned to port. And I instituted a requirement concerning this list: when we hit port, no one could leave the boat until the jobs were completed and all machinery was in working order. Only then could the guys, and myself, go on liberty.

I heard some grumbling about the posted job list and my rule that all tasks be accomplished before liberty was granted, and I knew that these requirements were not increasing my popularity among the engine room gang. But this was a submarine, and I was never comfortable until everything was in perfect working order—or at least as perfect as possible, considering the boat was more than twenty years old.

For some reason, my subconscious feelings of doom seemed to have lessened on the *Thornback*. Even though the spaces were much tighter and the living conditions far less comfortable than on the big nuclear boat, the fears that I might never return—though still lurking in the back of my mind—became easier to suppress. I don't understand why my hidden fears had diminished at that point, and I never will.

Puerto Rico, and several weeks of war games involving a fleet of diesel subs and a great number of surface ships, all going out to sea on Monday morning and returning Friday afternoon. I had about five guys working for me in the after engine room, most of whom still disliked my requirement that all equipment be in the best working order before they could go on liberty. On one of the Friday afternoons, shortly after we returned to port, our differences came to a head.

After the boat had been tied up, I walked into the engine room and found only one man at work—a young fireman who had crossed off one of the jobs on the list and was working on it by himself. The rest of the list had not been touched. "Where are the other guys?" I asked the fireman.

The young fellow was visibly upset and reluctant to speak. "I don't know," he murmured lowly.

"You don't *know*?" I inquired. "Come on, tell me where they are."

"I . . . think they left the boat, sir," he said. He didn't normally address me as sir, but he was in a difficult position, and he was scared.

Barney stepped into the engine room, looked around, and asked, "Where are the rest of the guys?"

"Looks like they decided to leave," I replied. "Guess they're tired of working for me."

Barney didn't like what he heard. "What you gonna do?" he asked.

"I'm going to go find them."

"Good," Barney said. "I'm going with you."

We found them only a few hundred yards from the boat, sitting in lawn chairs near an outdoor bar that jutted out over the water. There were four of them, all petty officers and all looking defiant. Big Berewski, the second-class, was seated closest to the front of the group, leaning back in his chair and doing his best to look relaxed.

"What you guys doing?" I asked.

"Just taking it easy," Berewski answered. The others said nothing.

"The work list isn't finished," I said.

Berewski smirked. "We know." The others began to look less defiant, even a little worried. They had reason to be.

Barney spoke up. "Come on, Berewski. You know that work list has to be done, and then we can all go on liberty."

Berewski looked at Barney for a long moment but didn't answer. They all sat in their chairs.

I had worked my butt off to qualify on the boat and learn the engine rooms, all in two months time. And now these guys seemed to think I was pushing them too hard. I'd had enough of this.

I looked each of them hard in the eye, one after the other, then I spoke directly to Berewski. "I've been in the navy more than six years, and I've never *yet* put a man on report—because I've never had to."

I turned and walked back toward the boat. Barney did the same.

I didn't look back until I reached the boat. They were all following, and they all climbed down the engine room hatch and went to work. I worked alongside them until the job list was finished.

That ended the problem. I think some of them, even Berewski, may have begun to like me a little better after that. I don't think they ever liked working for me.

Even war *games* can be hazardous to your health. One night while slumbering peacefully in my high bunk, I awoke to a terrific "Wham," the source of the noise being very close to where I lay. Awake in an instant, I became aware of a man running from the aft end of the compartment toward the forward hatch. It was the torpedoman on watch, and he was getting the hell out of there.

"What was that noise?" I yelled at him.

As he dove through the hatch and disappeared, he hollered back over his shoulder, "A torpedo!"

A *torpedo?* Hell, I was lying on top of a torpedo, in a room full of them. *Had one of them started up? Was it's motor running? Was one of the warheads heating up, getting ready to blow?* I got out of there myself.

Diving out of my rack, I charged forward out of the compartment, wearing nothing but my skivvies. I didn't slow down until I reached the control room. There I found a great number of officers and men, all crowded together with worried, puzzled looks on their faces. As I dove through the hatch into control and straightened up, I found myself face to face with the executive officer. He seemed less excited than the rest, and he hesitated long enough to look me up and down, noting that I had on only a pair of skivvies.

"What's going on, sir?" I practically hollered at the exec.

"We got hit by a torpedo," he said.

"I'll bet it hit in the after torpedo room, didn't it?"

"Yes, we think that's where it hit," he said.

"I'm sure of it," I answered. "I was sleeping back there when it hit."

To complete my shock, the exec broke into a grin. "Bet that woke you up, huh?"

I had to laugh at myself. "Yes, sir, it sure did."

"Maybe you ought to go get some pants on," he said. Then we laughed.

Back in the after torpedo room, the lights were on and some officers and men had set up a ladder and were inspecting a spot high on the pressure hull about ten feet aft of my bunk. A torpedo fired at us from another craft had malfunctioned and run at the wrong depth—our depth—and rammed into the side of us at full speed. The pressure hull sustained a slight inward dent, barely discernible, but it didn't leak.

We didn't win that round. Had the war been real and the torpedo armed, the fish would have blown us apart.

I went back to bed, and asked the guys to turn the lights out.

After several weeks of operating out of Puerto Rico, it came time to return to Charleston. I'd had my fill of war games, and certainly had enough torpedoes slamming into the pressure hull next to me to last a lifetime.

Back in Charleston, I felt great. I had overcome a number of obstacles on the *Thornback,* learned a lot, had some exciting times, and made some good friends. Six months to go in the navy, and then back to Colorado. Smooth sailing until my discharge, or so it seemed.

About two weeks after we tied up in Charleston, I was on liberty one weekday, having had the duty the night before. Happily driving down the street in my car, I looked in the rearview mirror and saw Arky close behind, honking madly and motioning me to stop.

I pulled over to the curb and Arky squealed to a stop behind me. Before I could even open my car door, he rushed up and said, "You better get back to the boat as quick as you can. They're getting ready to transfer you."

Chapter Seventeen

Terror Below

The *Amberjack*—that's all I could get out of Arky. When I tried to question him more he practically screamed in my face. "Get back to the boat! They're screwing you over, royally."

I threw my car in gear and headed for the base, breaking every speed limit on the way, my mind reeling. The USS *Amberjack* (SS 522), the same class diesel sub as the *Thornback,* was being outfitted for some sort of covert mission. Everyone in the squadron knew that, but no one knew much else, not even the crew. And why was *I* being transferred to it?

I passed through the main gate of the base, barely stopping to show my ID, then sped to the pier and parked. Still in civilian clothes, I ran down the pier, jumped aboard the *Thornback,* and slid down the ladder into the forward engine room. Chief Dick was there, looking concerned as soon as he saw me.

"What's happening, Chief?" I asked. "I heard something about me being transferred."

"Yes," he said with a sigh, "I'm afraid it's true."

"Can you tell me what the hell's going on?"

"Sure," he said, and proceeded to explain the situation to me. It was not good.

The *Amberjack,* which was nearly ready to leave on a top-secret mission, destination unknown, was short one engineman. And because their mission—whatever that might be—had such high priority, the squadron commander had given the boat permission to take an engineman from the *Thornback.* And since the engineering officer on the *Amberjack* had been given such free rein, he requested a first-class.

Here was the rub, and I could tell that Chief Dick didn't agree with it even as he told me. Earlier that same day, our engineering officer, Lieutenant Leischer, had selected a first-class from the auxiliary gang—enginemen who worked on auxiliary equipment throughout the boat and not in the engine rooms—to be transferred to the *Amberjack*. The man had practically broken into tears when he heard the news, pleading with Mr. Leischer not to send him on the long patrol because of the negative effect it would have on his wife. The engineer gave in and rescinded the order.

Directly following that fiasco, Mr. Leischer called another first-class auxiliaryman to his stateroom and told him that he would have to go to the *Amberjack.* The man refused! When the engineer reminded him that he couldn't refuse a direct order, the first-class told him he would disqualify himself from submarines before he'd go on the clandestine mission. Again, Mr. Leischer gave in.

Then the engineering officer went to Chief Dick and told him that he would have to select a first-class from one of the engine rooms. The chief apologized for having selected me, but explained that since I had less time left in the navy—six months—than either Arky or Barney, that if the chief was forced to lose a first-class, he had to choose me. I understood his position and told him so.

But I was mad, and I had reason to be. "You're telling me that those two auxiliarymen simply won't go? That one of them begged off because of his wife and the other just refused? And the engineer let them get away with that?"

"I'm afraid so," Chief Dick said. "I don't agree with it, but that's how it stands. So now you're the one that's going to the *Amberjack.*"

"Damn!" I said. "Nobody forced those guys to get married. They're in the same navy that I am, and *supposed* to take direct orders from senior officers."

"I know," Chief Dick said. "I can't believe it myself." Then he asked me, "Do you want to talk to the engineer?"

"Yes," I said, "I sure do."

The chief called forward and told Mr. Leischer that I wanted to talk to him. He hung up the phone and nodded, and I went steaming forward to officers' country. Lieutenant Leischer was waiting for me, standing in the doorway to his stateroom. He wasn't the only one waiting; I could see the captain and the executive officer, both standing half-hidden behind the curtains in the doorway to the wardroom.

Mr. Leischer looked harried and embarrassed. "Hello, Penley," he said, avoiding my eyes. "I understand you'd like to talk to me."

"Yes, sir," I said. "I hear I'm being transferred to the *Amberjack*."

"That's . . . uh, correct," the engineer answered.

"And I also understand that two other first-class enginemen—auxiliarymen—were ordered to go earlier today, and that they refused. And they were *allowed* to refuse."

"That's . . . correct, Penley. In their cases there were mitigating circumstances that wouldn't allow them to go on a long patrol."

"*Mitigating circumstances?*" I said. "I'm sorry, sir, but I have to disagree with that. Those guys are in the same navy as me, and when I get a direct order from a senior officer, I obey it. Isn't that how the military works, sir?"

Mr. Leischer's face reddened. "Yes, it is, Penley. But again, in their cases the circumstances were different from yours."

"I believe, sir, that the difference in their circumstances is that they refused a direct order, and they were allowed to do it."

The lieutenant didn't answer. I saw that the captain and the exec were still listening.

I went on. "I've been in the navy for six and a half years, sir, and in all that time, I believe the navy has treated me fairly and with whatever respect I deserved. But not this time. This time I'm getting screwed, sir."

Leischer looked down at the deck between us. "I wish you didn't feel that way, Penley."

"I wish I didn't feel this way too, sir. I'd love not to feel this way."

Again, no answer.

"I'll go," I said, "because I'm a good sailor, and I do my duty as ordered."

Leischer looked back up at me. "I know, Penley. You're a damn good sailor."

I wasn't finished. "Yes, I'll go, and I'll do whatever their top-secret mission requires of me. You knew I would. But remember, sir, you have two men under your command who refused to go. They're the kind of worthless characters you have to put up with in your division."

Before the lieutenant could reply, I said, "Give me my orders to the *Amberjack,* sir, and I'll be gone." I turned and left.

Back in the engine room, Chief Dick asked how my conversation with the engineering officer had gone. I told him exactly what I had told the lieutenant.

"My God!" the chief said. "You told him all that?"

"Yes, I did, Chief. And every word I said was true."

The chief shook his head, then offered his hand. "Good luck, Penley."

"Thanks, Chief."

Barney and Arky were nearly as mad as I was. Barney threatened to disqualify himself from submarines over the way I'd been treated, but the exec talked him out of it. The three of us went on a last big liberty together. Mom Rhino's, the Five-and-a-Quarter, the Candlelight Club, and all points in between. We even got a little belligerent, swaggering down the Strip like the invincible submariners we considered ourselves to be. Somehow we managed to avoid getting into any fights—probably a good thing for us.

Barney and Arky. In six short months, I had made two lifelong friends—the kind that one is fortunate enough to find only a few times in this life.

The Cold War had been the backdrop of my entire naval service, and something inside me had enjoyed it—holding the enemies of my homeland at bay. With this transfer, my Cold War was about to heat up, indeed, to grow very hot.

The *Amberjack* was a good-looking boat. Freshly painted and not a speck of rust in sight, the WWII-vintage sub looked almost new, inside and out. As we did our best to keep her operational during the six months I served on her, those good looks proved deceptive.

Admittedly, when I stepped aboard the *Amberjack,* I carried with me a negative attitude, my abrupt transfer and the way it had been handled having left a bad taste that would linger longer than I should have allowed it.

First, I met the chief of the boat, a broad-chested chief engineman with a square head and the eyes of a lion who looked like he could eat junior petty officers for breakfast. Besides being the boat's head honcho, Chief Boring was also in charge of the engine rooms. I decided right away not to give *him* any trouble.

Then to officers' country, and an introduction to the captain and the executive officer. The exec was a rather quiet, sharp-looking officer who appeared to be a bit shy. My first impressions of the man were positive, and would prove to be correct as we became more acquainted.

My impressions of the captain felt stronger and more conclusive, and would remain so as long as I served under him. A short, heavy man who raised questions within me at first sight, the captain shook my hand vigorously and told me with great enthusiasm how proud he was to have me on his crew, explaining that my reputation preceded me and that he considered me to be one of the finest enginemen in the submarine service.

To me, this one-sided exchange came across as a backslapping load of BS that lacked sincerity. But who was I to entertain such thoughts? He was the captain, and I was simply the greatest engineman who had ever set foot on a submarine.

Besides being a good-looking boat, the *Amberjack* was an extremely quiet machine, one of the reasons it had been chosen for the clandestine mission. When running silent and deep, she was reputed to be the quietest boat in the squadron, and thus best equipped to avoid detection by enemy sonar.

Indeed the *Amberjack* was a quiet sub, aptly demonstrated on submerged runs during the first weeks I rode her. However, the boat may have looked sharp, but it had more than its share of mechanical breakdowns. The big diesel engines, as well as innumerable other engine room machinery, seemed to give us problems of one sort or another every time we took her out to sea. I began to equate operating the boat with trying to drive a car that was a lemon; it looked nice, but I didn't trust it.

Even though the boat's commander had requested a first-class engineman—me—they didn't really need one. Each engine room had a first-class in charge, and both were senior to me.

I worked for Paul Carney, the man who ran the forward engine room. An easy-going, knowledgeable fellow with a fine sense of humor, Carney was aware of the circumstances under which I had been transferred. The two of us sat down and discussed this early on, and he told me that such an event would have given him a lousy attitude from the start. I thanked him for his understanding and told him he could expect my complete cooperation.

Carney and I worked well together. By this time, I could easily pull my weight in a diesel engine room, which was good, because there was always something that needed fixing.

My favorite bunk in the after torpedo room, perched high and identical to the one I'd had on the *Thornback,* was taken. The young guy who slept in it was a seaman, a would-be tough submariner whom I didn't particularly care for.

There was an unwritten rule on submarines that a senior man could trade bunks with one junior to him, whether the junior liked it or not. Out of courtesy, this rule was seldom used, and though I thought about invoking it in this case, I instead took a bunk in the torpedo room that lay near the back of the compartment at about waist level, directly below the upper hatch.

One night during a submerged operation, the hatch above me sprung a leak, dumping about a bucketful of seawater on me. After turning on all the lights and moving my bunk out of their way, the auxiliarymen put up a ladder and got the leak mostly stopped—but not altogether. Seawater dripped on my bed the rest of the night. The self-proclaimed salty seaman up in the high bunk woke up during this fiasco and bragged to me about how comfortable he was. I said nothing.

The following morning I found the seaman in the mess hall and told him that he and I were trading bunks. With great surprise, he puffed up indignantly and spoke loudly, for all to hear. "Oh, so you're going to take my comfortable bunk up high and make me take the one under the hatch that leaks, huh?"

As a mess hall full of men became quiet and listened to the exchange, I grinned at the kid and said, "You got it right, fellow. That's exactly what's going to happen."

And that's what did happen. Once again, I slept in peace, and the young seaman discovered a rule he hadn't known about, and maybe even learned something about keeping his mouth shut.

In April 1967, as the *Amberjack* was preparing to head across the Atlantic, our captain revealed that we were heading for the Mediterranean Sea. What part of the Mediterranean remained a mystery. We all knew that the boat had been outfitted with the latest state-of-the-art sonar equipment as well as high-tech cameras designed for photographing through the periscope. And that's all we knew.

Rumors flew that we were embarking on a spy mission into the Black Sea—a perilous journey into a Soviet-held body of water. The crew grew nervous and afraid—as in many walks of life, the unknown proving more scary than the known.

Around the same time, another American naval vessel, the USS *Liberty,* was heading for the mouth of the Mediterranean. The *Liberty,* a noncombatant, intelligence-gathering craft classified as a technical research ship, carried a crew of nearly three hundred men and was armed with only four .50-caliber machine guns.

Along with carrying a myriad of classified electronic and communication equipment, the ship's crew included of a number of naval intelligence personnel—commonly know as "spooks."

Like the crew of the *Amberjack,* the men on the *Liberty* were also nervous and afraid, but for a different reason. They knew where they were going—the Middle East.

The Middle East, whose countries never seemed to agree on anything—borders included—had been heating up for some time. The differences between Israel and several Arab countries—Israel's primary adversary being Egypt—looked to be coming to a boil. The USS *Liberty,* with virtually no armament and no armed escorts, had been ordered to steam to waters just off Gaza, in the far eastern Mediterranean. There the ship would operate, peacefully, in international waters.

Of course, we on the *Amberjack* knew nothing of this surface ship or its movements.

As the *Amberjack* left Charleston and headed across the Atlantic, into the unknown, we were told it would be a long patrol; it ended up lasting a total of three months. We who worked in the engine rooms, maneuvering, and the torpedo rooms, all felt sure that the men who worked in control—sonarmen, radiomen, quartermasters, and a few new faces—knew more about the mission than we did, but they would not discuss our impending operations, not a single word. In fact, they would hardly talk with us at all. And, as was to be expected, the officers were equally as closed-mouthed.

This was not a happy crew, and it never demonstrated the closeness that I had experienced on every other sub I had ridden. Not knowing where we were going or what we would do when we got there created an extremely uncomfortable environment, and this time I was unable to hide my old fears from myself; they could no longer be suppressed. I kept quiet about my personal feelings, but the future of the patrol felt dark, foreboding. A premonition? Perhaps.

Prior to the patrol, while the boat was spending some time in port and the married men were eating at home, the head cook got the chance to save up some of his allotted money for ship's meals. With these extra funds, he bought and stored a number of treats such as caviar, patés, and other fine foods never seen on submarine menus. The cook told us about the fine foods he was stockpiling and promised that on our upcoming unpopular patrol we would occasionally have a special meal composed of these delicacies. He was trying to give us something to look forward to at sea.

However, we would never see our fancy foods. When the captain heard about the cache the cook had put together for the crew, he scowled and told him that enlisted men would never appreciate such fine dishes, and he ordered him to serve them in the wardroom only. And that's what became of our special meals; they were served exclusively to the officers, by order of the captain.

The captain tried to appear friendly and buddy-buddy with the enlisted men. I went along with this act, of course, but I didn't believe it. In my mind, the captain considered enlisted men to be stupid, and easily duped by what I considered insincere shows of caring that insulted our intelligence.

It is a bad feeling when a submariner does not trust his captain.

The last time I'd crossed the Atlantic on a submarine had been several years before, in a nuclear boat. We had traveled at a depth of five hundred feet and traversed the great ocean at flank speed. Crossing in a diesel boat, on the surface, was a slower process, but it gave me a chance to spend some daylight hours on the bridge, a thrill that submariners seldom get to experience.

I would later learn that we had as many as four naval intelligence personnel aboard—spooks—who had been ordered onto the boat by the Office of the Chief of Naval Operations. These men were trained in foreign linguistics, Arabic and Russian languages being among them. The crew was not informed of the spooks' presence, let alone their purpose on the patrol, and we never would be. They were just faces, strangers who seldom ventured farther aft than the mess hall and hardly said a word to any of us. They slept somewhere up forward and spent their waking hours in the radio room, a small, tight space squeezed into a corner of control.

Rumors of our sneaking into the Black Sea still ran rampant through the boat. Sometime during the crossing, the captain gathered the crew in the mess hall, ostensibly to explain the purpose of our upcoming patrol. He first stressed the vital importance of our mission, and the absolute necessity that our presence in the Mediterranean be kept a secret from every country on Earth except our own.

The skipper didn't tell us where we would be operating, but our mission, he said, was to sneak in close to Soviet ships and record their sounds on sonar—a covert operation known as sonar fingerprinting. We would also be photographing enemy ships up close, through the periscope, of course.

This, according to the captain, was our mission, and we were never told otherwise.

Due to some mechanical or electronic malfunctions up forward—

problems that were never shared with most of us—the boat had to make an unscheduled stop for repairs at Rota, Spain. For once, we had no machinery problems in the engine rooms, so we spent the day cleaning and polishing equipment, or at least making a show of doing so.

The captain seemed in a great hurry to get on with our secret patrol, and he did not hide his discontent at the boat being forced to make an unscheduled stop at Rota. Repairmen from the tender worked on the boat most of one day and part of the night, and by the following morning, she was ready to go, or at least as ready as the *Amberjack* ever seemed to be. We fired up the three big diesels, left the shores of Spain, and headed for the Straits of Gibraltar.

The effectiveness of a diesel submarine in battle or in a covert operation—sneaking around where one is not supposed to be— is highly dependent on the boat's ability to achieve full speed on the surface. Why on the surface? Because of its limited range of travel when submerged. When the sub is in danger of being overpowered by the enemy during a battle, or when detected by the objective vessel(s) in a spy situation, the sub's life depends on its ability to retreat—fast.

A diesel sub can run submerged, on its batteries, for up to two days if it proceeds *very* slowly. However, when running at full speed submerged, the sub will totally expend its batteries in just forty-five minutes—and several hours are required to recharge. Because of this battery limitation, the boat must ultimately make its escape on the surface.

When the sub finds it necessary to escape hostile surface ships that have discovered its presence, it first must elude the enemy—at times while under a depth-charge attack—then slowly and silently sneak away submerged. Then, when the boat has put a mile or two between itself and the bad guys, it hits the surface and runs, at flank speed. With a head start and all three diesels churning at maximum RPM, a sub can outrun most surface ships. But, if even one of its diesels is out of commission, this type of getaway will not work. In this situation, instead of being able to make eighteen or nineteen knots per hour on the surface, the boat is slowed to a maximum of ten or twelve knots. At this diminished speed, it cannot escape a pursuing enemy. All three engines must be ready to go at all times, and capable of running at flank speed for as long and as far as needed.

On the way into the Mediterranean, we lost an engine.

The Fairbanks-Morse diesels on the *Amberjack* were each equipped with an air-driven starting motor, a vital piece of equipment without which an idle engine could not be started. Engines were shut down when running quiet and submerged, and they had to be started in a hurry when the boat hit the surface to make a run for it. One of our starting motors developed a problem, rendering the engine useless.

The news of the loss of an engine hit the captain hard. He stormed back to the engine rooms and asked the chief and all of us first-classes the details of the problem. We assured him that we had to have a new starting motor—that without it the boat could only run at two-thirds power.

The skipper obviously hated the idea of another delay, but he radioed a message that the *Amberjack* had to have another starting motor in order to proceed on patrol. We turned toward Italy, making all the speed we could, and tied up in the bay of Naples. There, for two anxious days and nights, we awaited the arrival of a new starting motor.

Naples was not the most impressive city I had ever set foot in, but sub sailors' tastes had never been described as discerning. Anytime we got the opportunity to go on liberty, wherever that might be, we went.

I had the duty the first night in port, and therefore could not leave the boat. I got my chance the second night there, and so after donning my dress whites I set out for whatever adventures awaited me in Napoli. I should have stayed aboard. After using up a great amount of luck and more help from my guardian angel than I deserved, I made it back to the boat late that night, alive.

It was early evening, still daylight, when I left the boat. After wandering the town alone for a while, I ran into a shipmate who was also by himself. We hooked up together and, as naturally as fish taking to water, began to hit a few drinking establishments. As night fell, the two of us found ourselves in a very out-of-the-way bar on a very dark street.

No street lights, no traffic, not even pavement. A shabby bar with one barmaid who could not speak English, and we the only two customers in the place. A risky setting in which to find oneself, but we thought nothing of it.

After we downed a couple of drinks, a rather nice-looking young lady sauntered in, scantily dressed and obviously flaunting her wares. My shipmate immediately invited the young prostitute over to our table and bought her a drink. She could speak a bit of English, albeit broken, but enough to communicate what she had to offer as well as the going price. My friend liked the deal, and soon the two of them left—off into the night.

Finding myself alone once more, except for the barmaid, I ordered another drink. She stood behind the bar, saying nothing, while I sat at a table across the room enjoying a few moments of solitude, a luxury that submariners seldom found.

A woman came screaming through the front door, literally. Somewhere in her thirties and poorly dressed, she was obviously not a prostitute. The woman spoke passable English, and she was very distraught. After shouting something in Italian to the barmaid, she ran over to my table and said, "You on the submarine?"

The answer was obvious; she was looking at my dolphins, and the *Amberjack* was the only U.S. ship in the port of Naples.

I nodded. "Yes, I'm on the submarine."

She whirled and ran for the door, motioning me to follow. "Come with me!" she said. "I have to show you something, submarine man."

I stayed in my chair, cautious, suspicious. The woman stopped at the door, madly waving her arms. "Come with me! Come with me! I have to show you something."

Against my better judgment, I stood up and followed her out the door. She ran down the front steps and turned left, hurrying off down the dark street.

"Come with me! Come with me!" she hollered. I followed. Not smart.

Moonlight cast a faint glow on the shadowy street, and as I followed the frantic woman, I began to get a creepy feeling—a feeling that she and I were not alone. I looked first to my right and then to my left. Two men had come out of the darkness. Both were stocky, broad in the chest, and both were closely flanking me—each walking slightly behind me and about two feet to either side. I kept moving and turned to take a long look at each of them. They were a bit shorter than me, and much stouter, reminding me of twin hit men. Neither turned his head nor made a sound; they just kept walking as if I weren't there.

The woman, still out in front, kept urging me to hurry. I tried to slow down, but the men crowded me, shoving me down the street with their shoulders. I sped up, to avoid contact with the silent bruisers who were herding me. I felt sure that I would soon be attacked, beaten, and robbed. I prayed that they wouldn't kill me.

We all kept walking, the woman forever urging me to move faster, the men saying nothing. Thoughts of home ran through my mind—my mother, my brother, the old ranch that I might never see again, and Dad. Maybe Dad was walking with me that night.

I knew I would fight if it came to that, but I also knew I would lose. They probably had knives, and even if they didn't, I surely couldn't take the two of them. I expected to die there on that dark street.

A shadowy building loomed out of the darkness—sitting off by itself, a small multistoried structure that looked to be made of cinder blocks. It was an apartment building, poorly built and poorly lit. The woman turned into the front door. I followed, along with my two burly shadows. There was no lobby and no elevator. The woman began running up an iron staircase, two steps at a stride. I hurried after her.

A few stories up, the woman opened a door and led us down a stark hallway. She stopped at an unmarked door and pushed it open. The men shoved me inside.

A small apartment, very small, and crowded with people. A dozen or more of all ages—men, women, young, old, even a few children. Some looked at me with hatred in their eyes; others looked away. No one said a word.

The little room was sparsely furnished—two or three chairs, a couple of small tables, and one narrow bed in a far corner. The English-speaking woman led me through the crowd to the corner bed. In it lay a young lady, not much more than a girl. She had been pretty earlier that evening; now she was not. Both eyes were blackened, her nose bloodied, her dark hair a tangled mess, her once smooth face covered in bruises.

I could see that the young woman had taken a terrible beating. Surprisingly, she had no broken bones. Two older women were holding the beaten girl, their arms supporting her while she cried. The women were crying too.

I looked around at the solemn crowd. *What was I doing here? Why had I been summoned to this tragic scene?* I soon learned the answer, and wished to God I hadn't.

The English-speaking woman turned to me. "You from the submarine?" she asked again.

"Yes," I said. "I told you I was on the submarine."

The woman pointed at the bruised and beaten girl. "A man from the submarine did this to her," she said.

I glanced around the room again, and realized that this was a family—the girl's family. *Oh, no!* I thought. *They know that a submariner did this to her, and now they want their pound of flesh.* The young men looked mad, vicious. I figured if one of the older men just said the word, the entire family would tear me apart.

But nobody moved.

I turned back to the woman and asked, "Is she sure it was a submariner?" I pointed at the dolphins on my chest. "Was he wearing these?"

She spoke to the sobbing girl in Italian. The girl looked up at me and nodded. Yes, her attacker had been a submariner. Again, I prayed they wouldn't kill me, but I had little faith in my chances of survival. The woman looked at the girl and spoke to me again, her voice filled with sadness. "A man from the submarine did this. Can you see how terrible it is? This thing that he did?"

"Yes," I said. "I can see what he did, and it is a terrible thing." I shook my head in despair. "The man did an awful thing to her, and I am sorry for what he did."

"Yes, you can see," she said. "We wanted you to see. We want you to know what the submarine man has done."

My heart was pounding, my fear palpable. "I can see," I repeated. "I can see what he has done."

I turned to the roomful of faces, some sorrowful, some angry. "I am sorry," I said to them, in the only language I knew. Mostly blank expressions, with a few nods of understanding from the older ones. I turned and spoke to the beaten girl. "I am very sorry." She dropped her head and sobbed.

I began to move toward the door. To my surprise, the family slowly separated, allowing me to pass. At the door, I turned and looked at them once more, then I opened it and stepped out, closing it softly behind me. I forced myself to walk quietly, normally, until I reached the stairs.

I took the stairs three and four at a time, charging down them so fast I nearly lost my footing. Outside, I didn't know where I was, but I knew the harbor lay downhill from where I stood. I ran in that direction as hard as my legs could carry me, instinctively pumping my way through dark streets and littered alleyways. Somehow, I reached the pier where the boat was tied.

I sat down on a piling and dropped my head between my knees, gasping for air. No one had come after me, either that or they hadn't been able to catch me. Whatever the reason, by some miracle, I was alive.

The next morning I told the chief engineman what I had seen, and that I was sure it had been a man off the *Amberjack* who had beaten the young lady so severely. The chief looked thoughtful for a moment, then nodded and told me not to tell anyone else. He appeared to know who was responsible, and I felt pretty sure that I knew, too. A young petty officer on the boat was known to go a little crazy when he drank too much. To my knowledge, the man was neither asked about the incident nor accused; he was simply told that he would have no more liberty—would not set foot off the boat in any port—until we returned to the U.S.

Sometime later, at sea, I confronted the young petty officer about the incident. He admitted that he had done it, explaining that the young girl had been a prostitute, and that he had passed out in her apartment. When he woke up, he found her rifling through his billfold. That's when he went wild, beat her up, and left her there.

His story didn't impress me. "You ought to stop drinking, you crazy bastard," I told him.

"Hell, she was a whore," he said.

"I know, and she was poor, and she had a family. You could have killed her, and you damn near got me killed in the aftermath."

He just looked at me with a crooked grin and said no more.

I avoided the man after that, and he avoided me. He was not a shipmate, just a loony who should have been court-martialed and thrown out of the navy.

I had had negative feelings about this patrol since the day I stepped aboard the *Amberjack*, and so far nothing had occurred to make me feel any better. If anything, I now had less faith in the success of our mission, whatever that happened to be. I hoped that my brush with violence and possible death in Naples had marked the low point of the patrol. At least I could still hope.

On our second day in Naples, the day after my late-night misadventure, a box was delivered to the boat—our anxiously awaited starting motor. All of the enginemen, along with the captain, were up on the main deck when the package arrived. The captain looked on as we eagerly opened it up, and he saw our faces fall when we looked inside. It was a starting motor, but the wrong one.

"What's the problem?" asked the captain.

We explained to him that it was the wrong starting motor. The captain didn't want to hear that any more than we wanted to tell him, but we assured him that the motor we had received would not fit our engine.

We were all squatting on the deck, looking at the box we had just opened. The captain stood over us. He was furious. "We received the starting motor," he bellowed, "and it *will* work!" We all looked at each other, unable to believe what we had just heard.

The captain continued, "Don't any of you forget that. Understand?"

After glancing at one another again, we looked up at him and said, "Yes, sir. We understand." The captain stormed away and went below.

I understood, all right. And as to forgetting, I would never forget the most frightening order I had ever heard a commanding officer give. The captain had waited as long as he was going to wait. Whether it was his decision alone or if he had orders from higher up, we would never know, but we immediately prepared to leave port, and proceed on our secret patrol. With great misgivings, we untied the boat, backed out into the bay, and left Naples on two engines.

A crippled predator should not pursue dangerous prey.

We traveled night and day, mostly submerged, running on batteries or snorkeling on the diesels during daylight hours, and snorkeling at night to recharge the batteries. We were generally aware of moving in an easterly direction, but most of the crew never really knew where we were. This was obviously according to plan, because nearly all of us were kept in the dark concerning our location. Somehow we managed to keep up with our movements in general, so that we had a fair idea as to what part of the Mediterranean we were in, but nothing more specific.

Tensions continued building in the Middle East, and as we would eventually learn, that's where we were heading.

We worked on those infernal engines all the time, trying to get the inoperable starting motor to work, or to jury-rig something that would allow the boat to achieve full power—to run on all three engines at once. A futile endeavor, but we never stopped trying.

I had never seen such a spiritless bunch of sailors. Submarine crews had always been the tightest and closest to serve on any craft in the navy. Not the *Amberjack*. We didn't even joke about the breakdowns, which would have been the norm for submariners. It felt unreal, like some sort of living fiction— riding a jinxed ship.

The captain would often walk through the boat, never failing to stop and talk to us in the engine room. Greasy parts spread everywhere, and we enginemen, shirtless and just as greasy, crawling around on the deck or in front of or behind an engine in 120-degree temperatures, and here would come the skipper, putting on his jovial, buddy-buddy act, smiling broadly and cracking jokes at which we all had to laugh. I didn't notice any jump in morale following his visits.

We did have good food and movies in the mess hall every night. One of the movies on board featured a naval scene that would later turn out to have some personal significance to all of us. In the movie, a floating target sled was being towed far behind a small tugboat, dragged across the water by a long cable. While a shore facility was firing at the target sled for practice purposes, an unsuspecting craft, either a submarine or a surface vessel, unknowingly found itself in the line of fire and was almost hit by the shelling—a near disaster from having wandered into another country's war games.

We thought little about this war game scene as we lounged in the mess hall watching the movie, but it would later come back as a grim and rather ridiculous reminder to many of us.

After a long trip submerged, without the benefit of showers, clean sheets, or fresh clothes, we reached the near-offshore waters of the Middle East. We all knew about what part of the Med we were in, but during our time there, most of us would never know our exact location.

We began carrying out some sort of maneuvers, remaining submerged at all times. Back in the engine rooms and maneuvering, we could tell that something was going on because the boat would make sudden turns, speed up, slow down, change depth, rig for silent running, stop, reverse, and take off again, all in various sequences and at odd times both day and night. Those of us back aft felt like blind men on a carnival ride.

I would later learn that at times the spooks didn't even know what the boat was doing. I also learned that the captain must have been a fan of the old television series *Get Smart*. In this sitcom, whenever the head spy wanted to speak privately with Max he would say, "Cone of Silence," whereupon a soundproof cone would descend over the two of them. When one of the senior spooks on the *Amberjack,* a chief petty officer, needed to speak on the secure phone line with the captain, he had orders to call the con over the nonsecure line and say, "Cone of Silence." When the captain received this laughable bit of code, he would call back on the secure line.

When the chief spook tired of the captain's little spy game, he made the mistake of telling him that he considered their "Cone of Silence" code to be ridiculous. The spook received a butt-chewing from the skipper for voicing his opinion, and the game continued.

Maybe it's just as well that most of us didn't know what was going on.

The environment in which we were conducting our spy operations began to change for the worse. We could tell this from the grim demeanor and worried faces on the guys who worked in control, and a few of them felt compelled to tell us, on the sly, that the *Amberjack* was engaged in extremely dangerous activities.

The Middle East continued to heat up. Israel was seriously rattling swords with several Arab countries, and we were nosing around in places where we'd best not be caught.

On June 5, 1967, war broke out—a violent conflict that would become known as the Six-Day War. Bitter enemies Israel and Egypt were major combatants, and up front the captain, the exec, the communications officer, the navigator, and the spooks discovered that the *Amberjack* was dead in the middle of a war zone.

Back aft, we kept working on and praying over engine number three, striving to get it to run. We didn't know what was going on or what might happen. Hell, we didn't even know that a war had erupted around us; but we did know that a boat with only two-thirds of its power, a capability of making a top speed of ten to twelve knots, would find itself in a tight spot if it encountered a serious enemy.

The *Amberjack* was not the only U.S. vessel in the war zone. The intelligence-gathering ship USS *Liberty*, with 294 men aboard and a total armament of four machine guns, was also in the area. And, according to later reports from a spook aboard the *Liberty,* as many as three other American submarines were operating there as well.

Early on the morning of June 8, 1967, according to eyewitness accounts from crew members on the *Liberty,* airplanes—flying boxcars displaying insignia of Israeli military forces—began flying low over the ship. And, according to all reports from the ship, the *Liberty* was conspicuously flying the American flag on its forecastle, as do all U.S. naval vessels. The menacing flyovers continued for several hours.

At approximately 2:00 p.m. local time, as the USS *Liberty* was sailing in international waters off the Sinai Peninsula, a number of Israeli jet fighters were seen heading directly for the ship. Suddenly, and without warning, the *Liberty* was attacked.

Israeli jets strafed the poorly armed *Liberty* with machine gun and rocket fire. Repeatedly the planes attacked, machine-gunning officers and men on deck, blowing football-sized holes in the hull with rockets, and dropping napalm—jellied gasoline that set inextinguishable fires all over the ship, rivers of it running across the decks and down stairwells into interior compartments filled with men. The gun tubs were taken out first and set ablaze with napalm, rendering the ship incapable of even slight retaliation. And the ship's superstructure, with its forest of antennae, was targeted in an obvious attempt to render it incapable of radioing for help.

As the assault on the *Liberty* ensued, a nearby periscope was spotted by several crew members. The identity of the submarine has never been revealed.

Shortly after the initial air attack, Israeli torpedo boats joined in the fray, machine-gunning the decks and firing rockets near the waterline in an apparent attempt to sink the ship. Two torpedoes missed the *Liberty,* but a third struck the forward starboard side, blowing a forty-foot hole in the hull and killing more than twenty men in below-decks compartments. Following the torpedo attack, the ship threatened to go under, but managed to stay afloat with a heavy list to starboard.

The jet fighters had blown up the motor whaleboat and all but three of the life rafts. When the remaining rafts were lowered into the water, the torpedo boats machine-gunned them, destroying the crew's last possible means of escape.

Sometime during the attack, the ship managed to transmit a radio message calling for help. The message was received by aircraft carriers attached to the Sixth Fleet; the carriers were operating in the Mediterranean within striking distance of the one-sided battle.

Four American jet fighters were launched from a U.S. aircraft carrier and sent on their way to defend the *Liberty*. Inexplicably, before the fighters could reach their destination, they were called back, forced to return to the carrier by order of the secretary of defense. Why was this recall order given? The reasoning behind it was not clear and, to my knowledge, has never officially been clarified by anyone.

The attack on the *Liberty* continued for approximately two hours. Then, leaving the ship battered, burning, filled with dead and wounded, and its decks awash in blood, the planes and torpedo boats left the scene.

Thirty-four men died in the surprise assault and 171 more were wounded. Sometime after the firing stopped, Israel signaled that they had made a mistake. They claimed that the USS *Liberty* was not flying its flag, and so they hadn't known it was an American ship. They apologized for the incident.

To the chagrin of most survivors, who disagreed with Israel's version of the attack, the U.S. government accepted their explanation and their apology. To this day, controversy remains concerning the motives behind the assault on the *Liberty* and the prior knowledge of its attackers.

The *Liberty* was not the only United States vessel to be fired upon in Middle East waters during the Six-Day War. Sometime, within two to three days of the *Liberty* attack or perhaps even the same day, hell itself hit the *Amberjack*.

We were submerged and running on batteries, as usual. Naturally, most of us knew very little, including our specific location. We did learn, however, what happened up forward when the Grim Reaper descended upon us.

We were running shallow, with the conning officer looking through the periscope. Suddenly, he hollered, "Oh, NO! Down periscope." He ordered the planesmen to take us deep. Down we went, steeper than even the conning officer had intended. One of the young planesmen spun the wheel so hard he locked the bow planes in full dive.

I was on watch in the forward engine room, which was also my battle station. I wondered what the hell was going on as we took a terrific down angle, somewhere between thirty and forty degrees. Next, the planesman whirled the wheel so hard the opposite way that he locked the planes in full up position. The boat tilted the other way, hard, and now I waited for us to broach the surface.

The battle station alarm began its Gong! Gong! Gong! while I fought with a four-hundred-pound hatch—trying to hold it open for the men to pass through on the way to their battle stations. All the while the boat teeter-tottered, first one way and then the other, whipping the heavy hatch, and me, back and forth—a ragdoll trying to cling to a monstrous pendulum.

Explosions, coming fast. Boom! Boom! Boom! All underwater and somewhere off to our starboard side.

We regained depth control.

Boom! Boom! More explosions, closer now.

As I held the hatch steady, the chief of the boat stepped into the engine room and hollered, "The game's over! Rig for depth charge!"

Then the same order blasted over the intercom. "Rig for depth charge! Rig for depth charge!"

My heart tried to pound its way out of my chest.

The chief charged on through, heading forward. As I tried to close the hatch, a young seaman stepped in, confused and rubbing sleep out of his eyes. "What's going on?" he whined. "What's going on?"

I screamed. "Get out of here! Get to your battle station!" The seaman's eyes about popped out of his skull. He ran on through the engine room, a good move.

All the enginemen made it to their battle stations. There were three or four of us in the forward engine room, and about the same number in the aft. We dogged the hatches and sealed the compartments, rigged for depth charge.

The charges kept coming.

The enemy vessels were making runs as they dropped their underwater bombs. A depth charge cannot be dropped directly off the side of a ship that is sitting dead in the water, as this will result in the charge going off beneath the ship, sinking itself instead of the target submarine. So the ship must drop its charges while making speed, to ensure that they explode somewhere behind it.

I could tell there were at least two surface ships after us, maybe three. During a run, dropping depth charges one after the other, they made a tremendous amount of noise—both from the explosions and from their roaring engines. At these times, we got underway on the batteries. Running just off the bottom, we tried to figure their direction and speed and evade the bombs exploding nearby.

Then they would stop, suddenly, and shut off their engines. We stopped, too. Sonar listening both ways. They listened for us, to see if they had killed us, and we listened for them, to try to find where they were.

Even back in the engine room it was easy to tell what was going on. I had been in numerous war games, wherein the pursuing surface vessels used the very same tactics as this real enemy, except in those cases they dropped harmless hand grenades.

Nothing on Earth sounds like a depth charge. And nothing could be more frightening. Sitting in the engine room, hardly daring to breathe, with even the clocks turned off to stop that bit of noise from being detected on sonar, all I could see in my mind was a depth charge coming straight down on top of us.

I didn't panic, but I learned why people do. I had never been so scared and would never be again. *If only I could shoot back,* I thought, *or even holler at them and call them dirty names.* But I didn't have that luxury. Just sit there in terror, trembling, like a mouse in a corner listening for the cat to find him. I looked at my hands. I had never before seen them shake.

We sent a young fireman down to the lower level to watch for leaks. Sitting in strained and terrifying silence, the rest of us couldn't even look at one another. Although I had been riding submarines for years, I had a thought that had never before crossed my mind. I looked all around me—up, down, forward, and aft—and thought *I'm under water, inside an airtight tube, and this is going to be my tomb.*

For several black minutes, I could not shake that vision of death, but I knew I couldn't afford to think that way. So I started calling those bastards up above every filthy, degrading name I could think of. I said the words in my mind, not daring to even whisper the names, but I thought them. That felt good.

The ship's engines roared to life, and in an instant, they began making runs, boiling the water around us with terrific explosions, bouncing the boat with shock waves. Holding the bench I sat on in a death grip, watching for leaks and thinking dirty names, again I felt our screws start up and the boat making turns as we strove to evade our determined pursuers.

They stopped again, and so did we. Quiet—an unearthly silence. Listening, fearing, praying, hating. Whoever was up there, I hated them. They were trying to kill me. I thought the fear and emotional strain might drive someone over the brink, but no one panicked. After about forty-five minutes or an hour, we managed to lose our enemy. When they abruptly stopped after a run, and we did the same, we found ourselves farther away from them. The ships appeared to have lost track of us. When they began another run, the explosions were clearly more distant. We sneaked away, praying that they would not find us again.

With only two engines operative, we didn't dare hit the surface to make a run for it. As soon as we exposed ourselves, the ships would have caught up with us and forced us down again, followed by more of those infernal bombs. I had had a lifetime dose of depth charges, and I hoped the captain had, too. *Please, Lord, don't let him hit the surface. Just help us keep sneaking away, no matter how long it takes.*

And that's what we did.

Our pursuers didn't give up easily. They continued to make runs, searching for us. Miles away, sneaking along deep, we could still hear the booms.

After we had made our escape and secured battle stations, I went looking for someone—the dopey seaman who had stopped in the engine room and asked me sleepily, "What's going on?"

I found him in the control room, just a few feet from a large plotting chart, which the captain, the exec, and several other officers were bending over in concentrated study. I didn't even notice who was in earshot; I was furious.

I grabbed the seaman by the shirt collar and pulled him an inch from my face. "What the hell did you think you were doing back there?" I yelled. "Rubbing your eyes and asking what's going on when you could clearly hear the battle stations alarm?"

Locked in my grip and too scared to speak, the kid just tried to shrug.

"This is a submarine, and you were worthless—just worthless. If you ever do something like that again, I'll grab a wrench or a hammer and knock you out. Then at least you won't be in the way. Understand?"

I was about to choke the young fellow, but he managed to nod. I let him go and shoved him away. It was then that I noticed the captain and all the officers. They had straightened up and listened to the entire exchange. I nodded at them, still in a rage. They smiled as I stomped away.

The crew's reaction to the attack on the boat was astounding, creating a weird atmosphere that I would not have believed myself if I hadn't seen it firsthand. No one would talk, not about the incident or anything else. Half the men on board suffered from insomnia—trudging back and forth from one end to the other, dead on their feet, but unable to sleep. A boatload of zombies.

Morale had been bad before; now it approached mass depression. A normal submarine crew would have laughed and carried on endlessly, raving about how we had handily escaped our bumbling attackers and left them wondering where we had gone. Not this bunch—they moved sullenly through the boat without even looking at one another, seeming not to care if we lived or died.

A day or so after the attack, the captain gathered us all in the mess hall to explain what we had experienced. He told us that what had sounded like depth charges had actually been something totally different. The boat had accidentally wandered into a war game and found itself near or under a target sled that was being towed. The explosions we heard were simply the shells hitting the water near us.

We all sat in silence. A few of us glanced at each other in disbelief, while some of the crew seemed to buy the story— maybe because they needed to believe something. I did not.

Given the circumstances—a high-security operation wherein we suddenly found ourselves embroiled in someone else's war—I cannot fault the captain for trying to calm us that day, but I didn't believe what he told us. I don't know if he had received any messages from his superiors between the time of the incident and the time that he addressed the crew, but I'm sure he was operating under severe security restrictions when he talked to us.

Several things didn't jibe with the captain's version of what we had encountered. One: why would either side be playing war games in the middle of a real war? Two: if those were simply projectiles hitting the water near us in a practice exercise, why were they exploding? Three: what were those vessels doing above us, starting and stopping their engines and sitting dead quiet in the water in between explosive runs? And four: how did our situation just happen to mirror a fictitious scene that took place in a movie that was aboard the *Amberjack?* The odds against such a coincidence seem astronomical.

Following the skipper's "explanation" of the incident, we were told, emphatically, not to breathe a word of it to anyone. I thought to myself, *Let's see now, supposedly nothing happened, but we're being warned not to talk about it. Hmmm . . .*

Nothing changed after the captain's address. Still nobody talked, and half the crew couldn't sleep. Neither his speech nor the incident itself was mentioned on the boat. It was as if we had all been struck dumb—almost as frightening as the depth charges themselves.

Over the years, various sources, inside the navy and out, have addressed the *Amberjack*'s presence in the eastern Mediterranean during the Six-Day War. Some of these sources made mention of the attack I have described while others refused to discuss it, choosing to treat the incident as if it never occurred. Some who spoke chose to remain anonymous even after many years had passed. Others talked more openly.

Four senior petty officers who were aboard the *Amberjack* at the time—men who chose to remain unnamed—believed that we were near the USS *Liberty* when she was attacked, and that the explosions we heard were perhaps echoes of the bombing and torpedoing of the ship.

However, years later a senior spook who had been aboard the *Amberjack* stated that we were never close to the *Liberty*. The same man said that we were operating off Alexandria, far to the west of the *Liberty*'s location. And the *Amberjack*'s captain, who swore that we were never within a hundred miles of the *Liberty,* also stated in a later interview that we were operating near Alexandria.

I have no reason to believe that the *Amberjack* was anywhere near the *Liberty* when the ship was attacked. So what about the explosions that went off around us and the surface vessels that we could clearly hear up above? Alternately moving at high speed while bombs detonated in the water around us, then stopping, shutting down their engines, and listening for us. And all the while, for nearly an hour, we on the *Amberjack* were sweating blood and taking evasive actions to escape the pursuing vessels.

An *Amberjack* sonarman, contacted years later, had this to say of the incident:

> During the Six-Day War we were stationed off of Alexandria. The reason you got bum dope from *Amberjack* crewmen is because most of the crew did not know where we were and in many cases did not know what we were doing other than spy stuff. We accidentally (so one of the officers told me) passed under a target sled that was being towed and subsequently got shelled. We went deep and manned battle stations. The shells could clearly be heard exploding outside the hull. The spook that was on board and in the sonar shack filled his drawers. I tracked two destroyers on sonar.

I was on board the *Amberjack* every day of June 1967. I do not believe that we were anywhere near the USS *Liberty* when she was attacked, and I certainly don't believe the target sled shelling story. Who attacked the *Amberjack* that terrible day? What nation? I don't know, and I probably never will.

What I do know is what I heard, what I felt, and what I experienced. I feel certain beyond a doubt that the USS *Amberjack* was detected and deliberately attacked by two or more surface vessels in the eastern Mediterranean during the Six-Day War, and I feel like the luckiest sailor in the world to have survived it.

Shortly after the captain addressed the crew, the boat was ordered to Suda Bay, Crete, in the Greek Islands. I didn't care where we were going—anywhere away from the violent Middle East and a war that I hadn't signed on for. I had two and a half months to go before my discharge, and now I knew I would make it.

At Crete we found what appeared to be the entire Sixth Fleet, all anchored in that one small harbor—a heavy cruiser, one or two aircraft carriers, smaller cruisers, and more destroyers than I had ever seen in one spot. Evidently, we had all been sent there to wait out the Six-Day War.

With all those thousands of sailors in the bay and only one small town, the admiral wisely restricted the number of men that could go on liberty at any one time. A very small percentage—approximately two percent—was allowed to leave each ship. For some reason the *Amberjack* got a special dispensation from this rule. I suspect the admiral had some knowledge of what we'd been through.

Not only were more of us allowed to go on liberty, we received permission for as much as half the crew to hit the beach if we participated in some sort of organized sporting event that would keep us out of the town. Planning that didn't take long.

Beer ball games had long been a navy tradition. Somehow our officers located a ball diamond on the outskirts of the town and borrowed balls, bats, and gloves from one of the larger ships that had room to carry recreational equipment.

It was a cloudless, hot afternoon in Crete, and instead of just one beer cooler standing behind the backstop, there were several. And it was not simply a beer ball game; it was a beer, whiskey, vodka, wine, and ouzo game. All this booze just seemed to appear magically.

We were dressed in navy dungarees, cutoffs, T-shirts, no shirts, white hats, and no hats. Even the captain participated. Wearing shorts and a T-shirt, the skipper easily kept up with the rest of us. Of course, we weren't difficult to keep up with; by the third inning, most guys were incapable of running between two bases without tripping over their own feet and falling down in the dirt—providing someone was lucky enough to get a hit, that is, an event that became more and more of a rarity as the afternoon wore on.

At the end of the game, we all looked like dirtballs, no one could walk straight, and two guys had passed out. We boarded the bus that came to take us back to the pier to catch the liberty boat, handing our two unconscious mates over our heads like fence rails and dropping them on the floor between the seats.

I had the feeling that the *Amberjack* crew could have gotten away with murder.

The big ships, the cruisers and the aircraft carriers, carried large liberty boats, and provided transportation back and forth to the pier for all ships in the bay. A number of surface craft sailors were waiting for the boat when we arrived on the pier. They were all dressed in sparkling white uniforms and mostly sober, it still being early afternoon and bright daylight.

Then there was us. We piled off the bus looking like farm boys at the end of a long day—some barefooted, some shirtless, some hatless, all dirty and dusty, and all enjoying a high state of inebriation. The skipper could not be identified from the rest of us. Our two unconscious guys were carried to the edge of the pier and plopped down on the hot concrete. They didn't complain.

The crowd of surface craft sailors took one look and moved away from us en masse.

The liberty boat glided up beside the pier—a large craft with every surface polished and glistening in the sun. We fell aboard, dragging along the two passed-out guys and dropping them in the bottom of the boat where they were repeatedly stepped on during the trip out to our anchored sub. The surface sailors, staring at us in horror, did their best to keep from touching us and soiling their uniforms.

The boat made a beeline for the sub so they could drop us off first. They got rid of us, all right, but the show wasn't over. Up on the main deck, the rest of the crew—those who hadn't gotten to go play ball and drink—had set up several makeshift barbecues. They were grilling steaks, chickens, hamburgers, and vegetables when we arrived.

We leaped from the gunwales of the liberty boat up onto the sub's main deck and immediately began terrorizing our shipmates. Having had much to drink but nothing to eat, we ran to their barbecues and started grabbing steaks and fistfuls of half-cooked food and gobbling them down. That didn't set well with our sober mates.

Fights broke out all over the main deck. Guys slugging it out and knocking each other off the side into the water while others were simply shoved off or staggered around and fell off without any help. The barbecues were overturned, spilling what food we hadn't already snatched onto the deck.

The liberty boat didn't leave; it just backed off about twenty yards and sat in the water—a ringside seat for all aboard. I'm sure we were more entertaining than anything they had found in town.

A boatload of men fighting over barbecue and throwing one another overboard had to be a hilarious sight. And, although it might not have appeared so to the untrained eye, this was an indication that morale was finally on the upswing—not a lot, but at least a positive sign.

I needed to get away, so the following day I put on dress whites and went to town by myself. Wandering the streets alone felt good, a bit melancholy, but good. It was a chance to reflect on past months and what we had endured at the hands of an unknown enemy in Middle East waters. The terror of fearing for my life without being able to fight back. In actuality, it would take years to fully resolve these issues in my mind, but for now it felt nice just to wander and think.

Cats. There were a great number of cats in the town, obviously without owners. Most of them were not wild, just neglected. Every now and then I stopped and petted one. After walking for hours, I saw a black and white kitten, about two-thirds grown, sitting alone in the doorway of a closed store. He looked half starved, both for food and for affection. I sat down in the doorway and began petting him and talking to him. He crawled into my lap and we quickly became friends, me talking and the kitten purring. A true victim and pure innocence, something I hadn't experienced in a long while.

After sharing an extended period of affection, which both the kitten and I badly needed, I decided that the two of us could use a good meal. I picked him up and hailed a cab. When the cab pulled over and I opened the door to get in, the driver frowned and wagged his finger, telling me I could not bring the cat with me in his cab. The man couldn't understand my words, but he quickly figured out that I was adamant about bringing my friend along. To the annoyance of the driver, the kitten and I crawled in. He probably charged me for two passengers.

We went to an expensive restaurant near the pier, a sunny place with a veranda where one could eat and drink at umbrella-shaded tables. Several formal waiters watched as I walked up the steps to the veranda, the kitten in my arms. When they figured out that I meant to share my table with a cat, they all shook their heads. It was not allowed.

"Yes," I said firmly. "My friend will eat with me." They pointed toward the street, telling me to leave. I refused.

One of them went and got the manager, a heavy, frustrated man who could speak a bit of English. He explained to me that cats were not allowed on the veranda, and I explained to him that neither I nor the kitten were leaving. "I'm going to buy a meal for each of us," I told him, "and you are going to serve us." At length the man gave in, shaking his head and muttering something about "Americans" as he walked away.

I ordered a meal for myself and one for the kitten—a bowl of their best meat, diced and deliciously raw. I had a beer and he had some milk. The other diners looked at us strangely, some smiling, some not. We enjoyed our dinner immensely. I don't know if that kitten ever got another good meal in its life, but it had one that day.

We pulled anchor and left Crete after a few days, and headed directly for Valetta, Malta. There we tied up near the fatally wounded USS *Liberty*. With more than eight hundred rocket and machinegun holes in her and a gaping torpedo gash in her starboard side, the proud ship had limped back to Malta, with a nine-degree list, under her own power. She was damaged beyond repair, however, and would later be sold for scrap.

Why did we stop in Malta? We were never told. Although we weren't aware of it at the time, a navy court of inquiry, hastily thrown together and hastily concluded, was held there concerning the attack on the *Liberty*. Perhaps that's why we were there. As usual, most of us didn't know, and we knew better than to ask.

From Malta, we sailed west and out of the Med, making one more stop in Rota, Spain. At long last, we received parts for engine number three—the correct parts—and were able to get it running. We engine men did not cheer as the big machine cranked over and started, the event coming long after it could have helped to save our lives.

Morale took a definite upward turn after we left port and sailed for home, and men began to sleep and laugh again. The human spirit, proving indomitable once more, saved us from ourselves.

As for me, I had spent years inside submarines, with few opportunities to actually view the awesome expanse of the sea. I passed long, pleasurable hours up on the bridge, gazing out over the endless Atlantic and wondering what adventures lay beyond the far horizon, beyond my own horizons.

I was twenty-six years old—and alive.

My fellow denizens of the deep ushering me home, June 1967.

Epilogue

I can still see them—working, sweating, daring, laughing—
Captain Bessac, Captain Summit, Captain Williams, Mr.
Rawlins, Mr. Chewning, Mr. Green, Mr. MacKinnon, Mr. Reed,
Mr. Dewhirst, Chief Kennedy, Bob Lee, Chief Spence, Whitey
Kutzleb, Donny Skelton, Leroy Lavender, Jim Nelson, Doug
Dunn, Don Durham, DeWayne Catron, Bob Cantley, Rich
Dominy, Ted Newell, Danny Dawson, Jack Kepler, Jack Wright,
Wild Joe Birkle, Chief Wabbit, Chief Dick, Gary Reynolds, Jim
Barnes, Paul Carney, Chief Boring, and countless others who
served our country and with whom I shared a great adventure.

Some have passed on, while many still remain. I see them
at reunions and in pictures they send, the ones who are still
here. They're getting to be old men now; some are old men.
But in my mind's eye they are young, wild, and brave. They are
magnificent.